Reimagining Prosperity

The historic task of the European Union (EU) today, this book argues, is to articulate and institute a new imaginary of prosperity. Imaginaries of prosperity integrate societies around the shared pursuit of a prosperous future, rendering 'political-economic' questions as the main preoccupation of politics. The new imaginary of prosperity in the EU must be able to provide answers to contemporary societal challenges while also conjuring a world in which people want to live. Through analyses of several policy fields, the book shows that the EU has already made modest strides in fostering more caring consumption, circular products and technologies, sustainable industry, and fairer corporate activity. But the EU must go further and faster if it hopes to respond effectively to Europe's problems, while arresting another descent into tribalism. This title is also available as Open Access on Cambridge Core.

Marija Bartl is Professor of Transnational Private Law at the University of Amsterdam. She is Director of the Amsterdam Centre for Transformative Private Law and a Principal Investigator of the N-EXTLAW Project .

Cambridge Studies in European Law and Policy

The focus of this series is European law broadly understood. It aims to publish original monographs in all fields of European law, from work focusing on the institutions of the EU and the Council of Europe to books examining substantive fields of European law as well as examining the relationship between European law and domestic, regional and international legal orders. The series publishes works adopting a wide variety of methods: comparative, doctrinal, theoretical and inter-disciplinary approaches to European law are equally welcome, as are works looking at the historical and political facets of the development of European law and policy. The main criterion is excellence, i.e. the publication of innovative work, which will help to shape the legal, political and scholarly debate on the future of European law.

Joint Editors

Professor Mark Dawson
Hertie School of Governance, Berlin
Professor Dr Laurence Gormley
University of Groningen
Professor Jo Shaw
University of Edinburgh

Editorial Advisory Board

Professor Kenneth Armstrong, *University of Cambridge*
Professor Catherine Barnard, *University of Cambridge*
Professor Richard Bellamy, *University College London*
Professor Marise Cremona, *European University Institute, Florence*
Professor Michael Dougan, *University of Liverpool*
Professor Dr Jacqueline Dutheil de la Rochère, *University of Paris II Pantheon-Assas, Director of the Centre for European Law, Paris*
Professor Daniel Halberstam, *University of Michigan*
Professor Dora Kostakopoulou, *University of Warwick*
Professor Dr Ingolf Pernice, *Director of the Walter Hallstein Institute, Humboldt University of Berlin*
Judge Sinisa Rodin, *Court of Justice of the European Union*
Professor Eleanor Spaventa, *Università Bocconi*
Professor Neil Walker, *University of Edinburgh*
Professor Stephen Weatherill, *University of Oxford*

Books in the Series

Reimagining Prosperity: Toward a New Imaginary of Law and Political Economy in the EU
Marija Bartl

Open Strategic Autonomy in EU Trade Policy: Assessing the Turn to Stronger Enforcement and More Robust Interest Representation
Wolfgang Weiß and Cornelia Furculiță

Trilogues: The Democratic Secret of European Legislation
Giacomo Rugge

The European Union, Emerging Global Business and Human Rights
Aleydis Nissen

The European Central Bank and the European Macroeconomic Constitution
Klaus Tuori

The Procedural and Organisational Law of the European Court of Justice: An Incomplete Transformation
Christoph Krenn

The New Economic Governance of the Eurozone: A Rule of Law Analysis
Paul Dermine

Digital Constitutionalism in Europe: Reframing Rights and Powers in the Algorithmic Society
Giovanni De Gregorio

Can the European Court of Human Rights Shape European Public Order?
Kanstantsin Dzehtsiarou

The Constitutional Boundaries of European Fiscal Federalism
Brady Gordon

Private Selves: Legal Personhood in European Privacy Protection
Susanna Lindroos-Hovinheimo

Fissures in EU Citizenship: The Deconstruction and Reconstruction of the Legal Evolution of EU Citizenship
Martin Steinfeld

The Boundaries of the EU Internal Market: Participation without Membership
Marja-Liisa Öberg

The Currency of Solidarity: Constitutional Transformation during the Euro Crisis
Vestert Borger

Empire of Law: Nazi Germany, Exile Scholars and the Battle for the Future of Europe
Kaius Tuori

In the Court We Trust: Cooperation, Coordination and Collaboration between the ECJ and Supreme Administrative Courts
Rob van Gestel and Jurgen de Poorter

Beyond Minimum Harmonisation: Gold-Plating and Green-Plating of European Environmental Law
Lorenzo Squintani

The Court of Justice of the European Union as an Institutional Actor: Judicial Lawmaking and its Limits
Thomas Horsley

The Politics of Justice in European Private Law: Social Justice, Access Justice, Societal Justice
Hans-W Micklitz

The Transformation of EU Treaty Making: The Rise of Parliaments, Referendums and Courts Since 1950
Dermot Hodson and Imelda Maher

Redefining European Economic Integration
Dariusz Adamski

Human Rights in the Council of Europe and the European Union: Achievements, Trends and Challenges
Steven Greer, Janneke Gerards and Rosie Slowe

Core Socio-Economic Rights and the European Court of Human Rights
Ingrid Leijten

Green Trade and Fair Trade in and with the EU: Process-based Measures within the EU Legal Order
Laurens Ankersmit

New Labour Laws in Old Member States: Trade Union Responses to European Enlargement
Rebecca Zahn

The Governance of EU Fundamental Rights
Mark Dawson

The International Responsibility of the European Union: From Competence to Normative Control
Andrés Delgado Casteleiro

Frontex and Non-Refoulement: The International Responsibility of the EU
Roberta Mungianu

Gendering European Working Time Regimes: The Working Time Directive and the Case of Poland
Ania Zbyszewska

EU Renewable Electricity Law and Policy: From National Targets to a Common Market
Tim Maxian Rusche

European Constitutionalism
Kaarlo Tuori

Brokering Europe: Euro-Lawyers and the Making of a Transnational Polity
Antoine Vauchez

Services Liberalization in the EU and the WTO: Concepts, Standards and Regulatory Approaches
Marcus Klamert

Referendums and the European Union: A Comparative Enquiry
Fernando Mendez, Mario Mendez and Vasiliki Triga

The Allocation of Regulatory Competence in the EU Emissions Trading Scheme
Josephine van Zeben

The Eurozone Crisis: A Constitutional Analysis
Kaarlo Tuori and Klaus Tuori

International Trade Disputes and EU Liability
Anne Thies

The Limits of Legal Reasoning and the European Court of Justice
Gerard Conway

New Governance and the Transformation of European Law: Coordinating EU Social Law and Policy
Mark Dawson

The Lisbon Treaty: A Legal and Political Analysis
Jean-Claude Piris

The European Union's Fight Against Corruption: The Evolving Policy Towards Member States and Candidate Countries
Patrycja Szarek-Mason

The Ethos of Europe: Values, Law and Justice in the EU
Andrew Williams

State and Market in European Union Law: The Public and Private Spheres of the Internal Market before the EU Courts
Wolf Sauter and Harm Schepel

The European Civil Code: The Way Forward
Hugh Collins

Ethical Dimensions of the Foreign Policy of the European Union: A Legal Appraisal
Urfan Khaliq

Implementing EU Pollution Control: Law and Integration
Bettina Lange

European Broadcasting Law and Policy
Jackie Harrison and Lorna Woods

The Transformation of Citizenship in the European Union: Electoral Rights and the Restructuring of Political Space
Jo Shaw

The Constitution for Europe: A Legal Analysis
Jean-Claude Piris

The European Convention on Human Rights: Achievements, Problems and Prospects
Steven Greer

Social Rights and Market Freedom in the European Constitution: A Labour Law Perspective
Stefano Giubboni

EU Enlargement and the Constitutions of Central and Eastern Europe
Anneli Albi

Reimagining Prosperity
Toward a New Imaginary of Law and Political Economy in the EU

Marija Bartl
University of Amsterdam

CAMBRIDGE
UNIVERSITY PRESS

Shaftesbury Road, Cambridge CB2 8EA, United Kingdom

One Liberty Plaza, 20th Floor, New York, NY 10006, USA

477 Williamstown Road, Port Melbourne, VIC 3207, Australia

314–321, 3rd Floor, Plot 3, Splendor Forum, Jasola District Centre, New Delhi – 110025, India

103 Penang Road, #05-06/07, Visioncrest Commercial, Singapore 238467

Cambridge University Press is part of Cambridge University Press & Assessment, a department of the University of Cambridge.

We share the University's mission to contribute to society through the pursuit of education, learning and research at the highest international levels of excellence.

www.cambridge.org
Information on this title: www.cambridge.org/9781009236225

DOI: 10.1017/9781009236195

© Marija Bartl 2025

This publication is in copyright. Subject to statutory exception and to the provisions of relevant collective licensing agreements, with the exception of the Creative Commons version the link for which is provided below, no reproduction of any part may take place without the written permission of Cambridge University Press & Assessment.

An online version of this work is published at doi.org/10.1017/9781009236195 under a Creative Commons Open Access license CC-BY-NC 4.0 which permits re-use, distribution and reproduction in any medium for non-commercial purposes providing appropriate credit to the original work is given and any changes made are indicated. To view a copy of this license visit https://creativecommons.org/licenses/by-nc/4.0

When citing this work, please include a reference to the DOI 10.1017/9781009236195

First published 2025

A catalogue record for this publication is available from the British Library.

Library of Congress Cataloging-in-Publication Data
Names: Bartl, Marija, author.
Title: Reimagining prosperity : toward a new imaginary of law and political economy in the EU / Professor Marija Bartl, University of Amsterdam.
Description: Cambridge, United Kingdom ; New York, NY : Cambridge University Press, 2024. | Series: Cambridge studies in European law and policy | Includes bibliographical references and index.
Identifiers: LCCN 2024023204 (print) | LCCN 2024023205 (ebook) | ISBN 9781009236225 (hardcover) | ISBN 9781009236171 (paperback) | ISBN 9781009236195 (epub)
Subjects: LCSH: Law–European Union countries. | Consumer protection–Law and legislation–European Union countries. | Sustainable development–Law and legislation–European Union countries. | Welfare economics. | Economic policy.
Classification: LCC KJE947 .B379 2024 (print) | LCC KJE947 (ebook) | DDC 341.242/2–dc23/eng/20240528
LC record available at https://lccn.loc.gov/2024023204
LC ebook record available at https://lccn.loc.gov/2024023205

ISBN 978-1-009-23622-5 Hardback
ISBN 978-1-009-23617-1 Paperback

Cambridge University Press & Assessment has no responsibility for the persistence or accuracy of URLs for external or third-party internet websites referred to in this publication and does not guarantee that any content on such websites is, or will remain, accurate or appropriate.

Contents

Series Editors' Preface   *page* xiii
Acknowledgements   xv

1 Introduction   1
  1.1 On Prosperity   5
  1.2 On the Role of the EU   8
      1.2.1 Where Are We Now?   10
  1.3 Conceptual Framework   12
  1.4 Structure and Choices   15

2 Imaginaries of Prosperity   20
  2.1 Introduction   20
  2.2 Social Imaginaries   22
      2.2.1 Defining Social Imaginaries   22
      2.2.2 How Social 'Imaginaries' Change   25
      2.2.3 On the Problem of 'Institution': What It Takes to Change a Social Imaginary   28
          2.2.3.1 *The Trouble with Instituting Economy*   29
          2.2.3.2 *On the Translation Role of Democratic Institutions*   35
          2.2.3.3 *Between Ideas and Interests*   38
          2.2.3.4 *On the Role of Law*   40
  2.3 Prosperity   45
      2.3.1 On the Meaning of Prosperity (Today): More about Happiness than Consumerism   46
      2.3.2 Of Prosperity and Democracy   51
      2.3.3 Of Prosperity and Technocracy   53
      2.3.4 Of Prosperity and Europe   55

		2.3.5	The Prosperity's Other: Looming Tribalism	59
			2.3.5.1 *Dialectics of Prosperity: Between Privatised and Shared Prosperity*	59
			2.3.5.2 *The 'Other' Collective Imaginary: The Rise of Tribalism*	62
	2.4	Sustainable and Shared	65
		2.4.1	On the Constitutive Outsides: Renewing Imaginaries of Prosperity	66
		2.4.2	In the Search of Future: Credible Prosperity in the Twenty-First Century	68
		2.4.3	Can the EU Make a Difference?	69
3	**Reimagining Consumption**		**72**
	3.1	Introduction	72
	3.2	Consumption as a Matter of Contract Law	77
	3.3	A Hurried Decline of the Imaginary of Shared Prosperity (1975–1985+)	80
		3.3.1	1975: Consumer Protection as a Collective Project	81
		3.3.2	1981: First Cracks	84
	3.4	Towards the Imaginary of Privatised Prosperity (1985–1995)	86
		3.4.1	1985: 'New Impetus' for Consumer Policy	86
		3.4.2	1990: Breaking the Link between Consumer Rights and Policy Objectives	88
		3.4.3	1995: Privatising for Good Causes: Public Services and Sustainability	91
	3.5	The Transient Hegemony of the Privatised Prosperity (1998–2012+)	93
		3.5.1	1998: The Birth of Common Interest and the Death of Politics	93
		3.5.2	2001: Competitive Consumer Law	97
		3.5.3	2012: Out of the Crisis with Better Information	99
	3.6	Towards an Imaginary of Shared Prosperity after 2018?	101
		3.6.1	2018: First Cracks: What Is the Deal in the 'New Deal for Consumers'	101
		3.6.2	2020: A New Consumer Agenda: A Next Step?	104
	3.7	The Contours of the New Imaginary of Prosperity	107

4 Designing Technology — 112
- 4.1 Introduction — 112
- 4.2 Embedding the Product — 114
  - 4.2.1 Ecodesign Framework — 114
  - 4.2.2 Embedding the Product in Time (Life-Cycle) and Society (Circular Economy) — 117
- 4.3 Steering Growth — 121
- 4.4 Beyond Win-Win — 123
  - 4.4.1 Distributive Trade-Offs 1: Consumers — 123
  - 4.4.2 Distributive Trade-Offs 2: Businesses — 125
  - 4.4.3 Distributive Trade-Offs 3: Workers — 127
- 4.5 Shoring up Publicness — 128
- 4.6 Hardening Law — 132
  - 4.6.1 Rise and Fall of Self-Regulation — 132
  - 4.6.2 Toward a More Mandatory Law — 134
- 4.7 The Contours of the New Imaginary of Prosperity — 137

5 Reinventing Industrial Policy — 139
- 5.1 Introduction — 139
- 5.2 Greening Growth — 143
  - 5.2.1 EU Industrial Strategy — 143
  - 5.2.2 Making Europe 'Competitive' via Green Growth — 150
- 5.3 Law as Burden — 156
- 5.4 Resourceful Government — 160
- 5.5 The Contours of the New Imaginary of Prosperity: or *Im Westen nichts Neues*? — 165

6 Transforming the Corporation — 171
- 6.1 Introduction — 171
  - 6.1.1 'Corporate Governance File' — 175
- 6.2 New Problems, New Solutions — 183
  - 6.2.1 Wait a Bit – *What Problems?* — 187
  - 6.2.2 Wait a Bit – *What Solutions?* — 190
    - 6.2.2.1 How Capable Are Directors? — 190
    - 6.2.2.2 The Conflicting Imaginaries of Prosperity — 191
- 6.3 Paradigm Shift in Knowledge and Expertise — 193
- 6.4 The Contours of New Imaginary of Prosperity — 195

	6.5 Going Beyond: *Pluralising Economy, Transforming Imaginaries*	198
	6.5.1 Mainstreaming Non-extractive Organisations	200
	6.5.2 Transforming Imaginaries	202
7	**Conclusion: Towards a New Imaginary of Prosperity in the EU**	204
	7.1 Changing Background Assumptions	207
	7.2 The Road Ahead	211

Select Bibliography   215
Index   229

Series Editors' Preface

The last decade has seen a revival of interest in the ideas or 'constitutional imaginaries' underlying the European Union (EU) and its law.[1] To give one example, the rule of law crisis has re-enforced a changing narrative, forwarded, for example, by the current President of the Court of Justice, that protecting fundamental values is at the core of Europe's legal mission.[2] As a corollary, it has become less fashionable to see the functional goals of the internal market as the EU's law core.

This book, by Marija Bartl, both rejects and embraces this change. On the one hand, it is firmly about the importance of understanding European integration in terms of markets and prosperity and their ability to contribute to the lives of Europeans. It thus fits with a line of research connecting EU law to changes in political economy.[3] On the other hand, it urges a fundamental rethink of how we imagine prosperity. In Bartl's vision, the failure of privatised prosperity requires a new imaginary of prosperity, where democratic and collective institutions take greater control over economic goods and their distribution.

Such a reinvented shared vision for prosperity is important, so she argues, not just for economic reasons but because narratives of prosperity and of democracy co-constitute each other. There is, therefore, a connection between the neoliberal narrative of prosperity that has dominated the Union for the last decades and the erosion of trust in democratic institutions that has established a turn to tribal or populist

---

[1] See, for example, Komarek (ed.), *European Constitutional Imaginaries: Between Ideology and Utopia* (Oxford University Press, 2023).

[2] Lenaerts, 'New Horizons for the Rule of Law within the EU'. *German Law Journal* 21.1 (2020): 29–34.

[3] P. Kjaer (ed.) *The Law of Political Economy: Transformation in the Function of Law* (Cambridge University Press, 2020).

imaginaries as its political shadow. Bartl's book is thus fundamentally about how new ideas of the role of collective institutions in Europe's economic order are vital in reversing patterns of *democratic* decay.

In addition to its overall conceptual argument, the book carries a close interest in economic institutions, historically reconstructing how core elements of EU law, from corporate governance to industrial policy, consumer protection, and the regulation of new technologies, are shaped by underlying ideas on how they contribute to prosperity. In every chapter, Bartl is not content to revisit past debates but also engages with how new EU initiatives – from the European Green Deal to regulation of the circular economy – slowly attempt to embed collective institutions in their vision of how prosperity in Europe can be realised. Readers can therefore both engage with the book's overall argument and use it as a guide to understand how new collective goals are reshaping concrete areas of EU law and policy.

As a book that does not simply analyse EU law but makes compelling arguments about its future, Marija Bartl's monograph is an important contribution to the field. We are delighted to welcome it to the *Cambridge Studies in European Law and Policy* series.

Mark Dawson
Laurence Gormley
Jo Shaw

Acknowledgements

This book was long in the making. As 'life' continued to happen – from an expanding portfolio of professional responsibilities to a global pandemic – each successive iteration required ever more changes, more restructuring, discarding old chapters for more relevant new ones, and adding more than a few years to the whole process. While it is for the reader to judge whether the outcome merits the effort, there would be no outcome at all without the generous help from colleagues, friends, and family, as well as substantial institutional support.

During the years-long writing process, it was first and foremost the N-EXTLAW project, generously funded by the European Research Council (ERC), that has enabled me to dive deeper into the question of how law relates to, and can facilitate, social change. To get to the product you hold in your hand (or on the screen – again the courtesy of the ERC), special credit is due to N-EXTLAW research assistant Finn Sands Robinson, who has edited the entire manuscript – having read perhaps a bit too much of it. My other dear colleagues in N-EXTLAW – including Nena van der Horst, Mario Pagano, Vladimir Bogoevski, Kinanya Pijl, Angus Fry, and Amy Lazell – have been crucial interlocutors in getting closer to understanding the role of law as a vehicle of social change, all the while providing me with the most congenial intellectual home.

Three other institutions have been crucial on this path. First, my home, Amsterdam Law School (ALS), has generously granted me a significant research leave, without which this book would not have been possible. Beyond that, however, it was the extremely vibrant intellectual community at ALS, and in particular at the Amsterdam Center for Transformative Private Law and within the project Sustainable Global Economic Law, that provided caring criticisms at the junctures when I most needed them. While I can't mention all the names who deserve my gratitude, I want to specifically give thanks to a number of my marvellous friends and colleagues, in no specific order, Chantal Mak, Aukje van Hoek, Christina Eckes, Mirthe Jiwa, Olga Gritsai, Yannick van den Berg, Laura Burgers, Aart Jonkers, Selma de Groot, Marco Loos, Iris van Domselaar, Joti Roest, Francesca Episcopo, Anna van Duin, Rolef de Weijs, Solmaz Esmailzadeh, Jessica Turco, Marleen van Uchelen, Sjef van Erp, Alessio Pacces, Giuseppe Dari-Mattiacci, Göran Sluiter, Benjamin van Rooij, Nik de Boer, Kati Cseres, Ivana Isailovic, Giacomo Tagiuri, Ingo Venzke, André Nollkaemper, Andrea Leiter, Kiki Brölmann, Kristina Irion, and Balázs Bodó. Beyond ALS, I want to specifically acknowledge the important exchanges with Poul Kjaer, Isabel Feichtner, Jonathan Zeitlin, Vanessa Mak and her team in Leiden, 'TEGL community' and the fine people at ENLENS, and above all Bob van der Zwaan. At different stages, each of these colleagues has either made suggestions or shown care that made my heart and mind sing.

Second, the European University Institute (EUI) in Florence has always provided me with immense bounty. Not only did it surround me with the most inspiring intellectual and cultural environment in which to write a PhD, it did so again for the present book. Writing is always hard, but it was made easier by a wonderful office overlooking Florence, inspiring lunches, coffees, or drinks with brilliant EUI staff (Joanne Scott, Mathias Siems, and of course Martijn Hesselink), and having a chance to receive early feedback on my work during the faculty seminar, with Bruno de Witte's incisive comments. Finally, the Institute of Advanced Studies in Nantes, which kindly hosted me in 2018, was the place where the idea for the N-EXTLAW project, as well as the book that aims to flesh out its central theoretical aspect, emerged during inspiring interdisciplinary exchanges with colleagues from across the world, further articulated during long runs (at least for me) with Jocelyn Olcott (Duke University).

Scattered across countries and institutions, many other colleagues have made an important impact on this book journey. Intense and inspiring conversations with Joana Mendes, Harm Schepel, Agustin Menendes, and Rebecca O'Rourke, when launching European Law Open, have sensitised me to numerous concerns that otherwise might have escaped a private lawyer. The 'Green Academies' at Vis in Croatia, organised by the team at the Institute for Political Ecology – most prominently by Vedran Horvat, and frequented by many transformative political thinkers and social activists – have helped broaden my horizon beyond my (necessarily limited) disciplinary and social container. The yearly 'Mountain Seminar' organised by Jan Komárek and Marco Dani, with the regular presence of

Sacha Garben, Jacco Bomhoff, Elise Muir, Pola Cebulak, and many others, has been an inspiring setting for the discussion of various chapters of this book. The start of the new 'Society for European Law *Unbound*' project, together with Daniela Caruso, Joseph Weiler, and a number of other colleagues, has given me hope that we can work to avoid some of the scarier scenarios presented in the book through genuinely inclusive discussions about EU law and integration.

Perhaps my most important fellow traveller on this journey was my exceptional friend and colleague, Candida Leone, who alone has read countless drafts and revisions and spent hours patiently brainstorming appropriate titles or covers. Sidney Richards, my wonderful versatile partner, has also responded to numerous last-minute demands for reading, commenting, and editing – even if he always preferred to defer to Candida in aesthetic matters. Martijn Hesselink, dear friend and mentor, has made the most important intervention in the writing process, first by urging me to convene and then generously by helping to organise a 'manuscript workshop' at the EUI. Once I had committed to this event, a great deal of writing discipline necessarily (and nervously) ensued, as I wished to benefit from the characteristically brilliant comments from friends and colleagues who have endowed the book with their presence – including Hans W. Micklitz (my inspiring and caring PhD supervisor), Agustin Menendes (a brilliant mind and my European Law Open co-traveller), Daniela Caruso (a dear friend and leading contract law scholar), Jiří Přibáň (a great legal theorist, who was one of the first to use 'social imaginaries' in EU law scholarship), Evelyn Terryn (the authority on consumer law aspects of ecodesign and circularity – and the most committed train traveller), Paul Blokker (a political theorist with a lot of patience for law and lawyers, and the leading scholar on social imaginaries), Alice Pearson (a brilliant anthropologist of corporate activity and a fellow at the EUI), Or Rosenboim (an EUI historian who has generously offered comments even as a different generative process demanded much of her energies), and Mathias Siems (the EUI professor of comparative law and a wonderful host during my stay there). Anna di Biase, with her competent, warm, and resolute support, has ensured that we had two truly great days.

Finally, it was my Croatian and Dutch families, as well as close friends such as Dražen and Marija, who have cared for me during various holidays-turned-writing retreats and provided the most nourishing environment for writing. Throughout the writing process, my forever-young mum Đurđica has continued to instil in me (if not always with success) the sense that life is also about fun, sun, and music. My nephew Alex at the same time made sure I was also sufficiently challenged from the less compromising Left. In between these familial treats, my partner Sidney offered often much needed care in the moments of self-doubt and tiredness. Without all the continuous encouragement and patient support of all these people who were ready to provide care 'no questions asked', this would certainly be a far worse book – if it were a book at all.

1 Introduction

The European Union (EU) is living its Weimar moment. The growing number of crises we face – environmental and climate crisis, skyrocketing inequality, care crisis, housing crisis, migration crisis, and the return of war in geopolitics – has only been matched by the growing number of electoral successes of the far and extreme right in various EU member states (MSs).[1] Europe will not be able, however, to respond to these crises by rehearsing old neoliberal recipes: not only do they fail to offer credible solutions to the problems they have (often) themselves created, but their futility may further empower various extreme movements that embrace identitarian and anti-democratic platforms. At this turning point, we have to do better. That is what this book is about.

The gradual slide to tribalism and extremism that we are seeing today is a culmination of the era of the strange "non-death" of neoliberalism, post-2008 crisis.[2] Instead of starting a shift towards a different model of political economy in the aftermath of the great financial crisis, the EU and its MSs have doubled down on privatisation and austerity, making those worst off ultimately pay for the irresponsibility of the financial markets.[3] The resulting crisis of trust is then as much a consequence of the deteriorating material reality of the many, as of the accompanying narratives of recovery and economic growth, that were presented as a reality on the basis of often casually composed metrics.[4]

---

[1] The crisis has only grown more existential; see Agustín José Menéndez, 'The Existential Crisis of the European Union', *German Law Journal* 14, no. 5 (2013): 453–526.
[2] Colin Crouch, 'Privatised Keynesianism: An Unacknowledged Policy Regime', *The British Journal of Politics and International Relations* 11, no. 3 (August 2009): 382–99.
[3] Thomas Piketty, *Capital in the Twenty-First Century* (Harvard University Press, 2014).
[4] Andrew Haldane, 'Whose Recovery?', Speech at the Bank of England (2016), www.bankofengland.co.uk/speech/2016/whose-recovery, last accessed 13 January 2024.

Today, following a short window of COVID-19 "public extravaganza" and energy crisis-induced largess towards both firms and residents, a new wave of austerity politics is on the table.[5] Not taxation or borrowing, but financial austerity is supposed to 'pay' for COVID-19 and energy crisis measures, through further cuts to public services and curtailing the capacity for public (green) investment.[6] The reasons for austerity seem to be purely ideological: at this point, even the most orthodox financial institutions suggest that, historically, lowering public spending at inopportune moments increases rather than decreases public debt.[7] The question that every European must ask is, however, can Europe afford another wave of austerity, mounted as I argue later on the already historic levels of poverty and inequality, and still hope to remain democratic?[8] If the response to this question is no, are there other alternatives to consider?

In this book, I argue that the only way to counter growing tribalism and a loss of trust in democratic institutions in Europe is to articulate and institute a new *imaginary of prosperity*.[9] Imaginaries of prosperity integrate societies around the promise of a prosperous future, placing the problems (and struggles) of political economy in the centre of the

---

[5] Wester Van Gaal, 'EU Agrees to Cut Spending for 2024, Despite Investment Needs', *EU Observer* (2023), https://euobserver.com/green-economy/157270?utm_source=euobs&utm_medium=email, last accessed 16 January 2024.

[6] European Court of Auditors, 'Special Report 18/2023: EU Climate and Energy Targets – 2020 Targets Achieved, but Little Indication that Actions to Reach the 2030 Targets Will Be Sufficient', *ECA* (2023), www.eca.europa.eu/en/publications/SR-2023-18, last accessed 16 January 2024.

[7] International Monetary Fund, 'World Economic Outlook: A Rocky Recovery', *IMF* (2023), www.imf.org/en/Publications/WEO/Issues/2023/04/11/world-economic-outlook-april-2023, last accessed 16 January 2024.

[8] Ricardo Duque Gabriel, Mathias Klein, and Ana Sofia Pessoa, 'The Political Costs of Austerity', *Review of Economics and Statistics* (2023): 1–45, https://direct.mit.edu/rest/article-abstract/doi/10.1162/rest_a_01373/117705/The-Political-Costs-of-Austerity?redirectedFrom=fulltext; Gregori Galofré-Vilà et al., 'Austerity and the Rise of the Nazi Party', *The Journal of Economic History* 81, no. 1 (2021): 81–113; Jacopo Ponticelli and Hans-Joachim Voth, 'Austerity and Anarchy: Budget Cuts and Social Unrest in Europe, 1919–2008', *Journal of Comparative Economics* 48, no. 1 (2020): 1–19; Gregori Galofré-Vilà et al., 'Austerity and the Rise of the Nazi Party', Working Paper, Working Paper Series (National Bureau of Economic Research, December 2017), https://doi.org/10.3386/w24106; Manuel Funke, Moritz Schularick, and Christoph Trebesch, 'Going to Extremes: Politics after Financial Crises, 1870–2014', *European Economic Review* 88 (2016): 227–60.

[9] I do not deal in this book with the important aspect of 'globalisations' of social consciousnesses, in which law also partakes. See Duncan Kennedy, 'Three Globalizations of Law and Legal Thought: 1850–2000', in *The New Law and Economic Development: A Critical Appraisal*, ed. Alvaro Santos and David M. Trubek (Cambridge University Press, 2006), 19–73.

political. They stand and fall on delivering a mix of prosperity *today* and, perhaps even more importantly, the prospect of *future* prosperity.

Somewhat schematically, at this turning point of history, there are three different social imaginaries vying to (re)constitute neoliberal societies. The first imaginary continues to champion the privatised route to prosperity, as established in the latter decades of the twentieth century. While this imaginary takes on board some of the challenges we face today, such as the reality of climate crisis, it remains committed to preserving the primacy of private actors, (financial) markets, and market-driven technological innovation as the best vehicle to get us out of crises and into a prosperous future.

Ranged against this privatising, well-institutionalised but increasingly unstable imaginary of prosperity,[10] we find two contenders for change, each espousing a more *collective route* to a better future. On the one hand, we see the rise of what I will call *tribal imaginaries*:[11] that is nativist and conservative imaginaries emerging in response to grievances experienced by some groups due to economic and cultural changes over the past forty years.[12] This family of imaginaries combines nationalist, chauvinist, anti-immigrant, and sometimes racist discourses, making identity – rather than prosperity – the central axis of the political.[13] Above all, tribal imaginaries are contemptuous of democratic institutions, scientific knowledge, and the liberal rule of law[14] and bent on limiting the scope of these relics of modernity.[15]

---

[10] The imaginary of prosperity fails when it does not deliver on prosperity today and, even more importantly, cannot generate the trust that it will deliver in the future.

[11] David R. Samson, *Our Tribal Future: How to Channel Our Foundational Human Instincts into a Force for Good* (St. Martin's Press, 2023).

[12] Jan Willem Duyvendak and Josip Kesic, *The Return of the Native: Can Liberalism Safeguard Us against Nativism?* Oxford Studies in Culture and Politics (Oxford University Press, 2023).

[13] See also Yascha Mounk, *The Identity Trap: A Story of Ideas and Power in Our Time* (Penguin Press, 2023). Mounk is mainly concerned with the 'woke' identity politics and encroachments on free speech, which he criticises (to a certain degree justifiably) as not being a good strategy to pursue the very purposes of these movements. While I am open to the argument that the coincidence of the woke and extreme right identity politics is an expression of similar underlying social developments, the huge difference between these movements, and the reason why I do not see woke identity politics as tribalism in this book is that woke identity politics is (so far at least) not against democratic institutions, the rule of law, or aspiring to win elections in order to expel the foreign and impose its own reading of identity on the rest of society.

[14] Francis Fukuyama, 'Against Identity Politics: The New Tribalism and the Crisis of Democracy', *Foreign Affairs* 97 (2018): 90–114.

[15] In a recent anecdote, the whole convention of the German extreme right party AFD circled around discussing *deportations* of insufficiently German Germans, as the way to solve the

On the other hand, we find a slowly emerging imaginary of *shared prosperity* in the EU and some of its MSs. In terms of its content, the nascent imaginary of prosperity shares some traits with the imaginary dominant in post-war Europe, building on the understanding that economy and markets are human-made, social institutions, and (increasingly) placing democratic and public bodies – rather than markets, businesses, or profit – in the driving seat of prosperity. The new imaginary of prosperity ought to articulate a novel understanding of prosperity that is both credible (in the face of the current challenges) and attractive (a world where people want to live). To successfully reconstitute society, it ought to institute not only a different mix of macroeconomic relations (a different role for tax, public spending, or welfare provision) but also a different set of microeconomic institutions,[16] including a new role for *corporations* in society, how and for whose benefit we govern *technology*, what role *industry* should play, or how to make *consumption* more sustainable in a long term. In fact, the very preservation of democratic institutions in Europe may depend on whether the EU, together with its MSs, in the short term succeeds in generating sufficient *trust* that they have the means to get all Europeans into a liveable, or even prosperous, future.

This book builds on three underlying arguments. The first argument is that after periods of prolonged privatisation, when imaginaries of privatised prosperity (such as neoliberalism or laissez-faire before) can no longer fulfil their socially integrative function – that is providing reasonably good outcomes today and a hope for a better future – the imaginary of prosperity must change. Such shifts require that democratic and collective institutions take greater control over the distributive outcomes of the economy, at least for the time being.[17] If society does not have the institutional channels to enable such transformation, we will see a loss of trust in its governing institutions and eventually authoritarian alternatives to democratic institutions being sought.

The second core argument is that the imaginaries of prosperity – be they privatised or shared – are co-constitutive with democracy. To start

---

most important German problems. Ashifa Kassam, 'Scholz Urges Unity against Far Right after Mass Deportation "Masterplan" Revealed', *The Guardian* (2024), www.theguardian.com/world/2024/jan/11/germany-far-right-mass-deportation-masterplan-meeting-olaf-scholz-condemns, last accessed 16 January 2024.

[16] On which I focus in this book.

[17] Until also this kind of political economy fails to deliver prosperity, and a shift occurs – similar to what happened at the end of the 1970s and the beginning of the 1980s.

with the latter, democracy needs imaginaries of prosperity insofar as they create the *right kind* of social glue to hold pluralist democratic societies together. Making prosperity the anchor of the Political provides for an inclusive shared purpose, direction, and even vigour to democratic politics and collective action. But imaginaries of prosperity also need democratic institutions to maintain their (for lack of a better term) 'output legitimacy' and, ultimately, stability. Democratic institutions and processes, aided by scientific knowledge, are the most effective vehicles to uncover prosperity's constitutive outsides: that is problems, issues, grievances, and constituencies that have been left out of the definition of what prosperity means or how to get there. It is critical, however, that when these outsides are discovered, they are also genuinely incorporated via democratic process – otherwise, the imaginary of prosperity will cease to fulfil its integrative function and faith in democratic institutions will diminish.

Third, if we do not see a *democratic transition* to a new imaginary of prosperity, we may expect a gradual dissolution of democratic societies due to the rise of tribal imaginaries, which aim at a very different mode of social integration. Such imaginaries rely on specific identity markers as social glue, making identity – rather than prosperity – the anchor of the Political.[18] Pluralism, democratic institutions, checks and balances, scientific knowledge, and critical media will be often seen as obstacles to such a form of social integration, because they *disrupt* what should hold society together, such as long-held values, traditions, family, common sense, or the authority of a leader. Tribal imaginaries also do not need democratic process (broadly understood) as a means to improve their 'output legitimacy', as the *'failure to deliver real benefits to one's community is forgivable so long as the other side is faring worse'*.[19] What is more, I fear, war as a tool of diversion and/or a growth strategy is a far more acceptable option in this type of imaginaries.

1.1 On Prosperity

But is prosperity really what we need to hold onto going forward? This may seem like a dubious suggestion given that our current conception of prosperity implies very unsustainable forms of material consumption.

---

[18] Sergei Guriev and Elias Papaioannou, 'The Political Economy of Populism', *Journal of Economic Literature* 60, no. 3 (1 September 2022): 753–832.

[19] Fintan O'Toole, 'Review of *Defying Tribalism*, by Susan Neiman', *The New York Review of Books* (2 November 2023), www.nybooks.com/articles/2023/11/02/defying-tribalism-left-is-not-woke-neiman/, last accessed 16 January 2024.

I want to argue, however, that this is a historically specific and very narrow understanding of what prosperity has stood for, and still stands for, today. If anything, neoliberal imaginaries may have helped us forget that prosperity is more than (over)consumption.[20]

Prosperity, as 'the good that we hope for' (from the Latin *pro/sperare*),[21] has always been about more than just material affluence. While a certain degree of comfort and material affluence is important for a good quality of life, it is only a part of the story. Next to material goods, prosperity requires a plethora of social goods (such as healthy relations, social standing and recognition, having meaning and purpose, caring for others, and being cared for) as well as institutional goods (including personal security, a degree of autonomy and voice in collective matters, health and education, rewarding work and sufficient leisure, non-corrupt institutions, etc.). Fundamentally, more than any current level of such goods, prosperity is about collective *trust* that people have a prosperous future ahead, as society has both institutions and means to get there.

When 'millennials' complain today about the fact that they are 'worse off than their parents',[22] they don't ask for luxuries, but for the basic conditions for a meaningful social life being met, today and in the future. They demand a certain material basis for life (work, housing, healthcare, and transport), a certain social basis for life (conditions to start a family, healthy relations, and acceptance in a community), and an institutional basis (competent and trustworthy public institutions and services).[23] What seems less decisive for their discontent today is whether they are *actually* materially worse off than their parents were at the same age[24] and more that they seem to have lost faith that society has the means to secure a safe and prosperous future.[25]

---

[20] Robert D. Putnam, *Bowling Alone: The Collapse and Revival of American Community* (Simon & Schuster, 2000).

[21] Tim Jackson, *Prosperity without Growth: Foundations for the Economy of Tomorrow* (Taylor & Francis, 2016).

[22] Matthew Elliot, 'European Millennials Expect a Worse Life than Their Parents, Survey Shows', *Youth Time Magazine* (2018), https://youthtimemag.com/dashed-dreams-european-millennials-expect-a-worse-life-than-their-parents-survey-shows/, last accessed 30 December 2023.

[23] Kate Alexander Shaw, *Baby Boomers versus Millennials: Rhetorical Conflicts and Interest* (Sheffield Political Economy Research Institute (SPERI), 2018).

[24] Roula Khalaf, 'Millennials Are Not as Badly Off as They Think – But Success Is Bittersweet', *FT* (2023), www.ft.com/content/6f7d7522-42e9-43cb-bd73-36eeee6681f3e, last accessed 30 December 2023.

[25] Jean Twenge, 'The Myth of the Broke Millennial: After a Rough Start, the Generation Is Thriving. Why Doesn't It Feel that Way?', *Atlantic* (2023), www.theatlantic.com/magazine/archive/2023/05/millennial-generation-financial-issues-income-homeowners/673485/, last accessed 23 June 2024.

While the meaning – the expectations – as to what prosperity comprises may not have changed dramatically between different generations,[26] we have seen dramatic changes in *how* prosperity was to be realised over time. The most fundamental shift was in the understanding of how political economy works and which actors (public or private) were best placed to deliver prosperity. For instance, the post-war imaginary of prosperity can be tagged as 'public Keynesianism', with the state responsible for ensuring prosperity by safeguarding safe middle-class jobs and collectively delivering public services and social security. In contrast, the 'privatised Keynesianism' of the neoliberal era[27] aimed to deliver prosperity by reliance on private actors, markets, competition, and credit, which were meant to introduce dynamism in both the public and private sectors, while delivering an abundance of cheap consumer goods and services.

These modes of pursuing prosperity are not without consequence. The privatising push of the neoliberal era has seen many material and immaterial goods on which prosperity depends (from housing to care and transport) commodified, privatised, and financialised. The ethics of competition and market, while perhaps introducing more dynamism at first, has over time exhausted many of the social, institutional, and infrastructural resources, making the *security* of well-being in the future (care, trust, community, and safety) seem available only to those who have the resources to buy it.[28] Even if some of the social and economic strains produced by these trends were relieved by reducing the cost of consumer goods, this was only a temporary fix – which in turn heightened both social and environmental extraction across the world, accelerating the environmental crisis.[29]

The evaporating promise of privatised prosperity has brought us to a crossroads, with two collective imaginaries competing: the ultimate question is whether we will manage to stay "in the corridor"[30] with some version of shared prosperity or whether we will slide towards

---

[26] This is not to say that there were no changes, however, as some critics have pointed out. Putnam, *Bowling Alone*.

[27] Crouch, 'Privatised Keynesianism'.

[28] Robert D. Putnam, *The Upswing: How America Came Together a Century Ago and How We Can Do It Again* (Simon & Schuster, 2020).

[29] Hoesung Lee et al., 'IPCC, 2023: Climate Change 2023: Synthesis Report, Summary for Policymakers. Contribution of Working Groups I, II and III to the Sixth Assessment Report of the Intergovernmental Panel on Climate Change [Core Writing Team, H. Lee and J. Romero (eds.)], IPCC, Geneva, Switzerland' (2023), https://mural.maynoothuniversity.ie/17886/.

[30] Daron Acemoglu and James A. Robinson, *Why Nations Fail: The Origins of Power, Prosperity, and Poverty* (Profile Books, 2012).

tribalism, as the other collective imaginary holds – with the destination unknown. What will be decisive, I argue, is the role that the EU will play in the upcoming years and decades.

1.2 On the Role of the EU

The slide towards tribalism is in full course in Europe. In several European countries, far or extreme right parties are at present in power or in government. Where they are not, their electoral chances are considerable in any upcoming elections. They are also expected to become a significant force in the European Parliament in 2024,[31] all the while the EU is preparing for another round of austerity.[32] This constellation will remind many of the 1930s of the previous century.

But there is something different this time around. We have the EU. While certainly flawed, in terms of its democratic credentials,[33] constitutional asymmetry,[34] or overenthusiasm for the 'integration through law',[35] a perfect polity is not a serious expectation anyway.[36] The EU is, I would argue, well positioned to develop a new imaginary of prosperity

---

[31] The concerns about the outcomes of the 2024 elections are growing, especially given the electoral results over the past couple of years in Italy, Sweden, Finland, and most recently the Netherlands. This is not even to mention the polling lead of Marine Le Pen in France, of the growing popularity of the AFD in Germany.

[32] Gabriel et al., 'The Political Costs of Austerity'; Galofré-Vilà et al., *The Journal of Economic History*; Ponticelli and Voth, 'Austerity and Anarchy'; Galofré-Vilà et al., Working Paper; Funke et al., 'Going to Extremes'.

[33] Dieter Grimm, 'Does Europe Need a Constitution?', *European Law Journal* 1, no. 3 (November 1995): 282–302; Jürgen Habermas, 'Remarks on Dieter Grimm's "Does Europe Need a Constitution?"', *European Law Journal* 1, no. 3 (1995): 303–7; A. Føllesdal and S. Hix, 'Why There Is a Democratic Deficit in the EU: A Response to Majone and Moravcsik', *JCMS: Journal of Common Market Studies* 44, no. 3 (2006): 533–62; A. Moravcsik, 'The Myth of Europe's Democratic Deficit', *Intereconomics* 43, no. 6 (2008): 331–40; Marija Bartl, 'The Way We Do Europe: Subsidiarity and the Substantive Democratic Deficit', *European Law Journal* 21, no. 1 (2015): 23–43.

[34] F. W. Scharpf, 'The Asymmetry of European Integration, or Why the EU Cannot Be a "Social Market Economy"', *Socio-Economic Review* 8, no. 2 (2010): 211–50; Scharpf, 'Monetary Union, Fiscal Crisis and the Preemption of Democracy', LEQS Paper No. 36, 2011.

[35] Mauro Cappelletti, Monica Seccombe, and Joseph Weiler, *Integration through Law: Europe and the American Federal Experience* (De Gruyter, 1985); Daniel Augenstein, *Integration through Law Revisited: The Making of the European Polity* (Ashgate Publishing, 2012).

[36] Noam Chomsky, 'The Corporate Takeover of U.S. Democracy', PhilPapers (2010), https://philpapers.org/rec/CHOTCT; Jan Rosset, Nathalie Giger, and Julian Bernauer, 'More Money, Fewer Problems? Cross-Level Effects of Economic Deprivation on Political Representation', *West European Politics* 36, no. 4 (July 2013): 817–35; Sheldon Whitehouse, *Captured: The Corporate Infiltration of American Democracy* (The New Press, 2019).

for several reasons: it is a deeply diverse and pluralist polity, with a layer of democratic and expert institutions that require a considerable degree of deliberation, negotiation, and consensus to act. The EU is also an entity *constitutionally committed* to having questions of prosperity at the centre of the Political.[37] At the same time, the EU is not able to muster a credible *tribal imaginary* that could become the anchor of its internal politics.[38]

Importantly, embracing *shared prosperity* may also be the EU's only alternative. If the EU continues the (modified) neoliberal path, it will only further exacerbate already existing problems, while strengthening the far and extreme right. And the far and extreme right has no real use for the EU. The second path could be to wait it out and let tribalism play out at the national level. But judging on historical experience, this is a risky path – not to mention that the EU was established in order to prevent the horrors that preceded its founding. Finally, the EU can still attempt to make serious strides to articulate and institute an imaginary of *shared prosperity*, which can offer responses to the many excesses of neoliberalism, start a new phase in integration, and ultimately set grounds for the protection and deepening of democratic institutions in Europe.

But the likelihood of success will depend on the political courage among EU institutions and politicians, as well as the representatives of the EU MSs in the Council.[39] First, they will have to keep their "eyes on the ball", focusing on articulating and instituting the best route to prosperity, rather than letting identity themes become central. Second, the EU institutions will have to genuinely stand up for those pulling the short straw in the current economic constellation, be they peripheral EU MSs or less privileged groups in society. Third, the EU institutions will have to take the rule of law issues more seriously: the continuous degradation of democratic institutions and the rule of law in several MSs would make the EU increasingly unable to act.[40] This issue should

---

[37] Jiří Přibáň, *Constitutional Imaginaries: A Theory of European Societal Constitutionalism* (Routledge, 2021).

[38] The attempts to promote 'European way of life' have certainly fallen flat not only among its populace. At the same time, what can be mustered of tribalism externally can hardly become the anchor of internal politics, due to the degree of diversity and pluralism in the EU. See https://commission.europa.eu/strategy-and-policy/priorities-2019-2024/promoting-our-european-way-life_en.

[39] I discuss the institutional and political economic 'lock-ins' that stand in the way of a new imaginary of prosperity in Section 2.3.4.

[40] For the overview of possible options, see Carlos Closa, Dimitry Kochenov, and Joseph H. H. Weiler, 'Reinforcing Rule of Law Oversight in the European Union', *Robert Schuman Centre for Advanced Studies Research Paper*, no. 2014/25 (2014).

not be a question of political partisanship; all parties of the broad centre must see this as their political priority.

1.2.1 Where Are We Now?

The need to shift to a new imaginary of prosperity has not gone unnoticed in the EU. From 2018, we see first the proliferation of the language of "new deals" in the EU, including a 'New Deal for Consumers',[41] and then – more importantly – the 2019 European Green Deal (EGD).[42] The latter EGD sets out big goals: it aims to be a 'new growth strategy' that places environmental sustainability at the centre of *economic policy*. The EU thus aims to integrate one fundamental constitutive outside – nature – into how we think about political economy in the EU, requiring the transformation of the ways in which we both *'produce and consume'*.[43] Granted, the EGD still places a lot of trust in private actors and (financial) markets, as "partners" in the shift to a more sustainable future, while the more social aspects of sustainability remain too peripheral.[44] But what the implementation of the EGD did and still does is chip away at the neoliberal background understanding of political economy. The EU institutions have started to embrace a more institutionalist view of the economy, going beyond "win-win" politics of common interest, increasingly understanding the government (including themselves) as responsible also for distributive outcomes and using the normative power of law to reshape them.[45] And the EGD does not stand alone: the EU's response to the COVID-19 crisis and energy crisis related to the war in Ukraine was to put in place instruments based on solidarity between EU citizens and EU MSs (e.g. the Next Generation EU[46] or REPower EU[47]).

But these first 'gains' are anything but stable. The currently negotiated EU fiscal framework threatens to seriously undermine what still remains

---

[41] European Commission, A New Deal for Consumers, COM(2018) 0183 final.
[42] European Commission, The European Green Deal, COM(2019) 640 final.
[43] European Green Deal 2019, p. 4.
[44] See for both critiques 'EuroMemorandum 2020: A Green New Deal for Europe – Opportunities and Challenges', EuroMemo Group (2019), www.euromemo.eu/euromemorandum/euromemorandum_2020/index.html, last accessed 16 January 2024.
[45] The shift in such background assumptions appears in all empirical chapters, if to a different degree.
[46] European Commission, Europe's Moment: Repair and Prepare for the Next Generation, COM(2020) 456 final.
[47] European Commission, REPowerEU: Joint European Action for More Affordable, Secure, and Sustainable Energy, COM(2022) 108 final.

of solidarity within and among MSs, possibly further pushing people into the embrace of the extreme right.[48] Also support for the EGD policies is weakening, with hollowed-out nature law[49] and measures to limit the use of pesticides being pushed entirely off the table.[50] So why, if at all, should we still be hopeful that the EU could help articulate and institute a new imaginary of prosperity?

Over the past years, European institutions have taken steps to reshape the micro foundations of the economy. These steps have gone beyond 'market regulation', attempting to reconstitute corporation, reshape industry, and encourage new ways of production and consumption. These are in no way insignificant efforts. First, at the level of the *imaginary*, these efforts rest on a different understanding of political economy than the neoliberal one. They take a more institutionalist view of the economy, go beyond politics of common interest, adopt a more interventionist understanding of law, and see EU institutions as co-responsible for distributive outcomes. Second, at the level of the *institution* of a new imaginary, the EU has proposed legislation and provided (some) public resources to reshape important microeconomic foundations, with the aim of shifting us towards more caring consumption, more responsible corporations, cleaner industries, or more sustainable products.[51] Creating new ways for acting in the world, individually and collectively, is a fundamental precondition to instituting a different kind of political economy.

The real concern that one should have is whether the EU has gone far enough, quickly enough, in creating building blocks, both imaginary and real, that can help usher a new imaginary of prosperity. Is the 'right to repair'[52] or the protection against greenwashing enough to shift our (over)consumption patterns? Can the due diligence legislation[53] really

---

[48] Simone Cremaschi et al., 'Geographies of Discontent: Public Service Deprivation and the Rise of the Far Right in Italy', Working Paper (2023).

[49] Elena Sánchez Nicolás, 'Negotiators Finally Clinch Deal on Landmark Nature Restoration Law', *EU Observer* (2023), https://euobserver.com/green-economy/157677, last accessed 16 January 2024.

[50] Bartosz Brzeziński, 'Conservative Backlash Kills Off EU's Green Deal Push to Slash Pesticide Use', *Politico* (2023), www.politico.eu/article/european-parliament-kills-off-landmark-pesticide-reduction-bill/, last accessed 16 January 2024.

[51] I discuss those in the empirical chapters.

[52] European Commission, Proposal for a Directive of the European Parliament and of the Council on common rules promoting the repair of goods and amending Regulation (EU) 2017/2394, Directives (EU) 2019/771, and (EU) 2020/1828, COM(2023) 155 final.

[53] Proposal for a Directive of the European Parliament and of the Council on Corporate Sustainability Due Diligence and amending Directive (EU) 2019/1937, COM(2022) 71 final.

succeed in redesigning corporation, even if it does not engage with the fundamentals (power, ownership, and profit)? Can we develop a credible industrial policy in Europe, without making crucial choices about technological futures a subject of broader democratic debate? How much critical raw materials can we extract, and under what conditions, in order to make sure that the new imaginary of prosperity does not end up being just another form of "green" extractivism for those born outside EU borders?[54] And the million-dollar question, to what extent can the transformation of micro foundations in fact stand against major changes at the macro level, such as those concerning fiscal or monetary policies?

These questions have no easy answers. Clearly, these shifts are arguably too "fresh" to have entrenched more deeply a different imaginary of prosperity in the EU's political institutions and discourses, as various developments on the macro level (e.g. the currently renegotiated Stability and Growth Pact) make clear. They are also too shallow to have actually provided a basis for different microeconomic institutions to enable the emergence of a different political economy from the bottom up. But unless rolled back, they do create a springboard from which the EU can continue a democratic transition to shared prosperity. The rest will depend on the understanding of historical responsibility and political courage of the very institutions and actors that many have (often justifiably) grown distrustful of.

1.3 Conceptual Framework

Let me add a couple of words on my conceptual framework. This book relies on the concept of 'social imaginaries'. In one famous definition, social imaginaries denote *'the ways people imagine their social existence, how they fit together with others, how things go on between them and their fellows, the expectations that are normally met, and the deeper normative notions and images that underlie these expectations'*.[55] Social imaginaries are central to social integration, resting on cultural and institutional frameworks that enable understanding, cooperation, and collective action.[56] They integrate at the level of 'imaginary' (including stories, myths, ideas, theories, and

---

[54] Natacha Bruna, 'A Climate-Smart World and the Rise of Green Extractivism', *The Journal of Peasant Studies* 49, no. 4 (2022): 839–64.
[55] Charles Taylor, *Modern Social Imaginaries* (Duke University Press, 2004), p. 23.
[56] Paul Ricoeur, *Lectures on Ideology and Utopia*, ed. George H. Taylor, Reprint (Columbia University Press, 1986).

utopias) and at the level of 'institution' (for instance, via laws, governmental bodies, institutional processes, or social practices – such as economic practices, family, or travelling).[57]

Over the past 150 years (at least), I argue that it was the social imaginaries of *prosperity* that have most often performed this socially integrative function, at least in the countries of the Global North. Imaginaries of prosperity have integrated around the promise of a prosperous future, placing the problems (and struggles) of political economy in the centre of the political. Importantly, the demand for prosperity has over time made democracy and its institutions (such as pluralism, critical media, scientific knowledge, and 'inclusive public sphere') functionally important for the social order instituted around prosperity. Democratic institutions (broadly understood) created various channels through which prosperity's *constitutive outsides* could reshape the *meaning* and the *route* to prosperity.[58] Democracy in this sense becomes not only "nice to have" but (and increasingly so over time) also fundamental for continuous integration around imaginaries of prosperity.[59]

Importantly, every historical incarnation of the imaginaries of prosperity will only be able to provide a *temporary* foundation for social integration in modern societies.[60] We have thus seen the oscillation between two (ideal) types of imaginaries of prosperity over the past 150 years – I will call them *privatised* and *shared* – returning in different incarnations in different historical periods. The two basic imaginaries of prosperity embrace the opposite understanding of the relationship between the economic and the political, or the state and the market. In imaginaries of *shared prosperity*, economy and markets are understood as (human-made) social institutions that need to be shaped politically – if prosperity is to be delivered to all. In contrast, in imaginaries of *privatised prosperity*, economy and markets are seen as self-regulating, nature-like systems and processes that in principle function optimally and need

---

[57] Ngai-Ling Sum and Bob Jessop, *Towards a Cultural Political Economy: Putting Culture in Its Place in Political Economy* (Edward Elgar Publishing, 2013).
[58] On the concerns about the continuous capacity of democratic institutions today to provide this function, see Jürgen Habermas, *A New Structural Transformation of the Public Sphere and Deliberative Politics* (John Wiley & Sons, 2023).
[59] For an extensive general treatment, see Robert A. Dahl, *On Democracy* (Yale University Press, 2020).
[60] Oliver Marchart, *Post-Foundational Political Thought: Political Difference in Nancy, Lefort, Badiou and Laclau* (Edinburgh University Press, 2007).

little steering to deliver prosperity to all.⁶¹ The *route* to prosperity then, in either of these imaginaries, requires *empowering* different sets of actors (be it private actors and capital on the one hand or democratic institutions on the other) to drive us to prosperity. Such choices have important implications on a procedural level (what role is assigned to democratic institutions and law) and on a material level (the relation to economic outcomes and particular groups and actors (e.g. workers, financial capital, and trade unions)).

An instituted imaginary of prosperity has thus its "life cycle" so to say, which operates at the level of the *imaginary* and the level of the *instituted*.⁶² At the height of its life cycle, an instituted imaginary of prosperity has a quasi-hegemony, mustering large social consensus around its route to prosperity, while engendering optimism and hope in a better future among broad swaths of society.⁶³ At this point, its institution in various laws, bodies, and practices have already progressed enough to give people a sense that their social institutions know how, and are able to, deliver prosperity. If it so wishes, in these periods the government will be able to undertake massive transformations with significant social support.

Every such hegemony has, however, a limited lifespan. At a certain point, the aspects of reality that were left unattended by any particular imaginary of prosperity will rear their head. At such a point in time, the established imaginary of prosperity will slowly run out of steam if from within its understanding of political economy, no effective solutions to the emergent problems can be found, gradually eroding the trust in its route to prosperity.⁶⁴ Increasingly thus, the imaginary of prosperity will not be able to fulfil its socially integrative function. In these crucial moments, democratic institutions have to do their work, reinventing

---

[61] Such as limiting 'information asymmetries' or removing (rather selectively) 'market failures'.

[62] This operation at the level of the imaginary (stories, ideas, and utopias) and at the level of instituted (laws, bodies, discourse, and practices) may operate within a different time horizon, with the latter 'slowing down' the former. See Chapter 6.

[63] Neoliberalism is best understood as the last instituted 'imaginary of prosperity', a historically specific synthesis of how political economy *works together* and *should work together* in order to deliver prosperity. To institute a neoliberal society, neoliberalism provided a story that made the new interpretation of the political (economy, politics, law, and government) cogent, replacing the understandings present before.
Neoliberalism became hegemonic in the EU at the end of the 1990s; it reached a major blow with the great financial crisis in 2008.

[64] See Section 6.3.

and gradually instituting a *new, credible, imaginary of prosperity*.[65] If this does not happen, for the reasons of capture, for instance,[66] prosperity will cease to be able to ensure social integration, and societies will increasingly experience signs of *societal disintegration:* as we see perhaps most glaringly in the US,[67] but increasingly also in Europe and the rest of the world.[68] Eventually, we may see reintegration around some sort of tribal identity shared by the majority – with grim consequences for minorities, pluralism, inclusion, 'human rights', critical media, knowledge governance, and ultimately democratic institutions.

1.4 Structure and Choices

When writing a book such as this one, one has to make many choices, and even more concessions. In what follows, I will first outline the set-up of the book and then articulate some of the parameters and limits of the account presented. Chapter 2 presents the conceptual framework of the book. I start by discussing the main concept on which I rely, namely 'social imaginaries', trying to unpack when social imaginaries are vulnerable to change (Section 2.2). I turn then to discuss the imaginaries of *prosperity*, setting out the limits of the contemporary reading of prosperity, the dialectics between privatised and shared prosperity, and tribalism as the prosperity's *Other* (Section 2.3). The chapter concludes by discussing the kind of *constitutive outsides* that have reared their head as crises at the present moment and which will need to be integrated into the new imaginary of prosperity if it is to provide a credible prospect of a liveable future (Section 2.4).

After setting the scene, the book turns to study how the imaginaries of prosperity have been changing in the EU, as well as the contours that any new imaginary may be taking. In Chapter 3, I explore the transformations of EU imaginaries of consumption. I study systematically the changes in EU consumer policy, that is how the background understandings of the role of economy, law, government, and politics have changed from 1975 to the present day. The chapter allows us to observe a deep epistemic and ontological shift, from a more institutionalist understanding of consumption that typified the welfare state imaginaries of

---

[65] Such a conception of prosperity will have to start, however, from a different articulation of the relations between the state and the market, between politics and the economy.
[66] See Footnote 32.   [67] Ezra Klein, *Why We're Polarized* (Simon & Schuster, 2020).
[68] Polarisation is perhaps one of the most used words in the Dutch parliament.

prosperity to a more individualised, depoliticised, and naturalised[69] understanding that is typical of imaginaries of privatised prosperity. Theoretically, the chapter also allows us to appreciate what it takes to institutionalise a new imaginary of prosperity. It requires years for the new imaginary to reshape the background understandings of all the aspects of social order. But once such understandings become sufficiently dominant and settled, one can observe a qualitative shift in the narrative, which becomes both elegant and confident – as it needs to no longer pay lip service to normative concerns that were important under the previous paradigm.

Chapters 4–6 take up other important microeconomic foundations, that is technology (ecodesign), industry, and corporation. The chapters mostly focus on the transformations in the EU's laws and policies after the 2008 great financial crisis. We can observe that until long into the 2010s, the EU remained vested in the neoliberal imaginary of prosperity, but with ever less conviction and compass as the time passed by. This would change after the 2019 EGD and the COVID-19 crisis. The changes seem to have been driven mostly by the growing realisation that our consumption and production patterns are (foremost environmentally) unsustainable. Thus, the EU increasingly aims to steer production towards the principles of circularity, through clear public guidance on how products should be designed (Chapter 4). Equally, safe technological and climate futures cannot be delivered by market alone; therefore governmental and legal intervention and support are necessary to get industry into the twenty-first century (Chapter 5). Finally, the realisation that corporations are systematically pushed towards short-termism rather than a long-term perspective demanded intervention – not only in the interest of the public but also in corporations' own interest (Chapter 6). The conclusion looks back on the main findings and tries to both summarise the background shifts in understandings and values and distil some basic building blocks of the new imaginary of prosperity in the EU. The conclusion also presents the road ahead – outlining what it would mean for the EU institutions to take their historical responsibility at this point seriously.

Now to parameters and limits. While this book aims to discern certain patterns of change, it cannot predict the future. After doing the empirical research, I hold no doubt that the shifts and policy changes that we

---

[69] By *naturalising*, I mean seeing social phenomena as given (by God or (human) nature), and thus also stable, and perhaps even intrinsically good. See Section 2.2.

have seen over the past couple of years indeed start from a different synthesis of political economy, a different imaginary of prosperity. But one cannot conclude on this basis a) how broadly this new imaginary is shared and whether it can last in the face of the growing influence of the extreme right, b) how far the changes already instituted will enable a different type of private action, and finally c) whether the EU will take additional steps, even if just by addressing the low-hanging fruit I outline, that would help to render more viable the new imaginary of prosperity.

Second, this is a book written by a lawyer. This will usually mean that law and policy will serve as a very important heuristic tool. But this is also a book about law, I want to suggest, even if not on its face. Law – in the sense of the 'democratic rule of law' – is a central element of 'modern social imaginary'.[70] The three competing imaginaries that I discuss throughout the book have very different relations to law. Imaginaries of prosperity – privatised and shared – build on the modern conception of the democratic rule of law, but at the same time they give rise to very different legalities that are co-constitutive of different routes to prosperity. Tribal imaginaries, in contrast, do not share the same commitment to the democratic rule of law, which is often seen as an unnecessary impediment to the rule of (whatever sized) majority. Overall, law is seen in this book as central both at the level of the *imaginary*, allowing us to interpret the dominant social imaginaries, and at the level of the *institution*, being one of the most important tools that shapes how we (can) go about our lives.

In terms of the selection of empirical chapters, many more micro- or meso economic foundations could have been added. Just consider the centrality of finance, work, or trade and investment for the issues I discuss in this book. I have attempted to integrate some of the important considerations related to these fields in the chapters on industry (Chapter 5) and corporation (Chapter 6), but clearly a separate reflection on the changing imaginaries of prosperity in these fields would have added granularity to our understanding of the contours of the emergent imaginary of prosperity. Equally, choosing to focus on micro- and meso (in the case of industry) economic foundations of the economy, instead of on the macro level of political economy, is a limit, as the more 'political' or 'inter-governmental' aspects of the EU (such as the recently renewed

---

[70] Taylor, *Modern Social Imaginaries*.

regressive fiscal pact[71]) could undo many of the gains that have been made thus far. Finally, the discussion of tribal imaginaries is based mostly on secondary literature (theoretical and empirical), as the EUs focus in the selected fields does not easily allow for the study of tribal imaginaries empirically. Such limits of scope are, I would hope, excusable as inherent in any intellectual attempt that tries to make a theoretical and empirical contribution at the same time.

There are also other possible concerns with the choices I have made. For instance, I study in this book various policy fields. But clearly one could dispute whether certain policy fields themselves should be part of the new imaginary of prosperity. Just consider consumer law and policy – isn't the rights-based consumer law exactly the problem? And yet, as this book is trying to map the "actually existing" ways of doing things, and how they change, it cannot start from any ideal normative conclusions. As societies, we have to move from a rights-based consumer law and policy, for instance, to a different way of thinking about consumption – and this is, I am glad to report, exactly what we are starting to observe in the context of EU consumer policy.

Also, lawyers may object that law and legal institutions do not receive sufficient credit at times. For instance, if in Chapter 3 on consumption I already acknowledge that the Court of Justice of the EU has never fully *bought into* the Commission's attempts to neoliberalise EU consumer law, why give such prominence to policy rather than law and to the Commission instead of the Court? For two reasons, at least. First, given the Commission's lack of formal legislative power beyond agenda-setting powers, the Commission must tread carefully in order to convince the European legislator (Council of Ministers and the European Parliament), and numerous other stakeholders, of both what plays in society and what should be done about it. This means that when developing its policy ideas, the Commission is always trying to sway the greatest number of 'stakeholders', articulating therefore carefully what it sees as shared. Second, by focusing in one chapter on a single type of document, produced by the same actor, for the same purpose, over a long period of time, I could also study more systematically the core changes in the conceptions of economy, law, politics, government, subjects, or society in the EU, thus being able to identify trends and important turning points in the institution of neoliberal imaginary of prosperity. The focus

---

[71] Wester Van Gaal, 'EU Secures Last-minute Deal on New fiscal Rules', *EU Observer* (2023), https://euobserver.com/green-economy/157867, last accessed 16 January 2024.

on the Court would not allow for such an approach, as it comes into play much later and with regard to a limited number of issues, all the while being subject to selection bias problems of its own.[72]

Finally, as most books that aim to make a more general argument, this book may leave the reader with more questions than answers. My sincere hope is, that those will be the right questions.

---

[72] Deborah L. Rhode, 'Access to Justice', *Fordham Law Review* 69 (2000): 1785.

2 Imaginaries of Prosperity

2.1 Introduction

How does one study what comes after 'neoliberalism'? The challenge that one faces, I would suggest, is first to identify what (if anything) neoliberalism is, in order to articulate what it would take to change it. Neoliberalism is many things to many people: an ideology,[1] a paradigm,[2] a rationality,[3] a governmentality,[4] a conspiracy,[5] and more. And there shall be no doubt that there are aspects to what we call neoliberalism that squarely fit some of these concepts.

Yet at the same time, all these understandings undersell what has made neoliberalism *stick*. Critics understood its importance in having reshaped everything from state institutions, public services, the ways in which business is conducted, to how we understand ourselves as human beings. What they tended to overlook was its socially integrative function. As any 1980s or 1990s native would keenly remember, neoliberalism gave many people across the world a sense of optimism, while also providing a clear direction to democratic politics and governmental action (Section 2.2).

---

[1] David Harvey, *A Brief History of Neoliberalism* (Oxford University Press, 2005); Slavoj Zizek, *The Sublime Object of Ideology* (Verso Books, 2019).

[2] Poul F. Kjaer, *The Law of Political Economy: Transformation in the Function of Law* (Cambridge University Press, 2020).

[3] Marija Bartl, 'Internal Market Rationality, Private Law and the Direction of the Union: Resuscitating the Market as the Object of the Political', *European Law Journal*, 21, no. 5 (15 January 2015): 572–98.

[4] Michel Foucault, *The Birth of Biopolitics: Lectures at the Collège de France, 1978–1979* (Picador, 2010).

[5] Belen Balanya et al., *Europe Inc.: Regional & Global Restructuring and the Rise of Corporate Power* (Pluto Press, 2000).

There is little doubt, however, that neoliberalism (or any other imaginary of prosperity for that matter) has had a beginning and thus it will also have an end. In the EU, neoliberalism reached the peak of its integrative function between the end of the 1990s and the great financial crisis of 2008. It provided a temporary basis for societal integration around an imaginary of prosperity that advocated the empowering of capital, market, and competition as the best route to prosperity. As its integrative functions weakened after the 2008 crisis, we should have seen a democratic transition to a new imaginary of prosperity (Section 2.2).

Yet the democratic shift to a new imaginary of prosperity – the same one that took place in the 1970s and 1980s to neoliberalism – has not taken place (yet). Instead, in the years following the great financial crisis, political institutions and actors have doubled down on the neoliberal imaginary of prosperity, taunting its successes – while neglecting that there is a growing number of people whose reality had little in common with the official story of economic recovery and prosperity[6] (Section 2.2).

This institutional drift fostered a growing mistrust in the chosen route to prosperity, and the institutions that advocated it, with modern societies gradually losing the (always temporary) *shared* foundation around which they were constituted. The mistrust, however, undermines the basic constitutional structures and values of liberal democracies, through polarisation, conspiracies, and a growing sympathy for authoritarianism. Many new tribal imaginaries that are anti-democratic (nativism, supremacist thinking, revisionist imperialism, or religious fundamentalism) have emerged and even booked electoral successes, in Europe and elsewhere. But these imaginaries cannot provide, I argue, a stable foundation for modern societies, as they neither aim to provide solutions to problems they face nor deal with the inescapable pluralism of modern societies (Section 2.3).

What is needed to replace a neoliberal imaginary of prosperity is again a new, *credible imaginary of prosperity*. Fundamentally, we should not mistake prosperity for economic growth. Or material consumption. Prosperity, I want to argue, is an understanding of political economy that lays out a credible route to material and social basis of a good life, today and in the future, for oneself and one's children and grandchildren. 'Pro/sperare' – or that what we hope for – should thus *not* be reduced to the historically limited, and perhaps even empirically

---

[6] Andrew Haldane, 'Whose Recovery?', Speech at the Bank of England, 2016. Available at www.bankofengland.co.uk/speech/2016/whose-recovery, last accessed 14 January 2024.

incorrect, understanding of prosperity as mass consumption[7] (Section 2.4).

It is important to realise that the new articulation of prosperity has not emerged only due to the unwillingness of institutions. In fact, unlike the (relatively) peaceful and smooth shift[8] to the neoliberal imaginary of privatised prosperity in the 1970s and 1980s, the shift to what should be a new imaginary of *shared* prosperity has serious countervailing forces. On the one hand, big capital, well-resourced and well-integrated into law-making, has benefited and continues to benefit from neoliberal prescriptions. On the other hand, the measures to make the economy more environmentally sustainable have thus far focused to a large degree on consumers and consumption, creating another rift – both ethical and distributive – among those who can and who cannot pay for sustainability (Section 2.2).

In this chapter, I aim to do several things. First, I will articulate why we should think in terms of 'social imaginaries', rather than other compelling concepts, as the temporarily shared foundations of modern society. I then go on to argue why in modernity it was the imaginaries of prosperity that provided the most stable foundations of social integration. I will argue that imaginaries of prosperity are both capable of bridging the plurality of positions and identities and at the same time playing into the strength of modernity, namely democracy and knowledge governance. However, particular imaginaries of prosperity are only temporary hegemonic articulations, as they will sooner or later produce too many constitutive outsides to be able to fulfil their integrative role. In such a case, when contradictions become apparent, they become subject to their own dialectics, between privatised and collective imaginaries of prosperity. If such a transition is not enabled via democratic channels, we may see illiberal and undemocratic tribal imaginaries taking hold.

2.2 Social Imaginaries

2.2.1 Defining Social Imaginaries

The question of what holds societies together, after the demise of God, has been the core question in social theory. Some thinkers contemplated

---

[7] Tim Jackson, *Prosperity without Growth: Foundations for the Economy of Tomorrow* (Taylor & Francis, 2016).
[8] Of course, in the US and the UK, we have seen rather violent suppression of labour unions and collective action.

social cohesion under modernity;[9] others, in a more critical tradition, stressed that social integration relies on deception, as ideology[10] and hegemony.[11] Social imaginaries are one entrance point to this discussion, which does not immediately place itself in either of these traditions and requires an "open mind" to consider how societies are actually instituted and changed.

For Castoriadis, societies do not emerge as products of historical necessity, but rather as the result of a radically new idea of the world, which, when 'signified' and 'instituted', provides society with '*singular ways of living, seeing and making its own existence*' in each historical period.[12] While no society can exist without a social imaginary, which enables 'symbolic mediation of action',[13] Ricoeur argues that the imagination of alternative ways of living is never as radically novel as Castoriadis suggests. Rather, novelty is always socially embedded, constituted, or 'pre-figured', by the elements of the old.[14] This does not, however, turn (re)imagination into imitation, but rather imagination remains 'productive'[15] as long as it is producing new meanings and ways of being, with the intention of imagining radical alternatives to the status quo.

In Anglo-American tradition, Benedict Anderson explores the making of nations and nation states, showing how nations were produced as 'Imagined Communities',[16] via historical memory, museums, maps, language, and other sociocultural artefacts.[17] In fact, the long arch of modernity can be seen as the imagination and institution of a particular

---

[9] Emile Durkheim, *The Division of Labour in Society*, trans. George Simpson (The Free Press of Glencoe, London 2015), http://archive.org/details/in.ernet.dli.2015.126617, last accessed 5 January 2024.

[10] Karl Marx and Friedrich Engels, *The German Ideology: Including Thesis on Feuerbach* (Prometheus Books, 1 November 1998); Zizek, *The Sublime Object of Ideology*.

[11] Antonio Gramsci, *Prison Notebooks: Selections* (International Publishers, 1971); Ernesto Laclau and Chantal Mouffe, *Hegemony and Socialist Strategy: Towards a Radical Democratic Politics* (Verso Books, 2014).

[12] Cornelius Castoriadis, *The Imaginary Institution of Society* (MIT Press, 1997), 465.

[13] Paul Ricoeur, *Lectures on Ideology and Utopia*, ed. George H. Taylor (Columbia University Press, 1986), 258.

[14] Suzi Adams, *Ricoeur and Castoriadis in Discussion: On Human Creation, Historical Novelty, and the Social Imaginary* (Rowman & Littlefield, 2017).

[15] The reference to productive as opposed to reproductive imagination goes back to Kant. J. Michael Young, 'Kant's View of Imagination', *Kant-Studien* 79, nos. 1–4 (1988): 140–64.

[16] Benedict Anderson, *Imagined Communities: Reflections on the Origin and Spread of Nationalism* (Verso Books, 2006).

[17] Anderson's book is one of the central texts in nationalism studies. It has, however, also influenced Science and Technologies Studies, and in particular its American (Jasanoff's) tradition, who will develop the concept of 'co-production' of the social and technical.

(Western) 'modern social imaginary'.[18] What Taylor calls 'modern social imaginary' stands for a moral and institutional order, instituted via several crucial political boundaries: between economy and politics, the separation of the public sphere as a space for non-dominated political communication, and finally the idea and practice of (collective) self-determination.

It is the first boundary, between economy and politics, that will later become the central subject of the work of political economists Sum and Jessop in their exploration of how 'economic imaginaries' co-constitute social whole. That academic intervention is part of a broader trend that appropriates the concept of social imaginaries outside of the general theory of society, in the fields of political science,[19] science and technology studies,[20] law,[21] and political economy.[22]

---

[18] Charles Taylor, *Modern Social Imaginaries* (Duke University Press, 2004).

[19] Paul Blokker, 'The Imaginary Constitution of Constitutions', *Social Imaginaries* 3, no. 1 (2017): 167–93; Blokker, 'Populism as a Constitutional Project', *International Journal of Constitutional Law* 17, no. 2 (2019): 536–53.

[20] The concept of 'sociotechnical imaginaries', for instance, has been used to articulate how 'innovative technological projects' are turned into the future social order. Such sociotechnical imaginaries are made, or instituted, in the exercise of both public and private power, via '*the selection of development priorities, the allocation of funds, the investment in material infrastructures, and the acceptance or suppression of political dissent*'. From Sheila Jasanoff and Sang-Hyun Kim, 'Containing the Atom: Sociotechnical Imaginaries and Nuclear Power in the United States and South Korea', *Minerva* 47, no. 2 (2009): 119–46. See also David J. Hess and Benjamin K. Sovacool, 'Sociotechnical Matters: Reviewing and Integrating Science and Technology Studies with Energy Social Science', *Energy Research & Social Science* 65 (1 July 2020).

[21] Jan Komárek, *European Constitutional Imaginaries: Between Ideology and Utopia* (Oxford University Press, 2023); Päivi Leino-Sandberg, 'Constitutional Imaginaries of Solidarity: Framing Fiscal Integration Post-NGEU' (University of Helsinki Working Paper, 2023), available at https://helda.helsinki.fi/bitstreams/6c044fbd-a8ee-4bb1-a884-baf52446888a/download; Valeria Ferrari, 'The Platformisation of Digital Payments: The Fabrication of Consumer Interest in the EU FinTech Agenda', *Computer Law & Security Review* 45 (2022); Marija Bartl, 'Imaginaries of Progress as Constitutional Imaginaries', in *European Constitutional Imaginaries: Between Ideology and Utopia* (Oxford University Press, 2021); Komárek, 'European Constitutional Imaginaries: Utopias, Ideologies and the Other', *SSRN Scholarly Paper* (Social Science Research Network, Rochester, NY, 29 October 2019).

[22] Being part of a broader 'cultural turn' in political economy, exploring the performative role of practices, institutions, and devices in the making of a particular type of economy, or a particular type of capitalism. See, for instance, Michel Callon, 'Introduction: The Embeddedness of Economic Markets in Economics', *The Sociological Review* 46, no. S1 (1998): 1–57; Donald MacKenzie and Yuval Millo, 'Constructing a Market, Performing Theory: The Historical Sociology of a Financial Derivatives Exchange', *American Journal of Sociology* 109, no. 1 (2003): 107–45.

Sum and Jessop understand economic imaginaries as 'semiotic ensembles' that reduce the complexity of the social world by focusing on *relevant* economic problems, relations, practices, spaces, and subjectivities. Such a reduction of complexity operates at the level of *imaginary* and at the level of *structures* (technologies, institutions, and actors), shaping the grounds for possible futures by setting '*limits to compossible combinations of social relations*'.[23] What is more, while such a reduction of complexity may be necessary to enable action, it remains a reduction – constituting often invisible but ultimately *constitutive* outsides, which strike back as a source of crises.

2.2.2 How Social 'Imaginaries' Change

While the aforementioned paragraphs introduce the reader to some of the core uses of the concept of social imaginaries, they say little about how imaginaries actually change. To do so, I will rely on the work of Paul Ricoeur on utopia and ideology: the two faces of social imaginary.[24] In '*Lectures on Ideology and Utopia*', Ricoeur describes utopias and ideologies as the emanation of the symbolic:[25] '*where human beings exist, a nonsymbolic mode of existance, and even less a nonsymbolic kind of action, can no longer* [obtain]'.[26] Like Mannheim, Ricoeur suggests that both ideology and utopia are deeply *social*, in the sense of being shared cultural templates. What distinguishes them is their main orientation: the orientation of ideology is towards the preservation of the status quo, whereas the orientation of utopia is towards the transformation of power relations.

Ricoeur goes on to develop his theory of social imaginaries on the basis of his engagement with several different thinkers, over the past 200 years. He starts with Karl Marx, who argues that ideologies operate to distort the meaning of human action, in order to facilitate the power and

---

[23] Ngai-Ling Sum and Bob Jessop, *Towards a Cultural Political Economy: Putting Culture in Its Place in Political Economy* (Edward Elgar Publishing, 2013).
[24] Ricoeur, *Lectures on Ideology and Utopia*.
[25] Ricoeur argues that symbolic systems are both external to the human being, inasmuch as they predate them, 'pre-figuring' the space for meaning making. However, at the same time, this externality is only apparent, since these symbolic systems are *constitutive* of the human being, a sine qua non of human existence. It is the faculty of imagination then through which we relate to such symbolic systems, not only to reproduce them ('reproductive imagination') but also to engage with them creatively ('productive imagination'). It is through such creative, transformative engagement in productive imagination that humans transform symbolic systems and their shared imaginaries (Ricoeur, *Lectures on Ideology and Utopia*, p. 258).
[26] Ricoeur, *Lectures on Ideology and Utopia*, p. 12.

domination of the ruling classes. Indeed, Ricoeur agrees that ideologies will often, perhaps most of the time, be deceptive, inasmuch as they aim to provide the surplus of meaning that should legitimate the power of the rulers. But this, Ricoeur suggests, is only one possible function of ideology. In fact, we need to understand its prior functions in order to appreciate when and why deception creeps in. Two other functions of ideology, from a more superficial to a more original one, are that of *legitimation* and, further, that of *social integration*.

To discuss the legitimatory role of ideology, Ricoeur relies on Max Weber and his conception of 'Herrschaft', or domination. On this account, we need to understand ideology in relation to legitimation, that is as a way to *motivate* obedience. Ideology provides a set of understandings that bridge the gap between *the claim to power* by the rulers on the one hand and *the actual belief* in the (legitimacy of that) power by the ruled on the other hand – a gap, which is always bigger than those in power would wish for. Ideology thus aims to produce justifications for the status quo, and it is in this sense an exercise in reproductive imagination.

On a deeper level, however, Ricoeur suggests that ideology has an integrative function as well. If symbolic systems that mediate human action are constitutive of human life, then there must be a moment when they mediate *truthfully*, without deception. To develop the integrative function of ideology, Ricoeur draws on the anthropologist Geertz, who argues that sharing a symbolic system is the resource that integrates a community.[27] In turn, once any community develops the class of the rulers and the class of the ruled, the legitimatory function of ideology emerges, with a heightened possibility of it becoming deception.

What distinguishes ideology from utopia, even in its more innocent version, are the properties of imagination. As ideology either aims to justify the status quo or give meaning to what is, it remains within the ambit of reproductive imagination, that is of *'derivative presentation of the object, which brings to mind an empirical intuition that it had previously'*.[28] Utopia, in contrast, is an exercise in 'productive imagination', meaning here *'an original presentation of the object'* that creates the conditions for further thinking.

---

[27] Ricoeur, like Lefort, suggests that it may not be suitable to talk about ideology when it comes to pre-modern communities, since ideology – as utopia – is a modern phenomenon, whose emergence should be properly placed in conflict with other ideologies and utopias.

[28] Young, 'Kant's View of Imagination'.

Ricoeur sees utopia as a particular kind of 'critique' – a critique that does not focus on uncovering the deceptions of ideology, but rather orients itself towards imagining a different reality. It is a glance at our reality 'from nowhere'[29] that everything in the status quo starts to look strange, nothing more can or needs to be taken for granted. In terms of subject matter, *'Utopia introduces imaginative variations on the topics of society, power, government, family, religion'*, presenting alternative ways of living.[30]

To discuss utopia, Ricoeur draws mainly on the work of Mannheim, underlying three important characteristics of utopia. First, utopia is social in that it expresses a *'structural condition of a particular group, a "social substratum,"*[31] *which espouses it'*.[32] This social substratum does not have to be only a class but can also represent another substratum – such as women, racialised peoples, and ethnic or religious minorities. Second, utopia needs to be seen as a particular mentality, a *Geist*, that permeates a whole range of ideas and feelings. It cannot be expressed in a propositional form, but rather it presents a symbolic system, a social imaginary, of its own. Third, like ideologies, utopias are always expressed as antagonism with regard to other utopias; thus they are a particularly modern phenomenon.

Ricoeur concludes his lectures by drawing out some important parallels between ideology and utopia. As ideology operates on three levels – distortion, legitimation, and integration – so does utopia operate on three levels. Where ideology distorts, utopia is a mere fancy, lacking the core dimension of realisability, even bordering on madness. Where ideology is concerned with legitimation, utopia is an alternative to the present power. At this level, utopia is always concerned with hierarchy. Finally, where ideology is about integration, and thus about the present identity of a person and a group, utopia presents the exploration of a possible, the *'lateral possibilities of reality'*,[33] *'identities in suspense'*.[34]

The *imaginaries of prosperity* that I discuss in this book are potentially both ideologies and utopias: they may have emerged as utopias and, if successful, end up as ideologies. At the moment, however, when they fail to fulfil their integrative function, that is, when they fail to be able to

---

[29] Ricoeur here refers to Thomas Moore's *Utopia*. Ricoeur, *Lectures on Ideology and Utopia*, pp. 16 and 17.
[30] Ricoeur, *Lectures on Ideology and Utopia*, pp. 16 and 17.
[31] A concept of class is here replaced with a particular 'social substratum', a concept that could include a broader range of groups, such as women, racialised peoples, and ethnic or religious minorities.
[32] Ricoeur, *Lectures on Ideology and Utopia*, p. 310.   [33] Ibid.   [34] Ibid., p. 311.

provide the basis for the ideological integration of a society, they will have to be gradually replaced with other imaginaries. There is no guarantee, however, that new social imaginaries will necessarily be what Ricoeur understands as utopias: products of productive (rather than reproductive) imagination that present alternative ways of being and aim to transform any current power relations. In moments of interregnum such as the present moment, actors may try to maintain social integration by providing imaginable and realisable fixes (social or technological) to the existing "system". Or offer imaginaries that are explicitly not aiming to reimagine society but instead aiming to conserve identities and the ways of life, with a view to return to the (usually more glorious) past.

2.2.3 On the Problem of 'Institution': What It Takes to Change a Social Imaginary

If in the previous section, we focused foremost on the changes in social imaginaries at the level of the *imagination*, in this (longer) section we will grapple with the question of *institution* of social imaginaries. There is an ambiguity in the word 'institution' that is central to the entire conceptual framework of social imaginaries. Social institutions, on a most general level, are regularised ways of doing things. Sometimes they come with much more elaborate material and institutional elements – buildings, laws and procedures, employees, technologies, particular practices, discourses, etc. – all of which make such social institutions more stable and more entrenched. Yet, at the same time, any regularised way of doing things is always at least partially open, as smaller and bigger changes will take place over time, changing the social institution in the process.

But it goes further: the degree to which we are *open* as people to reshaping institutions and how far we can imagine transformative change, that is utopias and new worlds, has also changed throughout history. In the brilliant small book 'Institution', Roberto Esposito explores the changes in what he calls the *instituting praxis*, from Roman times onwards. Esposito argues that for Romans, law – 'ius' –was a tool that could *denaturalise* and *institute* even nature itself.[35] The Middle Ages,

---

[35] Esposito discusses here the legal institution of slavery, which was considered as unnatural by Roman jurists but turned into reality via law. Roberto Esposito, *Institution*, trans. Zakiya Hanafi, 1st ed. (Polity, 2022).

however, dispossessed 'man' from this world-making capacity.[36] Nature and various social institutions were seen as given by God and were thus both good and desirable by default. They were also not for 'man' (including a sovereign!) to change, but had to defer to God's natural order. The acceptance of institutions as 'given and immutable' will be, according to Esposito, challenged only in modernity, as modernity makes 'self-determination' into one of the central elements of the 'Western modern social imaginary', to paraphrase Taylor.[37] Yet, Esposito laments, even in modernity, societies have not truly come to terms with this inherent ambiguity of the instituting praxis, which requires living with the continuous tension between stability and change, if it is to fully thrive.

This ambiguity is particularly present, I argue, with regard to one specifically modern invention, namely the separation of (market) economy and politics. This separation, identified by Taylor as one of the crucial political boundaries making Western modernity and criticised by Karl Polanyi in its 'laissez-faire' institutionalisation as the most radical social experiment, has been the object of political struggles ever since (see Section 2.2.3.1). The struggles about the boundary between economy and politics have particular dynamics in democratic societies, which try to translate (without revolutions) the discontents into institutional change (Section 2.2.3.2). In democratic capitalism, however, such institutional change is always made more difficult due to the structural dependence of the state on industrial and financial capital (Section 2.2.3.3).

Finally, we encounter the ambiguity of *instituting praxis* once again with regard to the institution of law. Law is central to instituting praxis in a very practical sense of being the central vehicle for translating the imaginary into governing rules. But law also captures how society relates (or not) to its own power to *institute* itself, by developing different kinds of legalities. Lastly, being an institution in its own right, law, with its own imaginaries, edifices, and actors, works according to its own rhythm while it also enjoys the capacity to push or resist change (Section 2.2.3.4).[38]

2.2.3.1 The Trouble with Instituting Economy

Clearly, people have always materially reproduced themselves, and in this very basic sense, there has always been an economy. But what we

---

[36] Esposito refers to Saint Agustin's 'City of God'.   [37] Taylor, *Modern Social Imaginaries*.
[38] There are too many to name, going in both the direction of naturalising (Lochner line of cases in the US Supreme Court at the beginning of the twentieth century) and socialising economy (a growing number of climate cases at present).

refer to as 'economy' today emerged as a figure of thought – as an imaginary – only in modernity. The paradox of the economy's birth is that in order to be known and governed, the economy had to be seen as a sphere *separate* from society or politics.[39] The initial embarrassment of this separation has been recognised by early economists by using the term 'political economy' – 'the discomfort will later disappear within the discipline of economics.[40] The reason to separate, know, and govern (political) economy stemmed from the conviction that it is somehow fundamental for the 'wealth of nations',[41] for prosperity.

The meaning and degree of separation of the economy will become the object of intense political and intellectual struggle over the following centuries. How much 'economic freedom', and for whom, is beneficial? Shall power and resources be privatised, in the hope that market actors acting in their self-interest will deliver prosperity? Or shall the power and resources be (partially) collectivised and democratic and public institutions made responsible for the distributive outcomes? Who, if anyone, is answerable for the distributive outcomes of the economic 'system'?

With the progress of the industrial revolution, the first imaginary of prosperity that clearly places entrepreneurs – rather than state, government, or public institutions – into the driving seat of prosperity was tagged as 'laissez-faire'. This imaginary, the origins of which can be located according to Keynes in the period between 1750 and 1850 England,[42] sees prosperity as stemming from letting private actors 'do' as they deem fit, guided by their rational self-interest and personal morality. Whatever the social ill at hand, legislators and (democratic) politics, or state intervention more generally, were best left out of the economic process – as violating the boundary between state and market was either going to be futile or perverse.[43]

This first imaginary of prosperity has contributed to the expansion of economic activity in this period,[44] while also leading to a significant privatisation of power and resources. It was the entrepreneur himself

---

[39] Foucault, 'The Birth of Biopolitics'.
[40] Mariana Mazzucato, *The Value of Everything: Making and Taking in the Global Economy* (Penguin UK, 2019).
[41] Adam Smith, *The Wealth of Nations* (Aegitas, 2016).
[42] John Maynard Keynes, 'The End of Laissez-Faire', in *Essays in Persuasion*, ed. Keynes (Palgrave Macmillan UK, 2010), 272–94.
[43] Albert O. Hirschman, *The Rhetoric of Reaction* (Harvard University Press, 1991).
[44] Carl Benedikt Frey, *The Technology Trap: Capital, Labor, and Power in the Age of Automation* (Princeton University Press, 2019).

(at this time usually a man) who could decide how the accumulated surplus would be distributed, with little interference from the state in terms of taxation, health and safety rules, labour rights, or environmental standards. Entrepreneurs also had the power to decide what was being produced or done, how, and with what technologies: shaping thus the future in line with their own interest, without interference but the competition of other private actors.[45]

According to Keynes, several factors aided the institutionalisation of this particular imaginary of privatised prosperity in the relevant period.[46] First, the ineptitude of public administrators strongly prejudiced the 'practical man' in favour of *laissez-faire*. Second, other classes also had what appeared as their own idiosyncratic reasons to support this imaginary of prosperity. For instance, the class of lawyers readily embraced laissez-faire as it followed from, and cohered with, the highly formalist understanding of the institutions of property and contract that were developing around this time.[47] Ultimately, laissez-faire permeated even cultural institutions, entering into the educational books for the youngest, when, to quote Keynes, '*the political philosophy, which the seventeenth and eighteenth centuries had forged in order to throw down kings and prelates, had been made milk for babes, and had literally entered the nursery*'.

Yet just as Keynes was discussing the slow demise of laissez-faire, another fundamental invention emerged that will work to enforce the separation of the economy in social imaginary. Namely, the birth of the gross domestic product (GDP) measure enabled the representation of the economy with a single digit, containing the sum of all the processes of – commodified – production, distribution, and consumption in the formal economy of a particular territory.[48] And even if the makers of this measure realised the limitation of the GDP, the GDP soon became the

---

[45] This has not passed entirely without workers' protests. See Frey, *The Technology Trap*.
[46] It is not unthinkable that laissez-faire as a social imaginary was shared mostly by the middle and higher classes, the governing layer so to say. It was only imaginaries of prosperity post-WW2 (first shared and then privatised) that were shared throughout political communities – leading also to critique, however, of mass society, mass culture, consumerist society, pacification of working classes, and similar.
[47] This is, of course, not an accident: as I argue later, law is co-constitutive of imaginaries of prosperity. Each imaginary of prosperity produces its own legality, while law as an institution will continue to exercise some degree of independent influence provided that society adheres to the rule of law broadly understood. See this eminent Marxist historian for a cautious defence of the rule of law, E. P. Thompson, *Whigs and Hunters: The Origin of the Black Act*, 1st ed. [reprinted with a new postscript] (Harmondsworth [etc.]: Pantheon, 1975).
[48] Timothy Mitchell, 'Fixing the Economy', *Cultural Studies* 12, no.1 (1998): 82–101.

main measure of prosperity: the continuous growth of this magical number indicating the success of the government in delivering prosperity, while its decline meant recession and difficult times ahead for any political party in power.

The boundaries of (political) economy drawn by the GPD served to reinforce the commodified and patriarchal conceptions of prosperity. Until this very day, the GDP disregards unpaid care (work) as something that produces value in the economy, and thus worth growing or investing in – despite the fact that the whole economy depends on it.[49] The GDP also fundamentally devalues nature and in contrast fosters extraction, attributing value primarily to what is commodified and exchanged – rather than to what is cared for and preserved. Trees, waters, fish, and air have value only if (cut and) sold.[50] Finally, in the system of national accounts, public spending in public administration, health, education, infrastructure, or care is in this framework considered to be consumption rather than investment – and thus something of a luxury, to "save on" in every crisis.[51] These *constitutive outsides* will however come to haunt the imaginaries of prosperity, as care, environmental, and infrastructural crises that we are currently experiencing.

Now, it took two world wars until the argument that the economy is not simply a self-regulating system, working in the general interest, became powerful enough to lead to real-world changes across many continents. There are, of course, institutional and material reasons for that, which I discuss in the next section. Here it suffices to say that around mid twentieth century, we see a different family of imaginaries of political economy taking hold: from experiments with the "actually existing" socialisms in "the East" to the welfare states in "the West". What these approaches shared is that they saw the state, the public, and collective actors as the core drivers of prosperity – if in different measures. The East fully nationalised the 'means of production', dispensing

---

[49] Nancy Folbre, 'The Unproductive Housewife: Her Evolution in Nineteenth-Century Economic Thought', *Signs: Journal of Women in Culture and Society* 16, no. 3 (1991): 463–84, https://doi.org/10.1086/494679.

[50] Frank Ackerman and Lisa Heinzerling, *Priceless: On Knowing the Price of Everything and the Value of Nothing* (The New Press, 2005). A questionable response is commodification and assetisaton of 'environmental services'; see Diana Liverman, 'Who Governs, at What Scale and at What Price? Geography, Environmental Governance, and the Commodification of Nature', *Annals of the Association of American Geographers* 94, no. 4 (1 December 2004): 734–38.

[51] Mariana Mazzucato, *The Entrepreneurial State: Debunking Private vs. Public Sector Myths*, 1st ed. (Anthem Press, 2013).

with 'market economy' altogether (with the exceptions of Yugoslavia and Hungary in Europe).[52] The welfare states in the West nationalised considerable industries, owing often up to 25 per cent net national wealth in the 1970s (n.b. a number that today would be negative in countries such as the US or the UK[53]) and further focused on predistribution and redistribution, via tax, strong trade unions and democratic lawmaking.[54]

This period came to an end in the 1980s with another, this time peaceful democratic transition in the imaginaries of prosperity. Neoliberalism is best understood as a new imaginary of *privatised* prosperity, which postulated that the privatisation of power and resources – via deregulation, privatisation, liberalisation, flexibilisation, and financialisation – is the best route to prosperity. While many usually pinpoint Hayek and Friedman as the ideational leaders of neoliberalism, others have argued that far more consequential was a large infantry found among neoclassical economists and public administration graduates who have steadily introduced market-thinking into most fields of policymaking.[55]

This institutional transformation made 'efficiency' the central preoccupation of policymaking. First via the innocent objective of finding the most 'cost-efficient' way of realising public objectives, only to later turn efficiency itself into the public objective, by increasingly entrusting market mechanism ('allocative efficiency') to deliver on any remaining social or environmental objectives.[56] The central elements of the neoliberal policy recipe were the trio "deregulation, liberalisation, and privatisation", which rather than leaving private actors *alone* required governments to *expand* markets and competition to new areas, so that they could do their magic of delivering socially optimal (efficient) outcomes. Four central directions were taken: first was the privatisation and liberalisation of public utilities. Second, the support for the growth of finance via both deregulation and globalisation of finance. Third, the cutting of taxes as a means to introduce even more dynamism and

---

[52] Tony Judt, *Postwar: A History of Europe since 1945* (Penguin, 2006).
[53] For data, see this blog by Thomas Piketty. Thomas Piketty, 'Public Capital, Private Capital' *Le Monde* (2017), www.lemonde.fr/blog/piketty/2017/03/14/public-capital-private-capital/, last accessed 5 January 2024.
[54] Thomas Piketty, *Capital and Ideology* (Harvard University Press, 2020).
[55] Elizabeth Popp Berman, *Thinking Like an Economist: How Efficiency Replaced Equality in U.S. Public Policy* (Princeton University Press, 2022).Bram Mellink, Merijn Oudenampsen, and Naomi Woltring, *Neoliberalisme: Een Nederlandse Geschiedenis* (Boom Amsterdam, 2022).
[56] Berman, *Thinking Like an Economist*.

attract investment. Finally, the 'new public management' aimed at transforming public institutions themselves, in order to deliver more "customer value" and "choice" on the one hand and to behave more efficiently (outsource and cut costs) on the other.[57]

To become successful, the privatised imaginary of prosperity had to tell a credible story of prosperity. It was promised that markets and competition will raise all boats – and that convinced many. Neoliberalism also gave a free pass to governments not to worry about justice, fairness, power, or financial stability: in this new brave win-win world, all that one hopes for (pro/sperare) will be taken care of by the well-functioning markets.[58] Enabling access to such well-functioning markets, as Micklitz and Patterson argue, has thus turned into the vehicle of justice ('access justice'), while non-discrimination has become important both as a matter of justice and optimising market functioning.[59]

Many thought that the 'great financial crisis' of 2008, as it has come to be known in recent years, made clear that the neoliberal imaginary of prosperity had left too many issues unattended to. But curiously, with the exception of the regulation of the banking sector in Europe, not much has changed in the imaginary of prosperity embraced thereafter. The EU and its member states (MSs) still believed in the salutary effects of (international) competitiveness, privatisation, liberalisation, and deregulation– this time around, combined with austerity'.[60] The first shake-up of this "zombie neoliberalism" came only in 2016, with Brexit and the election of Donald Trump.

Returning to Esposito, we can see two opposing tendencies when it comes to the 'instituting praxis' in relation to the (representations of the) economy. The *naturalising* representations include, first, the deepening of the imaginary boundary between economy and politics/society, via various objectifying tools, such as GDP, or various indexes and measures. Second, the commitment to empowering private actors (via deregulation, tax breaks, and free hand to shape technological futures) also naturalises

---

[57] Vivien A. Schmidt and Mark Thatcher, 'Why Are Neoliberal Ideas So Resilient in Europe's Political Economy?', *Critical Policy Studies* 8, no. 3 (2014): 340–47.
[58] Berman, *Thinking Like an Economist*.
[59] Hans-W. Micklitz and Dennis Patterson, 'From the Nation State to the Market: The Evolution of EU Private Law', *SSRN Scholarly Paper* (Social Science Research Network, Rochester, NY, 1 June 2012).
[60] Schmidt and Thatcher, 'Why Are Neoliberal Ideas So Resilient in Europe's Political Economy?'

the economy as it leaves to chance – that is the whims of the individual self-interests – the responsibility of delivering prosperity, innovation, or better futures. Third, naturalisation also operates via *narrowing* of our understanding of humans and society: simple models, such as famous homo economicus, price systems, or self-regulating markets, are necessary to be able to imagine and represent social institutions as *nature-like*. Finally, the naturalisation of the economy also presupposes the unsuitability of collective and public institutions to govern, while in turn also bringing such incapacity about via privatisations, outsourcing, consultancies, austerity, etc.[61]

On the other hand, the instituting praxis of collectivising/socialising/democratising the economy (I use these terms interchangeably) implies, first, the assumption of the attitude of *collective self-determination* also vis-à-vis the economic institutions. Economy and markets are no longer seen as separate self-regulating systems, given to people by their own 'human nature', but instead as social 'institutions' made also through politics, law, and collective decision-making. Second, it is the empowered public, collective, or democratically governed actors – rather than private actors – who are seen as both responsible and able to bring about prosperity and better futures. Third, the socialisation of the economy will compel the *thickening* of our understanding of humans and society: humans, and their organisation, have (and can act on) a complex set of interests and values. Price systems alone cannot express or mediate those interests and values. Finally, the democratisation of the economy will require the spread of democratic processes beyond simple politics. As the economy is itself seen as being instituted, and thus political, some degree of democratic accountability and participation will be necessary throughout. Thus, for instance, the democratisation of power in the workplace (today, for instance, via worker participation, worker ownership, steward ownership, stakeholder governance, etc.), as well as the democratisation of decisions about technological futures, may be required.

2.2.3.2 On the Translation Role of Democratic Institutions

The struggles about the boundary between economy and politics have particular dynamics in democratic societies. Democracies try to

---

[61] Mariana Mazzucato and Rosie Collington, *The Big Con: How the Consulting Industry Weakens Our Businesses, Infantilizes Our Governments, and Warps Our Economies* (Penguin, 2023).

translate – without revolutions – the discontents into institutional change. In a healthy democracy, resistance and contestation at times when the imaginary of prosperity ceases to create trust in its route to prosperity should find sufficient expression in democratic politics and eventually penetrate policy and law-making. And this is exactly what happened when welfare state imaginaries became increasingly contested in relation to the economic crisis in the late 1970s and early 1980s, and we have seen what without much exaggeration may be called a democratic transition to neoliberal imaginaries of prosperity.

In Chapter 3, I unpack the mechanics of the institution of neoliberalism on the background of the transformation of the EU's consumer policy from 1975 until the present day. This systematic analysis shows how neoliberal ideas about state and market, public and private, continually 'trickled down' as 'bits and pieces' into EU policy-making, gradually introducing variation in how we understand the basic elements of our social ordering, be it consumer, economy, the role of government, the role of law, etc. For instance, we have seen how consumers were gradually turning from weaker actors in need of governmental protection to competent actors in the market, who first needed to become more mature (i.e. less conflictual), then had to accept trade-offs, to be finally called to act responsibly and shop around cross-border in order to 'reap' the benefits of the internal market. Even as these bits and pieces of the new thinking continued to accumulate, quantitatively, there was still much of the thinking that resisted. For instance, next to accepting trade-offs and improving their capacities to reap better prices, one could still find a passage, here and there, that suggested that consumers needed protection, the issue of fairness popped up, or the argument that consumer organisations need to be strengthened to represent consumers' collective interests.

At some point, however, these *old* ideas gave in. There is a moment of *radical transformation* in the EU policy thinking from around 1997, when we can observe a *qualitative* leap (rather than just a *quantitative* increase of neoliberal discourse as was the case before that) in the language that the Commission relied on in EU consumer policy. From this moment onwards, there was little hesitation, little lip service paid to the old normative concerns such as protection, justice, fairness, power asymmetries, and harshness of contractual terms. Henceforth, policy prescriptions are presented with a remarkable degree of coherence and confidence, elegantly and persuasively, as if assuming the unwavering social consensus underpinning the new vision of the world.⁶²

Of course, consumer law and policy were not – and could not be – the exceptions in the grounding of the new imaginary in the EU at the end of the 1990s. In fact, those studying different areas of law would notice this transformation independently in their own fields – be it in the area of tax law,⁶³ in the area of labour law,⁶⁴ in the area of company law,⁶⁵ as well as in EU institutional law.⁶⁶ At the level of the EU MSs, it is remarkably also a moment when the third-way social democrats of Tony Blair and Gerhard Schroder win elections in the UK and Germany – with the promise of unleashing the power of capitalism and individualism, seasoned by a dash of social democratic concerns. It is around this moment of *revolution* that the neoliberal imaginary of prosperity is, I believe, at the peak of its socially integrative function, being able to rely on strong social consensus about its route to prosperity, engendering broad trust in a prosperous future.

Now, one would expect the same gradual transformation to take place in the aftermath of the 2008 great financial crisis: democratic and expert institutions picking up on more fundamental criticism and slowly changing their (foreground and background) assumptions as to how the world (i.e. political economy) fits together, translating some of this hesitation in its law and policymaking. However, despite the

---

⁶² See Chapter 3. Clearly, the social consensus was never entirely perfect. The EU courts, for instance, have been less enthusiastic in adopting the same market language in consumer law. Its integrationist agenda, which was set to be filled by political institutions with market efficiency, still came paired with some degree of concern for interpersonal justice and the protection of weaker parties, especially in the wake of the 2008 economic crisis. See, for instance, Candida Leone, 'The Missing Stone in the Cathedral: Of Unfair Terms in Employment Contracts and Coexisting Rationalities in European Contract Law' (University of Amsterdam, 2022), available at https://pure.uva.nl/ws/files/48074023/Thesis_complete_.pdf.

⁶³ Jussi Jaakkola, 'Taming the Leviathan or Dismantling Democratic Government? Evolving Political Ideas on Spontaneous Income Tax Integration in the European Union', *European Law Open* 2, no. 3 (2023): 575–615.

⁶⁴ Ruth Dukes, *The Labour Constitution: The Enduring Idea of Labour Law* (Oxford University Press, 2014).

⁶⁵ Thomas J. Andre Jr., 'Cultural Hegemony: The Exportation of Anglo-Saxon Corporate Governance Ideologies to Germany', *Tulane Law Review* 73, no. 1 (1998): 69; Martin Gelter, 'EU Company Law Harmonization between Convergence and Varieties of Capitalism', in *Research Handbook on the History of Corporate and Company Law* (Edward Elgar Publishing, 2018), 323–52.

⁶⁶ C. Joerges et al., *Mountain or Molehill?: A Critical Appraisal of the Commission White Paper on Governance* (New York University School of Law, 2001).

considerable criticism and resistance to neoliberalism by this point, we do not see democratic and expert institutions changing perceptively their understanding of the role of law (is self-regulation really a panacea?), economy (is trickle down working well enough?), politics (do all groups in society really have only a common interest in "well-functioning" markets?) or government (should governments just facilitate markets?) until the end of the 2010s. The EU as well as its MSs instead doubled down on the privatised route to prosperity by adding austerity to the mix – making sure that the less privileged segments of society pay double the price for the excesses of financial capital. What is more, institutions also continued boosting the economic recovery that did not take seriously the lived experience of many,[67] and repeating neoliberal receipts that could hardly engender confidence in a "better future" among large segments of society.

The sequel to the 2008 great economic crisis is instructive because it allows us to see what happens if democratic and expert institutions do *not* turn to instituting a different, more credible imaginary of prosperity, despite a broadly felt crisis. As the neoliberal ideology at this point of time increasingly ceases to provide a symbolic framework within which many people could understand their socio-economic lives, we can observe a growing mistrust in most institutions that we connect with modernity – democratic institutions, but also science or mainstream media. Similarly to the 1930s, it is the incapacity of democratic institutions to articulate and represent the lived experience of many post-2008 that made those very institutions appear irrelevant or "rigged" to a growing part of the population.[68] If democratic institutions cannot *renew* imaginaries of prosperity to ensure that people feel connected to society via the shared hope in a prosperous future, many will turn elsewhere for meaning and connection. Yet the main alternative to prosperity – tribal imaginaries – as I discuss later in Section 2.3, do not need democracy, pluralism, science, or critical media.[69]

2.2.3.3 Between Ideas and Interests

Why did we not see the shift in the imaginaries of the political economy post-2008 – even if it was quite clear that neoliberal privatised prosperity

---

[67] Haldane, 'Whose Recovery?'
[68] Jeff D. Colgan and Robert O. Keohane, 'The Liberal Order Is Rigged: Fix It Now or Watch It Wither', *Foreign Affairs* 96, no. 3 (2017): 36–44.
[69] C. Joerges and N. S. Ghaleigh, *Darker Legacies of Law in Europe: The Shadow of National Socialism and Fascism over Europe and Its Legal Traditions* (Hart Publishing, 2003).

did not work (any longer)? It was certainly not the problem of the scarcity of ideas or alternatives. But ideas were not enough. I single out here three weighty reasons as to why the governing institutions did not face up to reality and attempt to change course – leaving, likely, a number of other powerful explanations unaddressed.

First and foremost, in capitalism, with mostly privatised money supply, a democratic transition to shared prosperity will be made more difficult due to the structural dependence of the state on taxation and thus also on the capital. States, and their governing elites, aspire to have a strong, well-resourced, internationally competitive, and technologically powerful "productive sector", as otherwise the state may face two problems: (a) weakening its geopolitical and geoeconomic relevance and (b) not having the means to fill its public purse, making it difficult for the state to "pay" for things people care for, today and in the future.[70] If this is what one believes – and that seems to be the case as this is what the parties on the political right argue strongly about each and every election –many policy choices will remain foreclosed by this (imagined or not) dependence.[71]

Second, this problem is made more acute by the fact that politicians and technocrats in democracies are generally *risk-averse*; thus proposals that seem radical or unpredictable may not fare very well – with the onus historically weighing more on the proposals that favoured sharing rather than the privatisation of resources and power.[72] Thus whenever politicians muster the courage to go for proposals aimed at a greater democratic control of the economy, for instance, inspired by their constituencies, social movements, or academic knowledge, the well-resourced finance and industry lobbies will mobilise to portray the changes as too dangerous or too risky.[73] Even the proposals that were a reality just a couple of years earlier, or are entirely "normal" abroad, may appear as outlandish ideas.[74]

---

[70] Sum and Jessop, *Towards a Cultural Political Economy*.
[71] The driver of the dependency is the set up of the monetary system, with the centrality of private money. See, for instance, Stephanie Kelton, *The Deficit Myth: Modern Monetary Theory and How to Build a Better Economy* (Hachette UK, 2020).
[72] Hirschman, *The Rhetoric of Reaction*.
[73] One of the best sources for insights into corporate lobbying in Europe is provided by Corporate Europe Observatory, with their flagship reports available at https://corporateeurope.org/en/reports.
[74] For instance, in the US the demand for universal health coverage may lead to the accusation that you are a socialist even if the entire Europe has such a system – without there being a threat of sliding to socialism (Bernie Sanders, *It's OK to Be Angry about*

Third, neoliberalism itself has benefited several groups, which in turn could exercise a growing influence on politics. Consumers *as* consumers benefited from the cheapness and abundance of consumer goods. (Over)consumption has at least partially compensated for the falling labour share of income in most 'developed' economies.[75] Today, many far and extreme right parties promote a conception of prosperity that relies on throw-away cheap goods, which "green elites" are allegedly trying to take away.

But neoliberalism has also benefited, and far more for that matter, some concentrated groups in society – for example the managers and shareholders of ever bigger corporations, inherited wealth holders, the managers of financial institutions, transnational lawyers, accountants, the finance industry, the consultancy industry, the real estate sector, etc. For most of these groups, their taxes decreased and their share of wealth increased, at times dramatically. Today, the level of inequality is past the nineteenth-century levels, thus being the highest in history.[76] With these levels of inequality, one should not be surprised that capital has exercised such a grip on power post-2008.

2.2.3.4 On the Role of Law

Law is vital to *instituting praxis* in a very specific sense of being the core vehicle for translating the imaginary into norms. But by looking at law, we can also understand how a given society relates (or not) to its power to *institute* itself. In political and social theory, law has always played an important role. The 'rule of law' has been seen as a core imaginary of modernity,[77] a facilitator of democratic governance,[78] and the main public tool to govern modern economy and society.[79] If anything, law's (practical) eminence has continued to expand over the past decades and

---

Capitalism (Crown, 2023). Or in Europe, suggesting that the rich need to pay more taxes – way below the post-war consensus – is still seen as 'tax threatening' even by those who put social security as the top issue on their political programme. For instance, a popular Dutch politician, Pieter Omtzigt, who has recently set up a successful political party 'New Social Contract' has made a statement to this effect in the RTL TV debate, in the context of the Dutch 2023 election campaign, www.bnr.nl/nieuws/politiek/10530449/bezuinigen-of-belastingverhoging-lijsttrekkersdebat-rtl-draait-om-deze-vraag, last accessed 5 January 2024).

[75] Branko Milanovic, *Global Inequality: A New Approach for the Age of Globalization* (Harvard University Press, 2016).
[76] Thomas Piketty, *Capital in the Twenty-First Century* (Harvard University Press, 2014).
[77] Thompson, *Whigs and Hunters*.
[78] Jürgen Habermas, *Between Facts and Norms: Contributions to a Discourse Theory of Law and Democracy* (Polity Press, 1997).
[79] Max Weber, *Economy and Society*, new ed. (University of California Press, 1992).

centuries, with law regulating an ever-growing number of social relations, in a process that has been sometimes critically called 'juridification'.[80] Today, the EU produces thousands of pages of law per year, to be added to all those pages produced at the national level. This is clearly not without consequence for law's self-understanding and for its function in society.[81] Law's normative sweep is not only related to its seeming omnipresence but more recently also to its political bite. As the world nears the climate catastrophe in an ever quicker tempo, there has been a growing body of environmental and climate court cases that give legal value and relevance to what previously was seen only as political and/or scientific claims. This politically contested development has nevertheless much to teach us about the law as both part of imaginaries of prosperity and an independent social institution.[82]

We can distinguish three ways in which law can be appreciated as an expression of modern social imaginaries. First, law has been an important discourse and a part and parcel of the story of political economy – that is what prosperity means and how to achieve it.[83] Second, law is a central tool for instituting ideas, translating them into norms, institutions, and ultimately practices – backed by coercive state apparatus. Third, and perhaps most easily recognised by lawyers, law is also a separate institution, with its own time, rationality, and values.[84] While not separate from society in any thicker sense, it is still an institution with its own actors, norms, and rationalities – which can work to resist,

---

[80] Jürgen Habermas, 'Legitimation Problems in the Modern State', in *Communication and the Evolution of Society*, ed. Habermas (Beacon Press 1979).

[81] Hans-W. Micklitz, 'The Measuring of the Law through EU Politics', in *The Politics of European Legal Research* (Edward Elgar Publishing, 2022), 223–38.

[82] Chantal Mak, 'Giving Voice: A Public Sphere Theory of European Private Law Adjudication', *European Law Open* 2, no. 4 (2023): 697–723; Chantal Mak and Betül Kas, *Civil Courts and the European Polity: The Constitutional Role of Private Law Adjudication in Europe* (Bloomsbury Publishing, 2023); Laura Burgers, 'Private Rights of Nature', *Transnational Environmental Law* 11, no. 3 (November 2022): 463–74.

[83] Chantal Mak, 'Giving Voice: A Public Sphere Theory of European Private Law Adjudication', *European Law Open* 2, no. 4 (2023): 697–723; Chantal Mak and Betül Kas, *Civil Courts and the European Polity: The Constitutional Role of Private Law Adjudication in Europe* (Bloomsbury Publishing, 2023); Laura Burgers, 'Private Rights of Nature', *Transnational Environmental Law* 11, no. 3 (November 2022): 463–74. Three Globalizations of Law and Legal Thought: 1850-2000" by Duncan Kennedy and Legal Thought: 1850–2000', in *The New Law and Economic Development: A Critical Appraisal*, ed. Alvaro Santos and David M. Trubek (Cambridge University Press, 2006), p. 19.

[84] Emilios Christodoulidis, *The Differentiation and Autonomy of Law (Elements in Philosophy of Law)* (Cambridge University Press, 2023).

soften, or push for change. Law is thus simultaneously a discourse, an instrument, and an institution.

Law as discourse is co-constitutive of the imaginaries of political economy. As I show in the empirical chapters, how we think about law, about its normative power, has been shaped by the prevailing imaginaries of prosperity. When the imaginaries of prosperity that favoured the privatisation of power and resources prevailed, law has tended to hollow out its own normativity, via deregulation, self-regulation, or deference, in order to leave world-making power to private actors. In contrast, when more collective imaginaries prevailed, law has assumed a more normative posture, instituting public decisions on how both power and resources should be shared via mandatory rules that aim to tackle the structural features of the economy and society.

Law is discourse in yet another, second sense: it has important legitimatory and normalising functions. Legal imaginaries – such as rule of law, positivism, formalism, materialisation, freedom of contract, and similar – add legitimacy to (different kinds of) political economy. For instance, freedom of contract has been important to imaginaries of privatised prosperity, adding veneer of legitimacy to the freedom to choose to work long hours, to enforce the acceleration clauses in mortgage contracts, or to shield a strong protection of intellectual property rights in the pharmaceutical industry. But freedom of contract has also been fundamental to justify large interventions on behalf of substantive rather than formal freedom and equality, as it concerns the protection of labour rights, tenancy, and similar.[85] This ambiguity or indeterminacy of law, which has ultimately enabled law to shift with social imaginaries, has also been one of the major reasons for both its praise and its criticism.[86]

The empirical chapters also speak to this legitimatory power of law in a twofold sense. We will see that the legal discourses that place values and concerns such as (in)justice, (un)fairness, power (asymmetries), bargaining power, and interdependence as central usually appear when imaginaries of 'shared prosperity' are more dominant. In contrast, legal discourses that stress choice, freedom of contract, self-regulation, formal

---

[85] Martijn Willem Hesselink, *Justifying Contract in Europe: Political Philosophies of European Contract Law* (Oxford University Press, 2021); P. S. Atiyah, *The Rise and Fall of Freedom of Contract* (Oxford University Press, 1985).

[86] M. Koskenniemi, *From Apology to Utopia: The Structure of International Legal Argument* (Cambridge University Press, 2006).

equality, or information (asymmetries) have been central to the legal discourses associated with privatised prosperity. Legal discourses of privatised prosperity were often amplified by discourses that profess deference to market or technology (law "lags behind"), while legal discourses in collective imaginaries have in fact stressed the public and democratic control over these other social spheres.

Second, law is one of the most important tools for instituting imaginaries into institutions and practices in modernity.[87] All social reformers, those on the "Left" and those on the 'Right", have used law to shape social reality to their liking. Consider, on the one hand, the welfare reforms including labour and tenancy law, European 'common agricultural policy', or the international proposals for the 'NIEO'.[88] Or consider, on the other hand, the large-scale *legal* projects of liberalisation and privatisation of public utilities over the past decades, which required large numbers of rules and regulations and thus were nothing short of major intervention.[89] Importantly, these processes of legal institution have *future effects*, by normalising the present and by shaping what may be accepted as a *"non-radical"* proposal in the future. Thus, by instituting certain norms, institutional arrangements, or modes of justification, law not only legitimises such present arrangements but also presents constraints on the *compossible futures*, as the divergence from outcomes, distributions, and values will always require more collective energy than maintaining the status quo.

Two examples. The ecodesign framework has over the last couple of years quite gradually expanded what 'product' stands for. It has expanded the understanding of the product as a set of relations – of production, distribution, consumption, and disposal – entrenching that the product cannot be seen in isolation from these relations. The recent expansion of the ecodesign framework to include certain circular economy principles – such as durability, recyclability, second-hand products, and repair – was made sufficiently imaginable by the previous iterations of law-making. These recent rules requiring a visible departure

---

[87] Much conversation in law is about whether one is 'instrumentalist' about law or not. But that discussion is mute, I want to suggest, as law is both a discourse, an instrument, and an institution.

[88] Ingo Venzke, 'Possibilities of the Past: Histories of the NIEO and the Travails of Critique', *Journal of the History of International Law/Revue d'histoire du droit international* 20, no. 3 (2018): 263–302.

[89] Hans-W. Micklitz, 'The Visible Hand of European Regulatory Private Law – The Transformation of European Private Law from Autonomy to Functionalism in Competition and Regulation', *Yearbook of European Law* 28, no. 1 (2009): 3–59.

from unqualified consumerism and economic growth were not only imaginable but even realised.[90] The contrasting example comes from the field of industrial policy.[91] Long seen as an unwanted child, over the past decade we have seen a growing policy focus on industrial policy, with more transformative ambitions post-European Green Deal. However, without a significant degree of legal institutionalisation, we have witnessed a relatively quick lapse into a publicly financed ("derisked") market approach[92] once the EU became concerned with lagging behind its competitors (US and China). The Net Zero Industrial Act not only commits public support in terms of subsidies and tax breaks to the clean technology industry but does so without many conditionalities in terms of social or environmental standards or continued public say. The law makes very few choices as to the kind of clean industries that should be publicly financed in this way: ultimately, everything goes according to this Act, from carbon storage to dirty hydrogen. The public discussion as to what kind of 'clean economy' we want (and can realistically get) has never really taken place.

Third (and final), as most lawyers know all too well, law is also a separate institution with its own time, norms, and rationalities. As such, law does not necessarily only *follow* the shifts in the imaginaries of prosperity, but at times can also act as an accelerator of shifts or a buffer of (sometimes negative) side effects. One of the reasons is that law is closer to the *ground*, making it an institution where contestation can take place before or next to political contestation.[93] This could be well observed during the great financial crisis, when the Court revived the unfair terms directive – the "Sleeping Beauty" to cite Micklitz and Reich – to strike down unfair provisions in mortgage contracts.[94] All the while, the European Commission and the other EU institutions, then still in the neoliberal mode, put in place a new mortgage directive mainly concerned with screening customers rather than protecting them against widespread misuse of power and harsh credit conditions. But as the recent work of Leone Niglia argues, the European Court of Justice running at its own tempo may have "caught up" with the neoliberal turn

---

[90] See Chapter 5.   [91] See Chapter 6.
[92] Daniela Gabor, 'The (European) Derisking State', *UWE Bristol WP* (2023).
[93] Irina Domurath and Chantal Mak, 'Private Law and Housing Justice in Europe', *The Modern Law Review* 83, no. 6 (2020): 1188–1220.
[94] Hans-W. Micklitz and Norbert Reich, 'The Court and Sleeping Beauty: The Revival of the Unfair Contract Terms Directive (UCTD)', *Common Market Law Review* 51, no. 3 (1 June 2014): 771–808.

in recent years[95] – exactly when the other institutions may be moving on.

Law has an intimate relation to modernity. Its various doctrines and principles have served to justify different types of political economy. At the same time, law goes beyond discourse only. It is one of the central tools, or instruments, for instituting ideas in social reality, and thus law shapes not only the present but also the imaginable futures. This law's role is further reinforced by its own institutional apparatus that operates in accordance with its specific principles, values, and persons, having thus also a *rationality* of its own that does not map one to one on political and economic discourses. And while law is certainly not without ambiguity,[96] the respect for the 'rule of law' – including its aspiration to justice and the limitation of arbitrariness – is something that sets imaginaries of prosperity, and democratic and pluralist societies, apart.

2.3 Prosperity

In 'The Crisis of Democratic Capitalism', a renowned Financial Times journalist Martin Wolf argues that democracy cannot survive without capitalism – and vice versa. Wolf suggests that democratic societies need a capitalist private sphere that rests on profit motive and a healthy degree of capital accumulation, as the necessary counterpart to democracy and collective self-determination.[97] Only if capitalism becomes too capitalist, so to say, will it undermine – rather than sustain – democracy.

While much can be challenged on his claim, Wolff does have an important intuition. That is, political economy has something to do with democracy, at least in large pluralist societies. Where Wolff, however, seeks the anchoring of democracy in a particular historical version of political economy, the capitalism[98] (of the mid twentieth century), my

---

[95] Leone Niglia, *The Structural Transformation of European Private Law: A Critique of Juridical Hermeneutics* (Bloomsbury Publishing, 2023).
[96] David Kennedy, *A World of Struggle: How Power, Law, and Expertise Shape Global Political Economy* (Princeton University Press, 2016).
[97] Martin Wolf, *The Crisis of Democratic Capitalism* (Penguin Press, 2023).
[98] I do not operate with the concept of 'capitalism' in this book, because I find the concept overdetermined. We have seen so many different variations of 'capitalist political economies', with fundamentally different understandings of profit or property, or fundamentally different distributive outcomes, so that putting them in one basket is analytically unhelpful. What is more, I do not think that overcoming capitalism should be the goal in itself, for many different reasons. Rather developing a realistic and inclusive conception of prosperity is what ought to keep people busy, both intellectually and politically.

contention is that various varieties of capitalisms have been central to democracy for another reason: namely because they present a subset of *imaginaries of prosperity*. Imaginaries of prosperity create a *right kind* of social glue, a sufficiently thin conception of good life that can be shared in large pluralist societies. This also means that there is no overcoming of (different varieties of) "capitalisms" without a different set of shared background beliefs and understandings as to what prosperity means and how a society can get there.

Importantly in my view, the *imaginaries of prosperity* are not an expression of simple politics – of being on the right or the left on the political spectrum. Rather they present background preconceptions as to the relations between economy and politics, between the market and the state. They in turn define how we understand left and right, public and private, as well as the individual and collective. Or, put differently, the whole political spectrum moves with the shifts in the imaginaries of prosperity. It is in this sense that they present a shared social imaginary: they can integrate societies exactly because they can bridge the divisions of "normal politics". That is, until they cannot – as we witness today with the shift to tribalism, which moves away from prosperity altogether and relies on some sort of dominant identity as a vehicle of social integration.

In what follows, I will first try to clarify what people in the Global North understand as prosperity. While many equal prosperity to consumerism or economic growth, we have good reasons to believe that what we hope for (*pro/sperare*) seems to be far more related to happiness and safety, today and in the future, than to SUVs and large mansions (Section 2.3.1). After, I turn to discuss the four central questions related to prosperity in Europe today: of prosperity and democracy (Section 2.3.2), of prosperity and technocracy (Section 2.3.3), what is the historical role of the EU at present (Section 2.3.4), and how to understand prosperity's other – tribalism (Section 2.3.5).

2.3.1 On the Meaning of Prosperity (Today): More about Happiness than Consumerism

What do people hope for? Is it an ever-larger amount of consumer goods that makes people (feel) prosperous? Or do they hope for something else? Most economists would link prosperity today to economic growth. Investment, innovation, and increases in productivity lead to a more capacious economy, producing more and cheaper goods, which in turn can be bought and enjoyed by an ever-bigger segment of the population, in ever-bigger quantities. More goods for less money, thus making everyone more prosperous: without ever having to rise the question of distribution. This "contestation free" prosperity, some suggest, is what grounds the current "addiction" of democracies to economic growth – people can have a more prosperous future without political struggles over the difficult questions of (re)distribution.[99]

The only problem with this economic understanding of prosperity is that it seems ever less credible in the context of the numerous crises we are facing. The logical solution has been to respond to environmental crisis by *greening* economic growth. If we make goods and services green, decouple growth from the use of material resources, and make the world net neutral, we can land in the green version of the present. This future seems like a non-brainer, as it relieves us from painful choices, while staying within the carrying power of Earth. The question remains whether it is a possible future: so far, this approach seems to be failing on both the environmental front (over the past couple of years, the use of material resources and energy has continued to rise[100]) and the social front, at least judging on the basis of the growing opposition to the green transition as envisaged by this programme.

The question I want to ask in this section is, however, whether our starting position is correct: is it consumption and, if so, what kind of consumption, that makes people thrive? Is there something essential in our present-day conception of prosperity that makes the permanent expansion of productive capacities a necessity? This is not only a theoretical question. If prosperity is central to democracy, and we cannot muster a credible conception of prosperity for a finite planet, we may be doomed to a violent autocracy or theocracy in the midst of climate collapse.

I want to explore this question of what we understand by prosperity today, not via any macroeconomic indicators but in a micro sense, that is how people themselves think about prosperity. To this end, I have settled for one political cleavage that has emerged in the wake of the 2008 crisis,[101] namely the complaints of the generation of the so-called millennials (born between 1981 and 1995) vis-à-vis the generation of

---

[99] John Barry, 'Green Republicanism and a "Just Transition" from the Tyranny of Economic Growth', in *Green Politics and Civic Republicanism* (Routledge, 2022), 59–76.

[100] See, for instance, Centre for Sustainable Research Factsheets, on Energy https://css.umich.edu/publications/factsheets/energy and on Material Resources https://css.umich.edu/publications/factsheets/material-resources.

[101] Kate Alexander Shaw, 'Baby Boomers versus Millennials: Rhetorical Conflicts and Interest' (Sheffield Political Economy Research Institute (SPERI), 2018).

their parents, 'baby boomers' (post-war babies). This short excursus is not aimed, however, at exploring in any detail the broader issues of intergenerational politics or intergenerational justice, but rather to attempt to distil more generally what prosperity may mean today, and any future expectations that may be connected to it.

The main concern raised by millennials has been that they have far worse chances of being prosperous than their parents. In general press, this conflict comes under titles such as 'Dashed Dreams: European Millennials Expect a Worse Life than Their Parents',[102] or 'Many Millennials Are Worse Off Than Their Parents'.[103] There are several interesting elements to this political cleavage. First, it has emerged post-2008 crisis, making it clear that the sense of the *loss of prosperity* spreads beyond the practically educated older population, and includes also a well-educated, younger generation. Second, this cleavage has been sustained by both the Left and the Right of the political spectrum, suggesting that there is some "common sense" about it.[104] Third, and finally, while broadly shared, the material comparison between millennials and their parent generation is not unambiguously in favour of baby boomers.[105] This also reveals that the concerns raised are located more in the sphere of future expectations, in the sphere of imaginary, so to say, than in the simple present.

In general media, the concerns of millennials are described as follows. Unlike baby boomers, millennials are said not to be able (as early or as easily) to afford housing,[106] to marry, or to have kids.[107] Millennials tend to be more indebted from the start, due to the costs of education, and they have to live with their parents, because housing is unavailable, which in turn makes it impossible to "grow up" and have a family and

---

[102] Matthew Elliot, 'European Millennials Expect a Worse Life than Their Parents, Survey Shows', *Youth Time Magazine* (2018), https://youthtimemag.com/dashed-dreams-european-millennials-expect-a-worse-life-than-their-parents-survey-shows/, last accessed 30 December 2023.

[103] Tami Luhby, 'Many Millennials Are Worse Off than Their Parents – a First in American History', *CNN Magazine* (2020), https://edition.cnn.com/2020/01/11/politics/millennials-income-stalled-upward-mobility-us/index.html, last accessed 30 December 2023.

[104] Shaw, 'Baby Boomers versus Millennials'.

[105] Jean Twenge, 'The Myth of the Broke Millennial: After a Rough Start, the Generation Is Thriving. Why Doesn't It Feel That Way?', *Atlantic* 2023, www.theatlantic.com/magazine/archive/2023/05/millennial-generation-financial-issues-income-homeowners/673485/; Roula Khalaf, 'Millennials Are Not as Badly Off as They Think – But Success Is Bittersweet', *FT* 2023, www.ft.com/content/6f7d7522-42e9-43cb-bd73-36eee6681f3e, last accessed 30 December 2023.

[106] Khalaf, 'Millennials Are Not as Badly Off as They Think'. [107] Ibid.

their own children.[108] They also enter the economic system that has made insecurity and competition the cornerstone of economic and social life.[109] At the same time, the chances that millennials will enjoy excellent health care and pensions similar to those of their parents are dubious at best[110] – a constellation made even more complicated with raising concerns about the long-term liveability of the planet.[111]

What is interesting about this list is that the complaints, or concerns about prosperity ("having it as good as parents") have relatively little to do with conspicuous consumption, such as big cars, luxurious furniture, fancy holidays, or powerful home appliances. Prosperity for millennials is about securing basic material, social, and institutional goods. This includes the capacity to afford a house, that is to put down roots in the way that previous generations did.[112] Furthermore, the stability of a housing situation is also one of the preconditions for forming many meaningful social relations – including those that signpost 'adulthood' such as marriage or having children. The other amenity to be able to have children is the accessibility and affordability of childcare and education – something that is ever more difficult in the context of privatised care. To thrive, many millennials further imagine an economy that would provide less insecurity and competition, and more security and cooperation (as it did for their parents). This connects to the overarching concern with the inequality of wealth and opportunity, often expressed in who gets a chance to buy a (first) house or not. Finally, having a liveable planet, and a prospect of good health (care) and a decent living at old age, presents long-term concerns that are fundamental for a sense of prosperity today as in the future.

So, what can we learn about the *content* of prosperity based on this list? Today, like in the past, prosperity will indeed require some material basics, such as a house or a means of sustenance. But to thrive, flourish,

---

[108] Patrick Collinson, 'UK Millennials Second Worst-Hit Financially in Developed World, Says Study', Guardian 2018, www.theguardian.com/money/2018/feb/19/uk-millennials-second-worst-hit-financially-in-developed-world-says-study, last accessed 30 December 2023.
[109] Alan France, *Understanding Youth in the Global Economic Crisis* (Policy Press, 2016).
[110] Andy Green, *The Crisis for Young People: Generational Inequalities in Education, Work, Housing and Welfare* (Springer, 2017).
[111] Brian Barry, 'Sustainability and Intergenerational Justice', in *Intergenerational Justice* (Routledge, 2017), 183–208, www.taylorfrancis.com/chapters/edit/10.4324/9781315252100-10/sustainability-intergenerational-justice-brian-barr, last accessed 5 January 2024.
[112] Green, *The Crisis for Young People*.

and prosper, a range of social and institutional goods remain necessary.[113] The sense of malaise today is related, on the one hand, to the systemic failure of the still instituted imaginary of prosperity – neoliberalism – to ensure that people have secure access to the basic basket of material, social, and institutional goods that are necessary for thriving. The commodification of many of these fundamental goods over the past forty years has made the financial insecurity created by neoliberalism much more dramatic for this generation, as their access to such goods is conditioned by their (strained) financial resources. On the other hand, the current prosperity also does not offer a convincing *route* to future prosperity, which would make clear how these goods will become (readily) available in the coming time: ever cheaper toasters cannot guarantee a safe and prosperous future.

The good news is that (over)consumption, or the availability of SUVs, is not what will cut it for the imaginary of prosperity. In fact, people want rather simple foreseeable things. A new definition of prosperity will have to provide a convincing story of how basic material, social, and institutional goods will be provided, not only today but also in the future, and in the face of all the challenges we face. Such a story will have to contain a new understanding of how macroeconomic and microeconomic institutions can effectively provide the mix of basic goods that prosperity requires. Anything less of that will *not* do: just consider that today (end of 2023) the economic situation in many European countries is not altogether grim, with the highest rates of employment in years.[114] And yet, loss of prosperity is what seems to drive many people to vote for extreme right parties, as only 'prosperity chauvinism' seems to provide a vaguely credible promise of securing prosperity also in the future.[115]

---

[113] Including healthy relations, social standing and recognition, personal security, a degree of autonomy in personal and collective life, having meaning and purpose, caring for others and being cared for, health and education, rewarding work and sufficient leisure, and so forth.

[114] See Eurostat statistics on (un)employment across Europe, from 2009 to the present. Eurostat, 'EU Labour Market Quarterly Statistics' (2023), https://ec.europa.eu/eurostat/statistics-explained/index.php?title=EU_labour_market_-_quarterly_statistics, last accessed 5 January 2024.

[115] According to Greve, economic insecurity correlates with the degree of support for multiculturalism in all European countries (with the exception of Hungary, at one, last measuring point in 2016). Bent Greve, *Welfare, Populism and Welfare Chauvinism* (Policy Press, 2020), p. 147.

2.3.2 Of Prosperity and Democracy

The core argument of this book is that prosperity is fundamental for democracy. That is, democratic institutions depend on the broadly shared *imaginaries of prosperity* as a *democracy friendly* ground for social integration. Imaginaries of prosperity – resting on the shared belief in a prosperous future – provide a necessary measure of societal glue even in widely pluralist societies, while giving objectives, direction, and vigour to their democratic politics and collective action. Democratic institutions are at the same time fundamental for prosperity, that is beyond just their moral appeal, for only the well-functioning democratic institutions can translate the resistance and contestation into the renewal of the imaginaries of prosperity, ensuring thus transformation and stability at the same time.

The imaginaries of prosperity, such as neoliberalism today or welfare state imaginaries of prosperity before, do several things for democracy. First, they are able to create an inclusive understanding of the 'we' (the political community, the institutions, and the people) that can encompass widely plural sets of values and worldviews. These imaginaries can provide a sufficient degree of sharedness and purpose necessary for social integration, for keeping societies together – without imposing what liberals call a "thick" conception of good life. Importantly, such imaginaries are also future oriented, rather than oriented towards the past or tradition; thus they aim to transform the conditions of life in order to land the polity in a better future.

Second, if the imaginaries of prosperity are to be able to fulfil their integrative role, they need to give rise to a social order that enjoys a specific kind of 'outcome legitimacy'.[116] That is, not only that the imaginaries of prosperity need to deliver a certain degree of prosperity today but they also need to have a credible claim that they can deliver prosperity tomorrow as well. To do so, within the imaginaries of prosperity, two main channels for 'updating' their empirical basis are crucial: democratic process and scientific knowledge.[117] Both channels are necessary in order to make sure that governing is based on a sound informational basis. This goes very much against the insistence on "common sense" governing, beloved by populists, which tends not only

---

[116] Fritz W. Scharpf, *Governing in Europe: Effective and Democratic?* (Oxford University Press, 1999).
[117] Michel Foucault, *Security, Territory, Population* (Springer, 2007).

to be bigoted but also based on "gut feeling" rather than on a sound empirical basis – hardly thus able to address various complex problems that societies face.[118]

Third, many political struggles in democracy are about the specific content and the meaning of prosperity, as well as – more importantly perhaps – the route to prosperity. For their credibility, if pressured by crises, imaginaries of prosperity will need to include their constitutive outsides. As this has to happen at least to some degree on the basis of sound knowledge and reasoned debate, the circles of prosperity can expand. Thus today, the environmental crises can force a community to rethink its relation to nature, the migration crisis can force people to rethink their geoeconomics (more prosperity abroad may limit one's exposure to the new waves of migration), or the care crisis can force a society to re-evaluate the place care gets in their socio-economic system. This process carries the potential for both inclusion and justice.

Democracy, in turn, can do several things for prosperity. If functioning at least reasonably well, democratic institutions are sensitive to the needs of the (constitutive) outsides in a polity, enabling the claims and grievances to shape and eventually reshape the meaning and route to prosperity. Three important qualities of democracy make it conducive to prosperity.

First, democracy is crucial for dealing with social conflict in a constructive or affirmative way.[119] Even in its "actually existing" forms, democracy gives itself the task of creating conditions for fostering resistance and opposition against any provisional hegemony, using thus the energies of conflict towards the transformation of social consensus – rather than exclusion and violence.[120] In democracy, the old should *always* be dying and the new should *always* be institutionalising.[121]

Second, democracy operates both on the level of politics and the level of the Political. Namely, democracy enables not only the change of policies but ultimately also the transformation of hegemonic, or constitutive, social imaginaries. The institution of neoliberal imaginaries of privatised prosperity is an excellent example of such societal

---

[118] For an influential sympathetic treatment, see Clifford Geertz, 'Common Sense as a Cultural System', *The Antioch Review* 33, no. 1 (1975): 5–26. For a more critical treatment, see Umberto Eco, 'Ur-Fascism', *The New York Review of Books* 22 (1995): 12–15.
[119] Roberto Esposito, *Politics and Negation: For an Affirmative Philosophy* (John Wiley & Sons, 2020).
[120] Neera Chandhoke, *Democracy and Revolutionary Politics* (Bloomsbury Publishing, 2015).
[121] Esposito, *Politics and Negation*.

transformation facilitated by the "actually existing" democracy. The gradual incorporation of what may seem politically attractive, *good ideas*, via policymaking, has ultimately prepared grounds for a peaceful *revolution*, making an entirely different relation between the state and the market, public and the private, as well as social and natural reality.[122] This should have also been the case in relation to the transition to shared prosperity, but for the reasons I discuss at least partially in Section 2.2.3, democracy has not delivered (so far).

Third, and importantly, the temporary hegemonies in democratic societies have an important function.[123] Namely, at the height of their integrative function, hegemonic social imaginaries create grounds for a more resolute action of public institutions as well as collective action in society more broadly – by showing the direction of travel, creating social support for political action, and fostering a certain shared optimism about the future. Hegemonic neoliberalism has transformed the entire society: the private and the public, the collective and the individual, the right and the left. In fact, today we may be in dire need of a new hegemonic social imaginary (of prosperity) that would provide social consensus for collective institutions to act resolutely to address the multiple crises that we are facing. Yet, such imaginaries always must be produced by and embedded in democratic institutions. Without the pluralising centripetal workings of democracy, the direction of travel may be instead towards fascist-like or soviet-like futures rather than towards actually solving social and environmental problems.

2.3.3 *Of Prosperity and Technocracy*

I noted above that prosperity requires reliance on scientific knowledge,[124] to ensure that policy choices are based on sound informational

---

[122] See Chapter 3.
[123] Oliver Marchart, *Post-Foundational Political Thought: Political Difference in Nancy, Lefort, Badiou and Laclau* (Edinburgh University Press, 2007).
[124] In this book, I do not discuss science as an institutional practice that itself requires certain condition to be able to fulfil its role of uncovering and analysing various 'constitutive outsides'. I (somewhat conveniently) assume that in the EU, certain minimum conditions of autonomy, resources, inclusion, independence, etc., are available for science to be able to fulfil this task. In Chapter 6, I spend some time discussing the difficulties, which emerge when science is used in policymaking. For a more general treatment of the question, see Sheila Jasanoff, *The Fifth Branch: Science Advisers as Policymakers* (Harvard University Press, 1998); I have myself discussed some of these problems in relation to the treatment of the science behind the precautionary principle, in the context of EU trade relations. See Marija Bartl, 'Regulatory

basis. To this purpose, modern states have increasingly relied on educated bureaucracies in order to help politics govern.[125] At other times, institutions were created that were meant to be entirely independent of political pressures and democratic process, as only "pure expertise" was deemed to be fit for the task.[126] Also in the context of international and transnational governance, the technocratic institutions have gained a greater role, as they were expected to solve problems (ranging from ensuring peace, facilitating trade, regulating labour, or solving climate crisis) and ensure output legitimacy – entirely without or with very thin democratic controls.[127]

Over time, it has become clear that technocratic institutions have their own deficits – not only obvious democratic deficits but also knowledge deficits.[128] Built often around narrow disciplinary expertise,[129] itself a part of a particular mainstream scientific paradigm,[130] and set within tight institutional and normative frameworks,[131] the technocratic institutions may also become incapable of seeing the full picture and incorporating *constitutive outsides* effectively. An illustrative example of this point comes from the UK. Andrew Haldane, the then Chief Economist of the Bank of England, has tried to reconcile Bank's post-crisis data, suggesting an exemplary economic recovery in the UK, with the much more negative picture shared with him by people and organisations during his visits to peripheral regions of the UK. After disaggregating the statistics regarding the changes in income, wealth, region, age, and housing situation after the crisis, what he discovered is that the recovery story had missed important distributive dimensions.[132]

Haldane was in this regard more an exception than a rule post-2008 crisis. The reason why populists can so easily maintain that the

---

Convergence through the Back Door: TTIP's Regulatory Cooperation and the Future of Precaution in Europe', *German Law Journal* 18, no. 4 (2017): 969–92.

[125] Weber, *Economy and Society*.
[126] Jeremy Leaman, *The Bundesbank Myth: Towards a Critique of Central Bank Independence* (Springer, 2000).
[127] Philippe C. Schmitter, 'Neo-Neofunctionalism', in *European Integration Theory* (1st ed.), ed. Antje Wiener and Thomas Diez (Oxford University Press, 2003), 45–74.
[128] Marija Bartl, 'Contesting Austerity: On the Limits of EU Knowledge Governance', *Journal of Law and Society* 44, no. 1 (2017): 150–68.
[129] Marija Bartl, 'Making Transnational Markets: The Institutional Politics behind the TTIP', *Europe and the World* 1, no. 1 (1 June 2017): 1–37.
[130] Thomas S. Kuhn, *The Structure of Scientific Revolutions*, 2nd ed. (University of Chicago Press, 1970).
[131] Bartl, 'Contesting Austerity'. [132] Haldane, 'Whose Recovery?'

institutions are "rigged"[133] ("we are tired of experts!"[134]) is that technocratic institutions have often remained stuck for too long with the neoliberal common sense, failing to incorporate real grievances on the one hand and keep up with the development of the scientific knowledge on the other. There are other problems as well. Technocracies can be captured, epistemically[135] and/or materially[136] by those who stand to lose from change. Supranational technocracy faces an additional set of challenges. As Hayek brilliantly observed long ago, it remains easier for supranational institutions to work to institute imaginaries that divulge power and resources to private actors, rather than imaginaries that aim to collectivise such power, as supranational institutions usually face their own institutional constraints.[137]

Technocratic institutions thus, just like democratic institutions, need to be able to incorporate the *constitutive outside* into the framings of social problems, while channelling real grievances into policy. Where it does not happen – for reasons of capture, incompetence, or distance – the trust in the entire governing system, the trust in *institutions*, will suffer. A possible consequence is that, like today, when knowledge is crucial for addressing various *constitutive outsides*, and supranational bodies may be better placed to address some of the global problems, a broad swath of people would rather trust YouTube influencers than institutions to provide answers to various social and environmental problems.

2.3.4 Of Prosperity and Europe

In his book 'European Constitutional Imaginaries',[138] Jiří Přibáň argues that prosperity is the core imaginary behind the EU and its internal

---

[133] Colgan and Keohane, 'The Liberal Order Is Rigged'.
[134] Henry Mance, 'Britain Has Had Enough of Experts, Says Gove', *Financial Times* 2016, www.ft.com/content/3be49734-29cb-11e6-83e4-abc22d5d108c, last accessed 1 January 2024.
[135] Wendy E. Wagner, 'Administrative Law, Filter Failure, and Information Capture', *Duke Law Journal* 59, no. 7 (2010): 1321–1432.
[136] Margarida Silva, 'The European Union's Revolving Door Problem', in *Lobbying in the European Union*, ed. Doris Dialer and Margarethe Richter (Springer, 2019), 273–89.
[137] Friedrich A. Hayek, 'The Economic Conditions of Interstate Federalism', *New Commonwealth Quarterly* 5 (1939): 131–49; Marija Bartl, 'Hayek Upside-Down: On the Democratic Effects of Transnational Lists', *German Law Journal* 21, no. 1 (January 2020): 57–62.
[138] Přibáň, Jiří. *Constitutional Imaginaries: A Theory of European Societal Constitutionalism* (Routledge, 2021).

market. Working within the framework of systems theory, while building his specific understanding of prosperity on the work of Friedrich Hayek and ordoliberals, Přibáň suggests that prosperity in Europe means foremost, and perhaps even only, privatised prosperity. To what extent is he right? Is the EU indeed doomed to privatised prosperity?

To start, one needs to acknowledge that the EU's institutions are not *symmetrical*, be it with regard to their competences[139] or macroeconomic structure.[140] It was thus also no accident that the EU was so successful in institutionalising a set of neoliberal policy prescriptions.[141] Neoliberalism gave the EU supranational institutions an opportunity to expand their own institutional power, by spreading markets, which in turn needed to be liberalised and Europeanised.[142] In this sense, neoliberalism has advanced the EU project via the push for liberalisation and privatisation, which came paired with a degree of re-regulation to remove the excesses that would stand entirely at odds with a commitment to 'social market economy'.[143] Yet, this still left the internal market asymmetrical (between social and economic), and often regressively distributive,[144] while further entrenching privatised prosperity.

But is the EU doomed to continue entrenching neoliberal imaginaries of prosperity – even if many of its technocrats and politicians, may realise that such a course does not make sense either in epistemic or democratic terms? The EU has not always been neoliberal. If anything, as I show in Chapter 3, neoliberalism became hegemonic in the EU only by the end of the 1990s, when we see the EU finally relinquish concerns with protection, structural inequalities, or asymmetries of powers that typified the previous welfare state imaginary of prosperity, and fully

---

[139] Fritz W. Scharpf, 'The Asymmetry of European Integration, or Why the EU Cannot Be a "Social Market Economy"', *Socio-Economic Review* 8, no. 2 (24 December 2010): 211–50.

[140] Fritz W. Scharpf, 'Monetary Union, Fiscal Crisis and the Preemption of Democracy', *MPIfG Discussion Paper, No. 11, 2011, Max Planck Institute for the Study of Societies, Cologne*.

[141] Nicolas Jabko, *Playing the Market: A Political Strategy for Uniting Europe, 1985–2005* (Cornell University Press, 2006); Bartl, 'Internal Market Rationality, Private Law and the Direction of the Union'.

[142] Ibid.

[143] Petersmann, Ernst-Ulrich. 'Neoliberalism, Ordoliberalism and the Future of Economic Governance'. *Journal of International Economic Law* 26, no. 4 (December 2023): 836–42.

[144] Damjan Kukovec, 'Law and the Periphery', *European Law Journal* 21, no. 3 (2015): 406–28. Also critiqued in terms of legal culture, see Rafał Mańko, Martin Škop, and Markéta Štěpáníková, 'Carving Out Central Europe as a Space of Legal Culture: A Way Out of Peripherality?', *Wroclaw Review of Law, Administration & Economics* 6, no. 2 (1 December 2016): 4–28.

orient towards facilitating markets and competition. It is only beyond this point that the narratives of international competitiveness, trade liberalisation, privatisation, deregulation, financial markets liberalisation, capital markets union, etc., became the tropes leading the day, not only before the 2008 crisis but also afterwards.[145] Similarly, Clemens Kaupa in his excellent book shows that much of the EU's neoliberal drift was contingent rather than necessary.[146] He argues that there is nothing inherently neoliberal in the EU treaties. Treaties could have been interpreted differently, and it was more a political decision – rather than any legal necessity – that turned the EU in the direction it went.

However, this is not to say that once neoliberalism has been institutionalised in the EU, a shift away would be easy. From a number of crucial institutional lock-ins of neoliberalism, perhaps the most relevant one is the Union's set-up that includes a monetary union without a fiscal union.[147] Stability is then enforced via control of public spending, thus permanently threatening austerity.[148] Furthermore, the lack of tax competences at the EU level, be it in relation to its 'own budget', limiting the EU's capacity to invest, or in relation to tax harmonisation, entrenching the EU's incapacity to limit tax competition among the EU MSs,[149] further restricts the space for developing a more collective imaginary of prosperity.

Beyond these institutional constraints, there are also particular political economic constraints that are not an explicit part of the treaties but create their 'real world' context. The first is the misalignment of interests between the European Core and the European Peripheries (Southern and Eastern). Namely, the countries of the European Core (Germany, the Netherlands, Nordic countries, and Austria), which are the 'exporters of capital' to the Periphery, have their interests clearly aligned with those

---

[145] See most specifically Chapter 5.
[146] Clemens Kaupa, *The Pluralist Character of the European Economic Constitution* (Bloomsbury Publishing, 2016).
[147] On the role of the CJEU in locking this constitutional settlement, see Harm Schepel, 'The Bank, the Bond, and the Bail-out: On the Legal Construction of Market Discipline in the Eurozone', *Journal of Law and Society* 44, no. 1 (1 March 2017): 79–98; Marco Dani et al., 'At the End of the Law: A Moment of Truth for the Eurozone and the EU', University of Luxembourg Working Paper, 2020, available at https://orbilu.uni.lu/bitstream/10993/45861/1/Weiss-VB.pdf.
[148] Clemens Kaupa, 'Has (Downturn-)Austerity Really Been "Constitutionalized" in Europe? On the Ideological Dimension of Such a Claim', *Journal of Law and Society* 44, no. 1 (2017): 32–55.
[149] Eloi Flamant, Sarah Godar, and Gaspard Richard, 'New Forms of Tax Competition in the European Union: An Empirical Investigation', Report, Eu-Tax, 2021.

of (their) capital.¹⁵⁰ This has impacted the way in which the EU has dealt with the 2008 crisis: saving mostly Western European banks was paid for by austerity, internal devaluation and large-scale unemployment in the Periphery.¹⁵¹ What is more, that same foreign capital (European, but also Chinese) has been able to acquire cheaply fundamental public infrastructure in the peripheral states (such as ports, islands, and public services).¹⁵²

The coalition building between the Southern and Eastern Periphery is difficult to achieve, however, because their 'models of development', and thus also their problems, differ. While Southern Europe is in a creditor–debtor relation with the countries of the Core, which in the EU monetary set-up makes them excessively dependent on the whims of the financial markets, the Eastern periphery has based its development on foreign direct investment, which keeps salaries low but leaves these countries somewhat more policy space,¹⁵³ at times misused by the likes of Orban.

Another "real world" complication for the project of de-neoliberalisation of the EU is the strong influence of industry and finance on European policymaking. Industry started lobbying Europe at least from the 1980s, when the European Roundtable of Industrialists was established.¹⁵⁴ Today, much power has been outsourced to industry and finance; via self-regulation, co-regulation, and generally massive degree

---

[150] Kukovec goes further and argues that the centre-periphery dynamics in the EU is built into the legal discourse. Kukovec, 'Law and the Periphery'.

[151] Emilios Christodoulidis, 'Europe's Donors and Its Supplicants: Reflections on the Greek Crisis', in *Constitutional Sovereignty and Social Solidarity in Europe*, ed. Johan Van Der Walt and Jeffrey Ellsworth (Nomos, 2015), 241–66.

[152] One of the demands of creditor countries, and in particular Germany, was for Greece to sell their islands as one of the means to pay back their creditors. See Spiegel report, 2010, www.spiegel.de/wirtschaft/soziales/schuldenkrise-cdu-und-fdp-fordern-verkauf-griechischer-inseln-a-681637.html, last accessed 5 January 2024. In a rather funny turn of events, the Greek minister of economy advises the same to Germany at the moment when the Constitutional Court uproots the spending plans of the Scholtz government, www.focus.de/politik/deutschland/um-schnell-grosse-summen-aufzubringen-griechischer-ex-minister-raet-deutschland-zum-verkauf-seiner-inseln_id_254033082.html, last accessed 5 January 2024.

[153] Visnja Vukov, 'Growth Models in Europe's Eastern and Southern Peripheries: Between National and EU Politics', *New Political Economy* 28, no. 5 (3 September 2023): 832–48; Laszlo Bruszt and Visnja Vukov, 'Making States for the Single Market: European Integration and the Reshaping of Economic States in the Southern and Eastern Peripheries of Europe', *West European Politics* 40, no. 4 (2017): 663–87.

[154] Bastiaan Van Apeldoorn, 'Transnational Class Agency and European Governance: The Case of the European Round Table of Industrialists', *New Political Economy* 5, no. 2 (2000): 157–81.

of consultations, giving industry the influence via well-established institutional channels.[155] Such coupling is difficult to wean out.

But this does not mean, I want to argue, that the EU and its institutions are not trying to bring about changes, despite significant constraints. And with some success. In the following empirical chapters, I explore the attempted transformations in four policy fields at the micro and meso level of the economy, where the EU enjoys the greatest competences and legitimacy. There we see the EU gradually trying to develop imaginaries of consumption, corporation, technological governance, and (to a lesser degree) also industrial policy that are both more sustainable and more shared. Even in the "macro sphere" some work has been ongoing. Consider the growing stress on the importance of public investment (European public goods), a stronger solidarity gesture behind the NGEU, and (if relatively weak) calls to at least align tax policy with the green agenda.[156] If nothing more, all these can be seen as preparing grounds for making the silent revolution eventually both imaginable and possible.

2.3.5 The Prosperity's Other: Looming Tribalism

2.3.5.1 Dialectics of Prosperity: Between Privatised and Shared Prosperity

Historically, the imaginaries of prosperity have oscillated between two main routes of prosperity. On the one side of that spectrum, we find a vision that prosperity originates from some social reality that is external to the public or collective domain, such as the market, technology, or individual strive. What pursuing prosperity requires in such an imaginary is to "untie the hands" of those who are rooted in these domains – that is to privatise power and resources – so they may be able to bring about better futures. On the other side of the prosperity spectrum, we find a story of prosperity that sees collective action, public and democratic institutions as central for delivering prosperity. What prosperity requires in such imaginary is to collectivise/publicise both power and

---

[155] In an excellent recent piece, Morvillo and Weimer argue that this problem of capture in food and safety has profoundly shaped the CJEU's decision-making, by the backdoor so to say. Marta Morvillo and Maria Weimer, 'Who Shapes the CJEU Regulatory Jurisprudence? On the Epistemic Power of Economic Actors and Ways to Counter It', *European Law Open* 1, no. 3 (2022): 510–48.

[156] See Chapter 5.

resources, not least by means of law, in order to ensure that all can partake in prosperity.

More specifically, the *imaginaries of privatised prosperity* place individual effort, self-interest, and self-reliance as central public values. Epistemologically, they tend to be naturalistic about many (hierarchical) social relations as well as the "economic system", seeing them as given by human nature and thus also good and mostly desirable.[157] These imaginaries of privatised prosperity stood behind both classical liberal and neoliberal conceptions of prosperity and society – both aiming to privatise power in order to bring about better futures. Needless to say, the privatisation of power and the 'untying' of the hands of private actors comes usually with a lot of legal and social engineering.[158]

The *imaginaries of shared prosperity*, in ethical terms, place solidarity, cooperation, and sharing as central public values. Epistemologically, they are more constructivist, seeing collective self-determination, law, and policy, as both ends and means to change economic structures, address power imbalances, and ensure fair distributions of wealth or voice.[159] The imaginaries of shared prosperity stand behind social-democratic, welfare state, and some socialist regimes, all of which placed more power and resources in public and collective hands in order to ensure that prosperity is more genuinely shared.

Overall, many of the political regimes that we have seen over the course of the past 200 years (laissez-faire, social democracy, welfare states, neoliberalism, some socialist regimes, etc.) can be placed somewhere on this spectrum between privatised and collective (route to) prosperity. What unites all regimes on this spectrum is that prosperity functions as the main anchor of the social imaginary, being a central device for social integration and a compass for the direction to collective

---

[157] See Section 2.2.3.1.

[158] Karl Polanyi, *'The Great Transformation: The Political and Economic Origins of Our Time'* (Beacon Press, 2001). For the implications of the embeddedness thesis in law, see Christian Joerges and Karl Polanyi, *Globalisation and the Potential of Law in Transnational Markets* (Hart Publishing, 2011); Aukje A. H. Van Hoek, 'Re-Embedding the Transnational Employment Relationship: A Tale about the Limitations of (EU) Law?', *Common Market Law Review* 55, no. 2 (2018): 449–87; Vladimir Bogoeski, 'The Aftermath of the Laval Quartet: Emancipating Labour (Law) from the Rationality of the Internal Market in the Field of Posting', PhD thesis, Hertie School (2021), https://opus4.kobv.de/opus4-hsog/frontdoor/index/index/docId/3717.

[159] For the outline of the ordo/neoliberal criticisms of this type of social or welfare 'constructivism', see Quinn Slobodian, *Globalists: The End of Empire and the Birth of Neoliberalism* (Harvard University Press, 2020), 212.

energies, while at the same time enabling a degree of pluralism and inclusion.

Clearly, this is not to say that imaginaries of prosperity are free of misogyny, racism, and a myriad of other social hierarchies. Far from that. Rather, this only means that they remain at the same time open to challenges on these same grounds. If the claim to power is based on the best route to prosperity, then the challenge that, for instance, empowering *only* white propertied men hampers prosperity will have to be, first, met by the considerations of prosperity – rather than some inherent supremacy of propertied white men. To do so, second, both the challengers and those to whom the claim is addressed will aim to substantiate as far as possible their claims by relying on (scientific) knowledge, empirical or theoretical. Arguments based on some sort of identity or theology, such as tradition, religion, ethnical belonging, race, gender, language, culture, or similar, cannot be decisive. Finally, such challenges will ultimately need an institutional framework that does not aim to suppress but instead aims to enable a sufficient degree of dissent – if for nothing else than because dissent is crucial for enhancing its informational basis.[160] It is in this sense that imaginaries of prosperity are at the *foreground* of Enlightenment ideology,[161] which values and aspires to – if certainly not immediately delivers – self-reflection, critique, scientific knowledge, inclusion, and ultimately democratic institutions. This aspiration is what distinguishes the imaginaries of prosperity – be it privatised or shared – from tribal imaginaries that place a group identity and/or a thick conception of good life as the anchor of Political. While tribal imaginaries can also provide a means of social integration, they relinquish, even as a pretext, the respect for many of the institutions and values that modernity, and Enlightenment, stand for.[162]

---

[160] Habermas, *Between Facts and Norms*.
[161] The 'background' of the imaginaries of prosperity at home was tribal imaginaries abroad that have justified colonial and neocolonial domination and extraction in various forms. For instance, "French civilisation" stood for a very specific group identity that was mobilised to justify all kinds of exploitation and extraction on the basis of postulated superiority. An interesting question to discuss is how the tribal imaginaries abroad related to the imaginaries of prosperity at home: this is, however, a huge historical question that in this book I cannot answer. It comes back only as a prospective question, namely what a credible imaginary of shared prosperity today, in the face of multiple crises – some of which are direct consequences of colonial and neocolonial relations – must mean for the EU's relation to the so-called third countries.
[162] Eco, 'Ur-Fascism'.

2.3.5.2 The 'Other' Collective Imaginary: The Rise of Tribalism

And the pretext does matter. As a person coming from a country, which has been the stage of much tribal violence (former Yugoslavia), understanding when and how societies descend into such ways of seeing and acting has been one of the major motivations to write this book. And however complicated the delivery of the aspirations of modernity is (such as publicness, institutions, truth, and science), I do not see how one is better off without such pretenses, at least in Europe.

It seems to me that both historically and at the present moment, we can see usually two different types of *collectivist imaginaries* developing after a previous period of dominant privatising imaginaries, which privatised both power and resources – and by their end date will have delivered vastly unequal and chaotic societies.[163] Also today, these two types of collective imaginaries aim to provide responses to neoliberalism's parasitic feeding on social norms and social support structures that it inherited from the previous period, but is unable to renew.

These two types of imaginaries, however, respond to the thinning out of social resources and support structures in very different ways, relying on different understandings of community and belonging. One type of collective imaginaries sees belonging as a *product* of institutions, shared purposes, and doing things together. Such collectives are, for instance, various voluntary associations (trade unions, social movements, eco-villagers, sports clubs, or religious associations) and less voluntary associations, such as neighbourhoods, cities, regions, nation states ('political citizenship'[164]), or the EU.[165] When *mobilised* as political imaginaries,

---

[163] In Europe, many argue that the turn to Fascism and Nazism can be understood as a response to extended periods of economic austerity and social contraction between the wars. Ricardo Duque Gabriel, Mathias Klein, and Ana Sofia Pessoa, 'The Political Costs of Austerity', *Review of Economics and Statistics*, 2023, 1–45, https://direct.mit.edu/rest/article-abstract/doi/10.1162/rest_a_01373/117705/The-Political-Costs-of-Austerity?redirectedFrom=fulltext; Jacopo Ponticelli and Hans-Joachim Voth, 'Austerity and Anarchy: Budget Cuts and Social Unrest in Europe, 1919–2008', *Journal of Comparative Economics* 48, no. 1 (2020): 1–19; Thiemo Fetzer, 'Did Austerity Cause Brexit?', *American Economic Review* 109, no. 11 (2019): 3849–86; Gregori Galofré-Vilà et al., 'Austerity and the Rise of the Nazi Party', Working Paper, Working Paper Series (National Bureau of Economic Research, December 2017); Mark Blyth, *Austerity: The History of a Dangerous Idea* (Oxford University Press, 2013).

[164] Thomas Janoski and Brian Gran, 'Political Citizenship: Foundations of Rights', in *Handbook of Citizenship Studies*, ed. Engin F. Isin and Bryan S. Turner (SAGE Publications Ltd, 2002), 13–52.

[165] Hanno Sauer, *Moral Teleology: A Theory of Progress* (Taylor & Francis, 2023).

this understanding of the collective is concerned with institutional belonging and any collective action is eventually aimed at transforming malfunctioning institutions.[166]

The other type of collective imaginaries relies on *tribal identity markers*, usually inherited or of "blood and soil" type, such as true Finn, people with white (or other colour) skin, 'native speakers', or Hindus. These *tribal imaginaries* foster a sense of belonging foremost by creating an outgroup, the other, the foreign.[167] Fintan O'Toole argues that *'perhaps the greatest advantage of tribalization is that it solves the problems of identity. (...) Tribal politics do not in fact deal in collective identities, which are always complex, contradictory, multiple, and slippery. They reduce the difficult "us" to the easy "not them." They set up some rough (and often arbitrary) markers of difference and then corral real collective experiences and histories within the narrow limits they define'.*[168]

Importantly, both collective imaginaries (tribal and shared prosperity) have analogous affective appeals, providing belonging, a sense of purpose, of being part of something bigger than one-self. A turn to such collective identities is a reasonable (emotional) response to the excesses of privatisation of both power and resources, of excessive individualism and marketisation. The central difference lies where the outlet of the collective energies is being sought: is the central problem of politics to deal with identity and group protection – against foreign(ness) –[169] or is the purpose the transformation of economic, legal, and political structures and institutions that have not served people well?[170]

The consequences of choosing one of these two collective imaginaries are dramatic. What is at stake are the most important signposts of Enlightenment including the fate of democratic institutions, pluralism, scientific knowledge and rationalism, and ultimately output (legitimacy). First, by making an inborn identity the anchor of social integration, exclusion becomes the defining feature of the polity, the state. *'All the group needs to hold it together is the conviction that it is being wronged by some*

---

[166] David Bollier and Silke Helfrich, *Free, Fair, and Alive: The Insurgent Power of the Commons* (New Society Publishers, 2019).
[167] Jan Willem Duyvendak and Josip Kesic, The Return of the Native: Can Liberalism Safeguard Us Against Nativism?, in *Oxford Studies in Culture and Politics* (Oxford University Press, 2023).
[168] Fintan O'Toole, Review of *Defying Tribalism*, by Susan Neiman, *The New York Review of Books*, 2 November 2023.
[169] Duyvendak and Kesic, 'The Return of the Native'.
[170] Kjaer, *The Law of Political Economy*.

real or imaginary enemy".[171] Government's main task is to make sure, to use Geert Wilders' winning speech, to *'deliver on the hope that the Dutchmen will come first again'*.[172] The main vehicle to achieve this is to devise an expanding set of means to exclude whoever does not fit the bill, making sure that the whole *'idea of the state* [as an institution] *becomes profoundly uncertain'*.[173]

In such a polity, the institutions that aim to foster critique, pluralism (of views or ways of life), or the dispersion of power – for example independent judiciary, freedoms of speech and association, protests, social movements, and trade unions – will increasingly seem to be useless annoyances, the tools for stoking unrest, giving space to 'particular interests' or serving as the propaganda machine of the outgroup.[174] Science and non-partisan media also don't fare well in tribal societies. Science will often come with information or positions that unsettle traditions, settled gender roles, or "heroes of our history".[175] Non-partisan media will take it as their *task* to be critical of various powers, practices, institutions, discourses, or technologies. Given that critique cannot be tolerated, science and serious journalism will become one of the first and most important "Others". All these anti-pluralist tendencies make it very difficult to maintain democratic institutions,[176] since authoritarian modes of government appear better placed to protect the tribe against all those who aim to disturb its own prosperity, values, history, tradition or gender roles, etc.[177]

Finally, in tribal societies, output legitimacy will suffer, for two reasons. First, those operating within tribal imaginaries focus usually only on certain aspects of problems, in one way or another linked to combatting foreignness or outsiders – leaving thus often far more significant causal mechanisms for solving problems outside the picture. At the same time, they also tend to weaken knowledge and democratic

---

[171] O'Toole, 'Review of *Defying Tribalism*'.
[172] From the victory speech of Geert Wilders, 22 November 2023: *'De hoop, dat de Nederlander weer op een komt te staan, waar te maken'*, www.youtube.com/watch?v=LuVZ_rEgj8k, last accessed 15 December 2023.
[173] O'Toole, 'Review of *Defying Tribalism*'.
[174] Antonis A. Ellinas, 'Media and the Radical Right', in *The Oxford Handbook of the Radical Right*, ed. Jens Rydgren (Oxford University Press, 2018), 269–84.
[175] PVV programme, 'Nederlanders weer op 1' (Dutch again first), at page 29, available at www.pvv.nl/?verkiezingsprogramma?.html, last accessed 2 January 2024.
[176] Jürgen Habermas, *A New Structural Transformation of the Public Sphere and Deliberative Politics* (John Wiley & Sons, 2023).
[177] Duyvendak and Kesic, 'The Return of the Native'.

institutions that could channel that *outside* back in and instead rely mostly on "common sense" to address the material reality their populations face. What should concern us most, however, is that in order to make up for the lack of output legitimacy in such societies, the new "Others" will have to be identified and possibly ever more extreme forms of othering and exclusion implemented. Ultimately, war as a *diversion mechanism* or even a *growth strategy* is never unconceivable in such an imaginary.

This is not to say that arguments based on identity, ethnicity, or religion have no place in democratic politics. There is always a degree of identification with the beliefs and arguments that we make, as well as traditions, nations, cultures, languages, or others. Such expressions belong to democratic politics as they express certain issues that people hold valuable. But the identification becomes a problem when it turns into overidentification: a simple tribal "us–them" imaginary that becomes the frame for understanding everything.

2.4 Sustainable and Shared

Many of the grievances of the disappointed citizens, who vote for extreme parties, are real. In a society that on the one hand seems to value only highly educated people,[178] and where a growing number of people find themselves sliding down the social ladder, while the future also does not hold any positive promise, the trust in the official institutions is bound to plummet[179] and various dubious solutions are sought in order to preserve 'our' resources.[180] Clearly, also other factors come into play. For instance, media, social and traditional, seem to thrive on spreading doom and often hate,[181] while numerous politicians and parties are the political entrepreneurs of exclusion.[182] Equally, some groups may see it as a grievance that their rights to dominate have been taken away.[183] Yet, I want to argue

---

[178] Michael J. Sandel, 'The Tyranny of Merit: What's Become of the Common Good?' (Allen Lane, 2020); Daniel Markovits, *The Meritocracy Trap: How America's Foundational Myth Feeds Inequality, Dismantles the Middle Class, and Devours the Elite* (Penguin, 2020).
[179] Wolf, *The Crisis of Democratic Capitalism*.
[180] Greve, *Welfare, Populism and Welfare Chauvinism*.
[181] Stuart Soroka and Stephen McAdams, 'News, Politics, and Negativity', *Political Communication* 32, no. 1 (2 January 2015): 1–22.
[182] Sergei Guriev and Elias Papaioannou, 'The Political Economy of Populism', *Journal of Economic Literature* 60, no. 3 (1 September 2022): 753–832.
[183] Debbie Ging, 'Alphas, Betas, and Incels: Theorizing the Masculinities of the Manosphere', *Men and Masculinities* 22, no. 4 (10 May, 2017): 638–57.

that both the economic and cultural reasons that drive tribalism can be addressed only if prosperity becomes once again the anchor of the political. What kind of prosperity it has to be this time around I discuss in the following section.

2.4.1 On the Constitutive Outsides: Renewing Imaginaries of Prosperity

Any successful imaginary of prosperity will have generated a degree of social consensus around what prosperity means and how to get there. But any such consensus will necessarily leave many issues unattended. As these issues become more urgent, and turn into serious problems, they will lead to crises that demand solutions. Such solutions, however, can be progressive: they can expand the circles of prosperity, making prosperity a tiny bit more shared, just, and stable.

Today, we are not short of crises, due to various *constitutive outsides* that our extractive economies have created. Perhaps the most immediate neglect in the neoliberal imaginary of prosperity was the distributive consequences of the privatisation of both power and resources. The attempt to "raise all boats", by empowering the capital, has ultimately led to a significant regressive shift in income between labour and capital and skyrocketing inequality within and among countries – in the Global North and some regions of the Global South.[184] For some time, the growing inequality was countered in the West via cheap consumer goods and borrowing, but the growing environmental degradation, real estate bubbles, privatisation of basic services, and financialisation have over time made basic material, social, and institutional goods – that is the basis for prosperity – unavailable to many.

But the problem has not been only that of raising inequality, but also that of losing grip on the technological futures. Having privatised the power over technological development, technological futures have been driven mainly by efficiency considerations of the capital, mostly, with a view of developing various labour replacing and labour disciplining technologies.[185] This has contributed in the West to the major shift of income from labour to capital.[186] The sense of existential insecurity created by technological development has in the meanwhile grown even further, with technologies such as AI not only promising to leave people

---

[184] Piketty, *Capital in the Twenty-First Century*.
[185] Simon Johnson and Daron Acemoglu, *Power and Progress: Our Thousand-Year Struggle Over Technology and Prosperity* (Hachette UK, 2023).
[186] Piketty, *Capital in the Twenty-First Century*.

jobless but eventually even threatening their very existence. Leaving the future of the world in the hands of this or that Silicon Valley entrepreneur is perhaps not where societies want to or ought to be. Rather, distributive and world-making capacities of technologies need to become a fundamental issue of democratic politics and intervention in any new imaginary of shared prosperity.[187]

These two dynamics take place on the background of three constitutive outsides that have at present turned into full-blown crises.[188] These constitutive outsides have been neglected in modern political economy from its inception in the eighteenth century – with neoliberal imaginary of prosperity mainly greatly accelerating the exploitation of the underlying resources, setting the ground for the present crises.[189] First and foremost, the casualty of our political economy has been 'nature', with the growing environmental degradation creating an existential threat today,[190] which we can see unfold with a "plain eye" in the multiplication of 'weather events'.

Simultaneously, we see another structural crisis of the modern economy unfold, namely the crisis of care.[191] In still rather patriarchal imaginaries of prosperity, the structural undervaluation of care work used to be borne by those whose time and effort counted for less – women – but has over time grown into a serious unavailability of care. For instance, privatising childcare, both via profit-based provisions and via the centrality of nuclear families, has aggravated many of the demographic problems that developed countries face.[192] At the same time, the care services are also struggling to find willing staff – as an increasing number of people make a rational choice to choose jobs that receive both more financial and social recognition than care work. These problems will only grow more urgent as societies age.

Finally, to complete the picture, the last big constitutive outside of the European political economy is its relationship with the 'developing countries', often former colonies. This extractive relationship has many aspects. I find most illustrative the problem of debt: some of the poorest countries in the world pay up to 20 per cent yearly interest rate on their

---

[187] Johnson and Acemoglu, *Power and Progress*.
[188] Nancy Fraser and Rahel Jaeggi, *Capitalism: A Conversation in Critical Theory* (Polity, 2018).
[189] The historical CO_2 emissions have doubled over the past 50 years, during the reign of neoliberal prosperity.
[190] Lee et al., 'IPCC, 2023'. [191] Fraser and Jaeggi, *Capitalism*.
[192] Amia Srinivasan, 'The Right to Sex. Feminism in the Twenty-First Century', *The Right to Sex: Feminism in the Twenty-First Century* (Farrar, Straus and Giroux 2021).

public debt, many of them spending as much as 50 per cent to 90 per cent of their budgets on servicing debts (instead of building infrastructures or paying for public or social services). The most lucrative of all trades, it seems.[193] But clearly, such exploitation of the developing world is coming back as a boomerang to Europe: as poverty, wars, and increasingly climate crisis are gradually displacing ever greater numbers of people, while the available places for a decent life are shrinking, Europe will face more uncontrollable migration pressures.[194] Thus perhaps rather than allowing European financial capital to continue extracting usury rate of interest from the poorest, keeping all of the plunder for itself and fuelling further inequality abroad and at home,[195] European citizens have every reason to demand that prosperity is more genuinely shared across its borders as this will lower the strain on our societies as well, while benefiting communities across the globe.

2.4.2 In the Search of Future: Credible Prosperity in the Twenty-First Century

I argued above that the rise of tribal imaginaries is not an accident. It is a response to decades-long privatisation of power and resources, which has created considerable inequality in the EU, exhausting at the same time societal, political, material, and institutional resources that were created in the previous periods. But instead of going down the path of tribalism that cannot solve the problems we face, we have another collective imaginary available: an imaginary of *shared prosperity*.

Such a genuinely shared imaginary of prosperity has to provide a credible prospect of a liveable future not only for a select few. First, the new imaginary has to move away from futures for the wealthy and university educated only and be able to present a convincing story also for practically educated, non-urban, "normal" people. This will require more democratic control over how power and resources (including technology!) are made and shared. Today, in a society where so much is left to

---

[193] Wester van Gaal, 'The Battle to Fix the "Rigged" Financial System Needs a Strong African Voice', *EU Observer* 2023, https://euobserver.com/africa/156991, last accessed 2 January 2024.

[194] There is some disagreement as to how big these pressures will be – much will depend on the liveability of the 'region'. Ingrid Boas et al., 'Climate Migration Myths', *Nature Climate Change* 9, no. 12 (2019): 901–3.

[195] Ugo Mattei and Laura Nader, *Plunder: When the Rule of Law Is Illegal* (John Wiley & Sons, 2008).

the whims of capital, it is the search for new ways of making a profit that shapes the future. Technologies that are labour disciplining or replacing not only lead to many people receiving an ever-smaller piece of the pie, but they also foreclose the prospect of prosperous futures.[196] Equally, subjecting basic material needs – like housing – to speculative investment produces an atmosphere of insecurity. In the scramble for last resources then, even a dispossessed war refugee may seem like a threat.

Second, the new imaginary of prosperity has to go beyond welfare state imaginary of prosperity in two important respects. Unlike in the 1940s or in the 1970s, it will be increasingly difficult to build a future as if environmental issues did not exist. With growing occurrences of weather events, and growing threats to human rights and property, most people (even those who advocate no action) realise that the world is facing a very serious, even existential problem. Moreover, given the irreversibility of environmental changes, eco-systemic balance, and tipping points, a credible future will only be possible if shared prosperity presents an actual route to a liveable planet.

Third, given the various crises that we are facing, the new imaginary of prosperity will have to take seriously (often capital-induced) global interdependence and match it with the actual commitment to sharing prosperity across borders. Unless European imaginaries of prosperity commit to more equitable relations with at least our most proximate neighbours in Africa and thus contribute to a more liveable life beyond its borders, the rising (real or perceived) migration pressures will feed the sense of threat, fuelling nationalism, nativism, racism, religious, and other forms of discrimination and hate. These responses may in turn diverge Europe from prosperity to tribalism, threatening its democratic institutions and problem-solving capacity, the proud signposts of European modernity.[197]

2.4.3 Can the EU Make a Difference?

The one thing that distinguishes Europe in the 1930s, from Europe today, is the EU. It is seventy years after its establishment, when its origin story is nothing but forgotten, that the EU is called to play the very role that its founders have intended for it. The *Communities* that were to gradually unite a deeply diverse polity, around the quest for prosperity rather than

---

[196] Johnson and Acemoglu, *Power and Progress*.   [197] Taylor, *Modern Social Imaginaries*.

identity,[198] with strong technocratic bureaucracy and eventually also stronger democratic institutions. Given the low probability of a shared tribal identity, European democracy, integrated only via imaginaries of prosperity, may prove central in shifting Europe to the imaginary of shared prosperity – without world wars this time around.

But this will require political courage on several fronts. First, the EU will need to maintain its commitment to knowledge governance – even in the face of the far and extreme right becoming a more dominant force in Europe. Second, the EU's supranational institutions will have to stand up for those pulling the short straws in the integration process – something they failed to do in 2008. Thus they will have to stand up to big capital, driven by short-term logic rather than long term (including their own) interest, as well as the influential EU MSs, which today insist on the new push for austerity, even if this is anything but prudent at this point in time.[199] Third, the EU will have to continue (co)developing and gradually institutionalising a new imaginary of shared prosperity that aims to strengthen the democratic control of the economy and ensure fairer sharing of the benefits of social cooperation, internally and externally. Only if such an imaginary delivers on the hope in a better, or liveable future, will the tribal imaginaries oriented towards "lost past glory" lose their grip on the future.

But instead of pondering once again the nature of EU, its constitutional structures, symmetries, and asymmetries, this book asks what shape the EU imaginary of prosperity is taking today, if any. This particular imaginary is emerging on the background of the EU constitutional structures, as well as particular material and social conditions in which we find ourselves in the first half of the twenty-first century. Any new imaginary will be then unavoidably partially restrained, but not fully determined by these constraints.

One important caveat before we turn to the empirical chapters. Not all important issues can be resolved fully at the EU level. Think of the housing crisis, for instance. Housing crisis is one of the central issues across Europe today, having most recently catapulted the extreme right to the biggest force in the Dutch parliament.[200] Yet the role of the EU in

---

[198] Jiří Přibáň, *Constitutional Imaginaries: A Theory of European Societal Constitutionalism* (Routledge, 2021).
[199] Wester van Gaal, 'EU Secures Last-minute Deal on New Fiscal Rules', *EU Observer*, https://euobserver.com/green-economy/157867, last accessed 2 January 2024.
[200] I&O Research, 'Negen Op Tien Nederlanders: Sprake van "wooncrisis"', www.ioresearch.nl/actueel/negen-op-tien-nederlanders-sprake-van-wooncrisis/, last accessed 2 January 2024.

relation to housing crisis remains limited and ranges from not getting in the way of solving such problems – which unreasonable fiscal rules would do – or by creating additional space and possibilities for solving such crises across Europe, for instance, by regulating financial markets.

But many other crises, however, cannot be solved but within the framework of the EU. The one that the EU itself has chosen to focus on and that in fact to a large degree can challenge all the constitutive outsides that I discuss above is environmental and climate crisis. In its landmark piece of policymaking, the European Green Deal, the EU argues that what ought to be done is nothing less than 'changing the ways in which we produce and consume' if we want to respond to the challenges we are facing.[201] The EU chose to act where it has most to say, where its competences are least doubtful, namely in the field of internal market regulation.

It is important to keep in mind that the continuing discontents with the EU policies may be related to the sidelining of *social issues* in EU's transformative agenda, even though they present the fundament of prosperity. Green growth on its own will not be sufficient to ensure good (sustainable, accessible, and affordable) transport or housing, without rethinking finance or public provision aimed at better distribution of access and control. Green growth may even aggravate the crisis of care, by continuing to prioritise traditional "productive" sectors and market-driven growth, all the while it is "unproductive" care sectors – such as health or education – remain underfunded despite being so crucial for people's sense of prosperity today and in the future.

I will draw attention to some of those social issues when discussing changing imaginaries of prosperity behind four important policy fields in the EU – consumption, the regulation of technology, industrial policy, and the transformation of corporation. The purpose of the empirical chapters is to identify what kind of *micro foundations* the EU has been trying to put in place over the past years, via various laws, policies, and institutional discourses, and what *compossible futures* these changes may make imaginable.

---

[201] European Commission, COM(2019) 640 final, The European Green Deal.

3 Reimagining Consumption

3.1 Introduction

Few would doubt that consumption is central to prosperity. We need housing, food, and clothes, but also health care, childcare, education, and transport, as well as places for socialisation, such as cafes and restaurants, playgrounds, or parks, to live a good life. While these needs have remained relatively constant over the past decades at least, and in some cases over centuries, *how* we consume, *how much* we consume, and *what is considered consumption* in the first place – as a matter of law and policy – has changed fundamentally.

Thus, while we have always needed a house to live in, how we have gone about the provision of housing has changed considerably. In the not-so-distant past, many people lived in multigenerational dwellings, with complex sets of rights and duties attached to them.[1] Over the course of the twentieth century, we have seen an important shift towards nuclear family dwellings, which were in large numbers provided by the state, with tenants over time having more rights and protections.[2] This changes again with the rise of neoliberalism and financialisation, when the collectively owned housing is increasingly privatised and purchased either by individuals via mortgage deals with banks or by (financial) investors.[3]

A similar transformation of *the how* of consumption – that is from community-based to public provision to private provision – has also

---

[1] Kristen R. Ghodsee, *Everyday Utopia: What 2,000 Years of Wild Experiments Can Teach Us about the Good Life* (Simon & Schuster, 2023).
[2] Ibid.
[3] Manuel B. Aalbers, 'The Variegated Financialization of Housing', *International Journal of Urban and Regional Research* 41, no. 4 (2017): 542–54.

taken place with regard to other fundamental services, such as childcare or transport. During the period of neoliberalism, a number of services that were provided collectively, be it via community or via the state, have been privatised.[4] The increasing individuation of consumption (consuming at the individual or nuclear family level) has increased not only private debt levels[5] but also the energy and material throughput of Western economies.[6] What is more, to get people to consume an ever greater number of vehicles, home appliances, clothes, holidays, etc., much had to be done in order to promote such spending – be it via a public route (e.g. law and policy) or the private (e.g. advertisement or cultural industry) route.

Since the 1980s, the European Union (EU) has become the main actor in regulating consumption, taking over much of the initiative from its member states.[7] The EU has produced a vast amount of policy and legislation that will gradually expand consumer protection from more exceptional situations (doorstep selling directive)[8] to buying offline (sale of goods)[9] and online (distance selling).[10] Two actors have played a central role in the EU consumer law and policy. On the one hand, the European Commission has shaped the horizons and agenda of law and policy in this field, setting up consumer policies and putting on the agenda legislation that the policy requires. On the other hand, the Court of Justice of the EU has been an important "corrector" of sometimes rather starkly instrumentalist EU legislation, which seemed to

---

[4] Frank Trentmann, *Empire of Things: How We Became a World of Consumers, from the Fifteenth Century to the Twenty-First* (Penguin UK, 2016).

[5] Moritz Schularick, 'Public and Private Debt: The Historical Record (1870–2010)', *German Economic Review* 15, no. 1 (1 February 2014): 191–207.

[6] Jason Hickel and Giorgos Kallis, 'Is Green Growth Possible?', *New Political Economy* 25, no. 4 (2019): 469–86.

[7] Hans-W. Micklitz, *The Politics of Justice in European Private Law: Social Justice, Access Justice, Societal Justice* (Cambridge University Press, 2018).

[8] Council Directive 85/577/EEC of 20 December 1985 to protect the consumer in respect of contracts negotiated away from business premises.

[9] Directive 2019/771/EU of the European Parliament and of the Council of 20 May 2019 on certain aspects concerning contracts for the sale of goods, amending Regulation (EU) 2017/2394 and Directive 2009/22/EC, and repealing Directive 1999/44/EC.

[10] Directive 2011/83/EU of the European Parliament and of the Council of 25 October 2011 on consumer rights, amending Council Directive 93/13/EEC and Directive 1999/44/EC of the European Parliament and of the Council and repealing Council Directive 85/577/EEC and Directive 97/7/EC of the European Parliament and of the Council.

forget parties in its zeal to promote the "well-functioning" of the internal market.[11]

In this chapter then, I explore how European institutions have imagined consumption, and consumers, within the changing imaginaries of prosperity. I do so by exploring systematically the discursive shifts behind the EU's consumer policies over the past 50 years, identifying how the background understandings of political economy have changed, including the role of the economy, government, law, politics, or nature, producing thus different imaginaries of consumers and consumption.

I rely on the Commission's consumer policies as a proxy for discerning European imaginaries. While certainly limited, as any proxy would be, the transforming consumer policies allow us to see the Commission's best guess as to what is broadly shared in European society and what would appear as appealing, credible, and necessary to the range of stakeholders it needs to convince in the process. I see the Commission's policies as good proxies for two reasons.[12] First, given the Commission's lack of formal legislative power beyond agenda-setting powers, the Commission has to tread carefully in order to convince the European legislators (Council of Ministers and the European Parliament) of what plays in society and what should be done about it. Second, by focusing on a certain type of documents produced by the same actor, for the same purpose, over a long period of time, I can also study more systematically the core changes in the conceptions of the economy, law, politics, government, and consumers in the EU, while being able to identify trends and important turning points in the institution of neoliberal imaginary of prosperity.

This chapter demonstrates several things. First, it shows that instituting a new imaginary of prosperity is both gradual and radical. Change proceeds by means of a variation in the understanding of the key elements of the social order, that is the economy, government, law, politics, and subjects behind consumer policies. These changes, or variations,

---

[11] Candida Leone, 'The Missing Stone in the Cathedral: Of Unfair Terms in Employment Contracts and Coexisting Rationalities in European Contract Law'. PhD thesis, University of Amsterdam (2022). https://pure.uva.nl/ws/files/48074023/Thesis_complete_.pdf.

[12] The new policies it proposes have to tap into the shared social imaginaries of the time – at least as they live in the heads of the EU's collective legislator – the Council, comprising EU member states ministers and high-level bureaucrats, the European Parliament, comprising of MPEs from all member states, as well as different 'stakeholders' who partake in the consultative process (consumer associations, business associations, the general public, etc.).

seem to cumulate; once new understandings of all the core elements of the social order have been sufficiently articulated, a new social imaginary can settle. Now, despite being born gradually through changes in the underlying conception of the social order, this settled imaginary is at the same time radically new. For unlike the previous variations, what emerges is something qualitatively different than the previous iterations: an articulation that is confident, coherent, convincing, and, one may even say, beautiful. The 1998 consumer policy, we will see, marks such a moment – the outing of a fully formed, perfect, privatising imaginary of prosperity that is confident in its conception of the world and the role of consumers within it.

Second, the neoliberal imaginary of prosperity has gradually replaced the world where consumer law and policy were much more collective and antagonistic.[13] At the time when the welfare state imaginary of shared prosperity predominated, next to consumers and businesses, also many other groups (e.g. workers, trade unions, small as opposed to big enterprises, and civil society actors) were seen as engaging in the struggle over the shape of consumption and economy. In this world, law and politics – rather than markets – were the main vehicles to articulate what prosperity means and how to bring it about. The role of government was to make sure that the outcomes of political battles were implemented, while it was expected to act with the principles of fairness and justice, as the main grounds of governmental accountability. In consumer policy, this meant that the protection of weaker parties took the central stage, with a view to ensuring that no groups (producers, distributors, or retailers) took advantage of each other. Legal institutions, with their discourses of justice and rights, were an important vehicle for not only implementing but also reasoning about the shape of political economy.

---

[13] The understanding of the *collective* that I propose in this book builds on the tradition in social theory that foregrounds conflict as the main driver or social change. While I recognise that other non-individualist social theories may provide an appealing consensual conception of the collective, my empirical work suggests that the negation of conflict in the past decades has usually coincided with the privatisation of power and resources. At the same time, conflict alone does not suffice to prevent the privatisation of power and resources – especially if the conflict is staged purely along cultural lines. Thus, some degree of *socio-economic* conflict seems to be necessary to stabilise imaginaries of shared prosperity. Within these not-so-exacting boundaries, I hope that the conceptual framework proposed by this book would be still of considerable interest to those who may entertain a different conception of social change.

The new neoliberal imaginary of privatised prosperity, which was ushered in from the 1980s onwards and became hegemonic around 1998, had a very different understanding of political economy and society. In this world, we find much more positive or naturalised conceptions of both the market and the actors that populate it. Standardised (rational) consumers and (innovative) businesses will drive economic growth forward in an economy that is mostly self-regulating, and win-win, provided that governments allow allocative efficiency to give shape to the market. The role of politics, and contestation, is limited as both businesses and consumers have an equal interest in the optimal functioning of the market. The role of law is mainly to facilitate a smooth market operation, which may require not only removing market failures but also at times chastening consumers into market-rational behaviour.[14]

This is, however, not where the story ends. After a long dominance of this privatised imaginary of prosperity in the EU consumer policy, we are witnessing a slow rearticulation of some elements of political economy that points in a new direction. This rearticulation shares some elements with the welfare state imaginaries of prosperity, while incorporating other concepts such as repair, longevity, maintenance, circularity, and sharing and embracing a more holistic concept of the consumer and their interests.

It is important to stress here that it took neoliberal imaginary almost two decades to become hegemonic. Thus, what we are seeing are only the first steps in the direction of a new imaginary, which needs both time and political will to take shape. The political will is, however, not emerging without constraint and pressure. The most important roadblock to change is the capital, which fosters the fear from shifting away from cosy neoliberal imaginary of prosperity where businesses are the "motor" of our prosperity, and which regulation or taxes will undermine. At the same time tribal imaginaries aim to compete with the emergent imaginary of prosperity by promising instead security by reaffirming old hierarchies and identities (be it national, ethnic, religious, or gender).

Two caveats are in order before we move to the empirical section. First, the chapter does not look at the other important actor in consumer law

---

[14] Marija Bartl, 'Internal Market Rationality, Private Law and the Direction of the Union: Resuscitating the Market as the Object of the Political', *European Law Journal* 21, no. 5 (15 January 2015): 572–98.

and policy – the Court of Justice – which has played a vital role in countering at times strongly instrumentalising moves of the European Commission. The reason is that the Court still remains constrained by the scope of its constitutional task of interpreting EU law, on the basis of cases that come before it. This means that its possibility to steer the transformation of imaginaries remains limited at best.[15]

Second, as the chapter follows the transformation of the Commission's consumer policies, it is also limited by what the Commission considers within the scope of consumer policy. Thus, for instance, the discussion on public services does not feature prominently in the Commission's documents after 1985 (with the exception of the 1995 policy), as the 'services of general economic interest' (SGEI) become a separate field of policy action. These previously monopolistic providers of public services had to be heavily regulated if the liberalisation and privatisation were not to end up in a social disaster. And still, at times the more 'voluntary' consumption that falls under consumer law and policy has provided consumers with more rights – a link recognised by the Court that extended some consumer rights to the field of SGEI.[16]

3.2 Consumption as a Matter of Contract Law

While we have always consumed, the institutional mix that ensured material reproduction of societies has transformed fundamentally. Industrialisation and the growing centrality of markets in the provision of goods and services have marked the past 150 years. It is both due to the growing importance of markets in providing goods and services for consumption, as well as a general increase in the quantities we consume ('mass consumption'), that consumption has started to resemble the patterns we are accustomed to today.[17] These transformations have been accompanied by the increasing importance of the 'law of contracts' in most European countries, where, as part of large 'civil codifications', contract formed the basic, background institutional framework against which the rise of consumption took place.

The history of contract law follows quite neatly changing social imaginaries. The ideological background of the nineteenth-century contract

---

[15] Leone, 'The Missing Stone in the Cathedral'.
[16] Candida Leone, 'Transparency Revisited – On the Role of Information in the Recent Case-Law of the CJEU', *European Review of Contract Law* 10, no. 2 (1 January 2014): 312–25.
[17] Leone, 'The Missing Stone in the Cathedral'.

law was in principle progressive. Contracts freed people from the chains of 'status' and enabled them to participate in the emergent market economy freely, as equals.[18] The rich and poor, the strong and weak, all had the freedom to conclude contracts with whom they wanted, on the subjects they wanted, and on the terms they wanted.[19] Landlords and tenants, industrialists and workers, adults and minors, debtors and creditors, could all enjoy their freedom in the market. The state, in the service of the new order and its subjects, was then bound to respect private autonomy and recognise and enforce these freely concluded contracts.[20]

Before long, however, many realised that the core contract law principles of private autonomy and formal equality materially played out rather differently for the rich and the poor, for those of "better" and "worse" backgrounds, for men and for women, etc.[21] Those who had more (bargaining) power and knowledge were able to impose their own terms on those who had less power, under the threat of state enforcement. A very broad range of contracts could be concluded and enforced, such as agreements for 7-day working weeks, 16-hour workdays in mines, and/or for children under the age of 9.[22]

Given the apparently unfair effects of this newly acquired freedom, the regulation of market relations – reliant on contract law and private law more generally – became a space of political struggle in the late nineteenth and throughout the twentieth century.[23] "Freedom of contract" was to take significant hits as time passed, with new fields of law (labour law, tenancy law, and later consumer law) being carved out of the private law domain, which itself remained subject to relatively unconstrained freedom of contract.[24]

When it comes to consumption, in the course of the nineteenth-century goods that were transferred through the market fell under the background rules of classical (liberal) contract law. Yet, in those early

---

[18] Max Weber, *Economy and Society: An Outline of Interpretive Sociology*, vol. 2 (University of California Press, 1978).
[19] Of course, "all" often excluded women and racialised groups.
[20] R. L. Hale, 'Coercion and Distribution in a Supposedly Non-Coercive State', *Political Science Quarterly* 38, no. 3 (1923): 470–94.
[21] Ibid.
[22] P. S. Atiyah, *The Rise and Fall of Freedom of Contract* (Oxford University Press, 1985).
[23] In an early critique of this trend, Weber speaks of 'materialisation' of contract law. Weber, *Economy and Society* Part IV, 4.
[24] Ruth Dukes, *The Labour Constitution: The Enduring Idea of Labour Law* (Oxford University Press, 2014).

days, both the number and complexity of such consumer contracts were comparatively low, barely presenting an issue of larger societal concern.[25] Areas where consumers' interests found their way to court were most often related to the health and safety of consumer products, for instance, the question of the contractual relevance of advertisements for quack medicines, the so-called puffs.[26]

Consumer contracts emerge as a *problem* with the rise of adhesion contracts.[27] These so-called boilerplate contractual terms were incorporated into contracts without negotiation, under the radar so to say, shifting most rights to sellers and leaving buyers without much protection. The critique of this practice came from several different directions. Some argued that sellers used standardised contract terms to take advantage of buyers, who were in a structurally weaker position.[28] Others feared the usurpation of legislative power, whereby sellers produced quasi-legislation applicable across a broad range of contracts.[29]

While adhesion contracts clearly presented a problem for contract law and contract theory, they were also a sign of new times. Leone argues that adhesion contracts only became an issue in the first half of the twentieth century because a growing number of people gained access to a broader palette of consumer goods. Yet the rising number of transactions, which anything but resembled the arm's length business negotiations that classical contract law had in mind, took liberal contract law out of its comfort zone.[30]

It was only post-WW2 that consumers' interests, and contracts, became a matter of both broader social mobilisation and governmental action in Europe. Different countries had very different social and legal trajectories when it came to both. For instance, in France, the consumer question was first taken up by trade unions in the 1960s, with consumer bodies and associations only developing later. The particular focus of

---

[25] In most continental legal systems, contract law does not require a particular form.
[26] Anat Rosenberg, 'Exaggeration: Advertising, Law and Medical Quackery in Britain, c. 1840–1914', *The Journal of Legal History* 42, no. 2 (4 May 2021): 202–31; Trentmann, *Empire of Things*.
[27] Leone, 'The Missing Stone in the Cathedral'.
[28] Friedrich Kessler, 'Contracts of Adhesion – Some Thoughts About Freedom of Contract', *Columbia Law Review* 43 (1943): 629; Roscoe Pound, 'The Role of the Will in Law', *Harvard Law Review* 68, no. 1 (1954): 19.
[29] Ludwig Raiser, *Das Recht Der Allgemeinen Geschäftsbedingungen* (Hanseat. Verlag-Anst., 1935), as cited in Leone, 'The Missing Stone in the Cathedral'.
[30] See also Trentmann, *Empire of Things*.

governmental intervention was to regulate the prices of consumer goods, as well as ensure health and safety.[31] In the UK, the Melony Report (1960) outlined all kinds of problems faced by citizens and consumers. However, it was not until the 1970s that the first piece of legislation in the field of consumer protection was produced in the UK.[32] In the Netherlands, the social movement preceded governmental intervention by a long haul,[33] with the first legislation appearing shortly after the 1962 Kennedy's Consumer Bill of Rights.[34]

Micklitz argues that the rise of the importance of consumer protection in the 1970s coincided with the crisis of the welfare state and may be seen as one of the early signs of privatised Keynesianism, that is (debt-driven) consumption as a replacement for the diminishing public provision. This, he further argues, made the EU member states much more ready to hand over the initiative and power in the field of consumer protection to the European communities when they became interested in the field.[35]

3.3 A Hurried Decline of the Imaginary of Shared Prosperity (1975–1985+)

As the EU entered the field of consumer protection with a consumer policy in 1975,[36] most of its member states already have some substantive provisions on consumer protection in place, as well as consumer bodies taking care of collective consumer interests. However, the EU makes a new overture in that it attempts a more systematic approach to consumer protection: a comprehensive consumer *policy*. With growing complexity and juridification, a policy seems to promise more coherent or rational governance, starting from an overview of the field governed and articulating how a wide range of issues and problems are interrelated – setting thus a proper basis for any future intervention.[37]

From the 70s, each EU consumer policies starts by carefully outlining the state of (political) economy, and continues with the articulation of

---

[31] Peter van Dam, 'The Entangled Consumer: Rethinking the Rise of the Consumer after 1945', *Journal of Nonprofit & Public Sector Marketing* 33, no. 2 (2021): 212–38.
[32] Fair Trading Act 1973; Consumer Credit Act 1974. The Labour government also created the Department of Prices and Consumer Protection in 1974, only to be abolished by the Conservative government in 1979.
[33] van Dam, 'The Entangled Consumer'.
[34] Micklitz, *The Politics of Justice in European Private Law*, Part II, 2.   [35] Ibid.
[36] Christoph U. Schmid, 'The Instrumentalist Conception of the Acquis Communautaire in Consumer Law and Its Implications on a European Contract Law Code', *European Review of Contract Law* 1, no. 2 (July 2005): 211–27.
[37] Christoph Knill and Jale Tosun, *Public Policy: A New Introduction* (Red Globe Press, 2020).

the subject of the intervention – the consumer – and their needs vis-à-vis other economic actors and systemic pressures. The commission also articulates what it deems to be the role of government (itself in particular), what politics has to say in the shape of consumer rights, and what the appropriate ways in which law could, and should, intervene are. Content-wise, this makes consumer policies an excellent proxy for mapping the changing imaginaries of prosperity, and the role of consumption within.

3.3.1 1975: Consumer Protection as a Collective Project

The 1975 consumer policy opens with the section '*The consumer and the economy*', in which the European Commission describes the economy in which it is to intervene. In the Commission's view, the transformation towards a consumer society is nothing but finished: '*The discovery of new materials, the introduction of new methods of manufacture, the development of means of communication, the expansion of markets, new methods of retailing* [that] *have had the effect of increasing the production, supply and demand of an immense variety of goods and services*'.[38]

As a consequence of these ongoing transformations of market conditions, '*the balance between suppliers and customers has tended to become weighted in favour of the supplier. ... The consumer, in the past usually an individual purchaser in a small local market, has become merely* **a unit in a mass market***, the target of* **advertising campaigns** *and of pressure by* **strongly organized production and distribution groups***.*'[39] In this new constellation, producers and distributors have an upper hand, which they abundantly use in order to pursue their interests and goals. Thus, producers and distributors have '*a greater opportunity to determine market conditions than the consumer*', while at the same time mergers, cartels, and abuses of competition '*create imbalances to the detriment of consumers*'.[40]

The social whole that the Commission portrays is that of the economy as an ever more complex market offering many goods and services, but also presenting a space for conflict and abuse. The main actants, the subjects in this complex market, are the producers and distributors who, through aggressive advertising strategies, for instance, may exercise

---

[38] Council Resolution of 14 April 1975, on the 'Preliminary programme of the European Economic Community for a consumer protection and information policy' (the programme itself is added as the annex to the resolution), No. C 92/3.
[39] Consumer Policy 1975. All emphases in the quotes, in this and the following chapters, were added by the author of this book.
[40] Consumer Policy 1975.

excessive power over the consumers' choice. These groups, the Commission claims, have a structural advantage in this new complex market. Consumers, in contrast, have lost much of the control they once had in their local, overseeable market.

In order to remedy this, two pathways are envisaged: on the one hand, consumers need to organise – collectively – to fight and defend their interests. On the other hand, government also needs to take responsibility for consumer *protection* – as due to structural asymmetries, the collective action of consumers will not always suffice. Thus, the role the European Communities is to safeguard consumers' interests, by taking *'full account of consumer interests in the various sectors of Community activity, and to satisfy their collective and individual needs'*.[41]

As guidelines for legal and political intervention, the European Commission identifies *five basic rights* of consumers,[42] on the grounds of

Five Consumer Rights

(a) the right to protection of health and safety,
(b) the right to protection of economic interests,
(c) the right of redress,
(d) the right to information and education,
(e) the right of representation (the right to be heard).

Five EU Policy Objectives

A. protection against hazards to consumer health and safety,
B. effective protection against damage to consumers' economic interests,
C. adequate facilities for advice, help and redress,
D. consumer information and education,
E. consultation with and representation of consumers in the framing of decisions affecting their interests.

---

[41] Consumer Policy 1975, No. C 92/4.
[42] Inspired by J. F. Kennedy, 'Special Message to the Congress on Protecting the Consumer Interest', www.presidency.ucsb.edu/documents/special-message-the-congress-protecting-the-consumer-interest, last accessed 3 January 2024.

which it develops *five policy objectives* for the EU consumer policy (those will also find their way into later consumer policies of 1981 as well as 1991).[43]

Consumers are bearers of rights, and the task of government is to ensure the fulfillment and protection of these rights. Furthermore, these consumer rights, and the policy objectives that follow from them, are not conceptualised by the European Commission as individual rights only. Rather, they are also collective rights, relevant for consumers both as individuals and as a group in the struggle against producers and distributors.

This language of protection, alongside the stress on individual and collective rights, is one of the signposts of a welfare state imaginary of shared prosperity. There is nothing natural about the ways in which the market allocates and distributes either resources or power. Instead, government is responsible for the shape the market takes as well as its distributive outcomes. If there are groups who seem consistently getting the short end of the stick – as established through the political process – they need to be protected by government. It is by means of law, and rights, that such protection takes place.

Indeed, this protection required rather far-reaching legal interventions from today's point of view: '*Purchasers of goods or services should be protected against **the abuse of power** by the seller, in particular against **one-sided standard contracts** (*), the **unfair exclusion of essential rights in contracts, harsh conditions of credit, demands for payment for unsolicited goods** and against **high-pressure selling methods**'.*[44] By changing the rules of contract, that is curtailing the contractual freedom of stronger actors, the legal infrastructure of market (relations) – that is the markets themselves – is changed. The core concern of (consumer) law in this period is to remedy power asymmetries, the abuse of stronger bargaining positions, and remove any resulting unfairness from market transactions. In terms of legal imaginaries, law is seen as constitutive of markets, making clear that there is little which is natural, or apolitical, about market's distributive consequences.

Furthermore, the recognition of both government's capacity to govern and its responsibility for market outcomes is discernible when it comes to the protection of health and safety. '*Substances or preparations which may form part of or be added to foodstuffs should be defined and their use regulated, for example by endeavouring to **draw up in Community rules, clear and precise positive lists**'.*[45] Government, in this social imaginary, has a sufficient

---

[43] Consumer Policy 1975, No. C 92/1 and No. C 92/4.
[44] Consumer Policy 1975, No. C 92/6.   [45] Consumer Policy 1975, No. C 92/5.

knowledge to identify such harmful substances and regulate them authoritatively by placing them on lists of prohibited substances. "Government failure" is still nowhere to be seen.[46]

The 1970s are often identified as the period when the neoliberal privatising imaginary of prosperity started taking hold across the world.[47] Yet, as the analysis of the 1975 consumer policy makes clear, the institutionalisation of neoliberalism did not actually even start in many fields of law and policy. The imaginary of the political economy that prevails here is still that of a place of struggle between different classes or groups. Government is not seen as a neutral arbiter between these different groups but instead has an obligation to intervene, remedy power asymmetries, and redress any abuses of power. Interventionist law and policy – rather than a reliance on market processes – is a crucial instrument to shape economic and social reality. The collective imaginary is, however, going to show its first cracks only a couple of years later. Starting with the destabilisation of the concept of politics, and the role of government, which characterise it.

3.3.2   1981: First Cracks

As a consequence of the economic downturn in previous years, the 1981 consumer policy starts with a much more gloomy picture: '*in the current difficult economic situation, a situation characterized by a **slowdown in incomes growth**, continuing unemployment (...), consumers are obliged to pay more attention to the way in which they use their income (...)*'.[48] The Commission then sees as the task of consumer policy to enable *the consumer to act with full knowledge of the facts*', while making sure that consumers are able to '*hold the balance between market forces*'.[49] Thus, unlike a couple of decades later, when the Commission sees expanding consumer demand as the main driver of economic recovery and consumers as instrumental to economic growth, during the economic crisis at the beginning of the 1980s, the task of consumer policy is still to

---

[46] Joseph E. Stiglitz, 'Government Failure vs. Market Failure: Principles of Regulation', in *Government and Markets: Toward a New Theory of Regulation*, , ed. Edward J. Balleisen and David A. Moss (Cambridge University Press, 2009), 13–51.

[47] David Harvey, *A Brief History of Neoliberalism* (Oxford University Press, 2005).

[48] Council Resolution of 19 May 1981, on a second programme of the European Economic Community for a consumer protection and information policy (the programme itself is added as the annex to the resolution), No. C 133/2.

[49] Second Programme 1981, No. C 133/12.

strengthen consumers as a class that holds and should hold a certain economic power in the market.

The main change from the previous consumer policy lies in the conception of politics, that is in the understanding of how the Communities are to achieve the abovementioned objectives. '*In the course of the implementation* [of the 1975 consumer policy], **the idea gradually developed** *that the consumer should be increasingly seen as having a part to play in the preparation of economic and social decisions concerning him*'.[50] The Commission continues: '[W]*ithout in any way ceasing to ensure that the rights listed above are complied with, the consumer policy, which has hitherto been mainly defensive, should become* **more positive and more open to a dialogue** *in order to establish the conditions in which the* **consumer can become a participant** *in the preparation and implementation of important economic decisions which concern him first and foremost as a buyer or a user, and which very largely determine his individual or collective living conditions*'.[51]

The Commission suggests that two consequences follow from this attempt to make the decision-making about consumer policy more 'open and positive'. First, the consumer movement will be expected to '*progressively* **take into account the economic and social implications of the decisions** *on which it might wish to be consulted*'.[52] Second, while it is still the case that the action taken '*by the individual consumer is not likely to have much effect on the mass market where he exercises his choice, the excessive growth in regulatory powers can only serve to* **over-institutionalize** *the relationships between the parties concerned*'.[53]

Several things are going on here. While the Commission acknowledges consumers' interests as different from those of producers, as their interests must be pursued collectively, it restricts this collective action to a kind of cooperative relationship, rather than an agonistic struggle, with suppliers. However, in contrast to full-blown privatising imaginary, the Commission still does not postulate a fully "common interest" between the different groups in the smooth market operation. Instead, it proposes a more collaborative type of politics.

The perception of the appropriate role of government is also changing. When the Commission warns against the growth of regulatory powers that could "over-institutionalise" the relationships between the parties, we see an important privatising move. Government needs to guard against being too steering and too interventionist, so as not to

---

[50] Second Programme 1981, No. C 133/2.
[51] Second Programme 1981, No. C 133/2.
[52] Second Programme 1981, No. C 133/3.
[53] Second Programme 1981, No. C 133/12.

crowd out the space for private initiative. This is one of the early announcements of the "de-regulation" narrative that becomes a trademark of the new imaginary of privatised prosperity.

While these two shifts are significant, in many other aspects the 1981 consumer policy simply takes over the framings from the 1975 consumer policy, maintaining relevant aspects of the imaginary of collective prosperity. Government still has enough knowledge to act on public health and safety, putting harmful substances on blacklists or handing out *prior* authorisations for potentially hazardous products and services.[54] Equally, the document maintains the language of protection and envisages that private law rules should *protect* consumers against all kinds of abuses, such as unfair trading practices, unfair terms, misleading advertisements, or obliging sellers to supply spare parts for consumer goods.[55]

3.4 Towards the Imaginary of Privatised Prosperity (1985–1995)

3.4.1 1985: 'New Impetus' for Consumer Policy

By the mid-1980s, the private route to prosperity was becoming the more dominant imaginary across EU policy. In 1985, the Commission published one of its most influential policy papers in its history – the 'White Paper on the Completion of the Internal Market'[56] – which portrays the internal market as a matter of technical interventions and articulates some 200 measures necessary for the "completion" of this internal market. The White Paper precedes a new European Treaty – the 'Single European Act'[57] – whose main contribution was introducing majority voting in several important areas of EU policymaking, among which the single market. It is then the combined operation of the various technical measures required for completing the market, enabled by the newly established majority voting, which would also bring a 'new impetus to consumer policy'.[58]

An important epistemic shift takes place in the New Impetus to Consumer Policy. The objectives of the consumer policy change: it is *citizen welfare* (i.e. citizens should benefit from the well-functioning

---

[54] Second Programme 1981, No. C 133/4.   [55] Second Programme 1981, No. C 133/7.
[56] European Commission, Completing the Internal Market: White Paper from the Commission to the European Council, COM(85) 0310 final.
[57] Single European Act, 1986.
[58] Commission Communication to the Council, New Impetus for Consumer Protection Policy, COM(85) 314 final.

3.4 TOWARDS IMAGINARY OF PRIVATISED PROSPERITY

internal market) and *productive efficiency* (consumer confidence in the safety and quality of products increases sales) that are to become the axis of the Commission's thinking about consumer policy.[59] The Commission challenges member states who see consumer policy as a *'fair weather'* policy.[60] Claiming that when *'seen from this twin standpoint of citizens' welfare and efficiency of production, consumer protection assumes its proper dimensions as an indispensable part of the fabric of Community policy'*.[61] The internal market thus gradually becomes a justification for consumer policy, while consumer policy is understood as central for the smooth operation of the internal market. The world of the EU consumer policies hereby ceases to be constituted at the meso level of groups, with conflicting interests, and instead reveals itself as constituted at the macro level of the (well-functioning) market.

This changed perspective is linked to the new ways of delivering old objectives. Thus, when it comes to the Commission's approach to health and safety, we see a shift in the understanding of the role of government. Namely, the Commission proposes *'a programme of legislation which would set out clearly for manufacturers and suppliers the health and safety levels which their products must meet in order to ensure the protection of the consumer'*.[62] By implication, the implementation of this seems to be left to businesses themselves. This approach also strongly resembles the 'new approach to technical regulation', which starts in the same year and expects the regulator to set the standards while businesses and their associations decide on the best way to deliver them.[63] Both present a move to partially privatise formerly public competences.

The Commission's changing imaginary of the economy reveals itself in its renewed approach to the protection of consumers' economic interests. The Commission, for the first time, sees consumers' economic interests, rather than the protection of consumers, as explicitly linked to the participation in the European cross-border market: *'If the common market is to be fully effective, it must be made easier for consumers to buy goods in other countries (...) Consumers generally are unaware of their existing rights or the advantages to be obtained by exploiting differences in prices prevailing between Member States and on the operation of customs controls for Community citizens at Member States' frontiers within the common market'*.[64] The Commission

---

[59] 'New Impetus', p. 8.   [60] 'New Impetus', p. 3.   [61] 'New Impetus', p. 8.
[62] 'New Impetus', p 10.
[63] Jacques Pelkmans, 'The New Approach to Technical Harmonization and Standardization', *JCMS: Journal of Common Market Studies* 25, no. 3 (1987): 249–69.
[64] 'New Impetus', p. 16.

foregrounds in this policy what will be the guiding star of the privatising imaginaries of consumption, namely that *'Better information for consumers is a prerequisite for the improved operation of competition'*.[65]

However, in terms of concrete legal measures, it is only in the upcoming "Consumer Credit Directive" where information is the central paradigm; other proposed legal measures on the basis of this policy, and the imaginary behind them, remain collective. Thus, the Commission pushes through relatively wide-ranging legislation providing substantive protection to consumers against unfair terms in consumer contracts. A measure that would endow public courts with a capacity to strike down unfair contract terms – therefore curtailing freedom of contract (of suppliers). And while the justification for this measure is the fact that consumers will often be faced with contracts in foreign languages and thus may not be able to familiarise themselves with the terms, the measure is not limited to only cross-border contracts. If anything, the unfair terms protection will be mostly invoked in a national context.[66] Unfair terms protection is a legal tool that belongs to the (welfare state) imaginary of shared prosperity, and it will prove in the future,[67] as it did in the past,[68] to be fundamental for dealing with *unequal bargaining power* in contractual relations.

In terms of the representation of consumers' interests, and thus the concept of politics behind the New Impetus, the cooperation between consumers and businesses remains central. The Commission returns to the 1981 consumer policy and contemplates the reasons for the lack of success in the dialogue between consumers and businesses (jointly 'operators') in bringing about private standards that could replace governmental intervention. As it often comes, the Commission realises that it must use public power – the law – in order to successfully privatise that same power: *'Backed up by Community law, however, codes of business practice have an analogous position to product safety standards'*.[69]

3.4.2   1990: Breaking the Link between Consumer Rights and Policy Objectives

After years of economic trouble, the consumer policy of 1990 clearly set out a more optimistic tone. Things are getting better, also for consumers.

---

[65] 'New Impetus', p. 16.
[66] Hans-Wolfgang Micklitz and Norbert Reich, 'The Court and Sleeping Beauty: The Revival of the Unfair Contract Terms Directive (UCTD)', *Common Market Law Review* 51, no. 3 (1 June 2014): 771–808.
[67] Ibid.   [68] Leone, 'The Missing Stone in the Cathedral'.   [69] 'New Impetus', p. 19.

The previous shift to a macro perspective of the market seems to have been entrenched in the Commission's thinking, helping it to articulate a path forward: '*The construction of the internal market is expected to be greatly to the advantage of the consumer. To gain the benefits, it is necessary that consumers be sufficiently confident to use the opportunities*'.[70] Not only is the Commission confident that the internal market is good for consumers, but also that consumers are good for the internal market: '*Attention to consumer interests*', *not only for their own sakes, but also for the benefits of producers, distributors and enterprise in general.*[71] This newly found alliance between consumer protection and market objectives seems to put consumer policy on firmer ground – giving rise to new confidence on all fronts.

How then is the Commission going to advance the interests of both consumers and businesses, in this newly found alliance? '*Four main areas of focus are identified because of their importance in* **building the consumer confidence necessary to support the implementation of the internal market**. *(1) Consumer Representation; (2) Consumer Information; (3) Consumer Safety; (4) Consumer Transactions*'.[72] Consumer *rights*, a regular occurrence in the previous policies, are nowhere to be seen. The shift from subjective rights thinking to objective thinking in consumer policy reinforces a more "global", or macro, view of consumer policy, where rights become one of the elements of a broader internal market policy mix.

When it comes to the understanding of the role of government and of consumers, it is the *information paradigm* that becomes the main tool to "harmonise" consumer interests with those of the internal market in the emerging imaginary of privatised prosperity.[73] However, at this point of time, this subject matter is still approached rather cautiously by the European Commission. Suggesting that '*Sales promotion information is not of itself a sufficient basis for decision making for significant purchases. Consumers need access to* **factual information and advice** *right across the range of supply*'.[74] Therefore, the public or collective provision of information still

---

[70] European Commission, *Three Year Action Plan of Consumer Policy in the EEC (1990–1992)*, p. 2.
[71] European Commission, *Three Year Action Plan*, p. 3.
[72] European Commission, *Three Year Action Plan*, p. 5.
[73] Note that the project is to harmonise the interests of the consumers with the logic of an abstract entity, the internal market.
[74] European Commission, *Three Year Action Plan*, p. 15.

has an important role to play. The provision of factual information should come '*from various sources*', and purely market provision is thus insufficient.[75] This hesitance will, however, be abandoned in the course of the 1990s.

Importantly, while a withdrawal of government is announced in many different ways within this and previous policies, we can still see the role for the government in at least one way – namely the European Communities that will *make* the European internal market. For the first time, the Commission indicates that the differences in contract law between member states may present a problem for the internal market, insofar that they inhibit consumers from engaging in cross-border transactions: '*The differences in conditions of sale in contracts across the twelve Member States are such as to inhibit consumers from purchasing significant items or services away from his or her place of residence. (...) It is necessary to identify the elements in the existing contract laws of Member States which are likely to inhibit consumer purchasing and as far as possible eliminate them*'.[76] This framing that the Commission adopts,[77] facilitated with the move from unanimity to majority voting, will set the grounds for a battle for full harmonisation in the 2000s.[78]

When it comes to its conception of politics, the Commission continues to ponder how to facilitate cooperation between businesses and consumers. At the same time, however, it does not seem to have entirely embraced the politics of common interest. Instead, the Commission is still concerned with the creation of strong consumer groups, providing them with both technical assistance and financing, in order to set the grounds for the negotiation of relations between businesses and consumers.

By 1990, we have still seen relatively few pieces of consumer legislation. The doorstep selling directive and product liability directive both came into force in 1985, but their implementation was planned years later. In 1987, the Commission also adopted the first Consumer Credit

---

[75] '*Sales promotion information is not of itself a sufficient basis for decision making for significant purchases*', European Commission, *Three Year Action Plan*, p. 8.
[76] European Commission, *Three Year Action Plan*, p. 14.
[77] This trend is best articulated in the famous 'Sutherland Report', published in 1992, and available at http://aei.pitt.edu/1025/1/Market_post_1992_Sutherland_1.pdf.
[78] M. B. M. Loos, 'Full Harmonisation as a Regulatory Concept and Its Consequences for the National Legal Orders. The Example of the Consumer Rights Directive', *Centre for the Study of European Contract Law Working Paper Series*, No. 2010/03 (2010).

Directive. These three pieces of legislation provide a blueprint for some of the most innovative legal tools that originate from the EU consumer policy: withdrawal rights, strict liability for defective products, and finally the central role of consumer information as a tool of consumer policy. Importantly, while the first two measures are still about market shaping – remaking the infrastructure of market transactions by redistributing power, rights, and obligations between different market actors – the Consumer Credit Directive is different. As an early announcement of the imaginary of prosperity to come, the Consumer Credit Directive is mainly focused on the provision of information, thereby finding a "golden balance" between pursuing consumer policy objectives and at the same time improving market functioning without the risk of "over-institutionalisation".

3.4.3 1995: Privatising for Good Causes: Public Services and Sustainability

In 1995, the Commission published perhaps one of the most interesting documents in the recent decades, titled 'Priorities for Consumer Policy 1996–1998'. Unlike previous and later policies – at least until the 2020 consumer agenda – this document has very different aspirations and structure. It lists a number of issues that the Commission considers of crucial importance for consumer policy, which certainly go beyond simple "completing the Internal Market"[79] considerations. *'Virtually every policy in the European Community has some significance for consumers. Faced with this situation and given the resources available for redeployment, the Commission must choose priorities from a range of options'.*[80]

This programmatic document, for the first and, until recently the only time,[81] very openly engages with a broad range of issues that touch consumers and consumer policy and will be later retired into special, siloed, policy domains and legislations.[82] These topics include, for instance, financial services, consumers' interests in the supply of public services, measures to improve consumer confidence in foodstuffs, encouragement of a practical approach to sustainable consumption,

---

[79] From 1992 Treaties, we officially begin to use the term 'Internal Market' to denote a new level of market integration.
[80] European Commission, Priorities for Consumer Policy, COM(95) 519 final, p. 3
[81] The 2020 Consumer Policy is a similarly wide-ranging document. See Section 3.6.2.
[82] Hans-W. Micklitz, 'The Visible Hand of European Regulatory Private Law – The Transformation of European Private Law from Autonomy to Functionalism in Competition and Regulation', *Yearbook of European Law* 28, no. 1 (1 January 2009): 3–59.

strengthening and increasing consumer representation, and international relations and development.

Perhaps the most remarkable element of the document is a discernible transformation of the imaginaries of both economy and government. The document announces a push for the *liberalisation* of *public* services – a push to introduce the principle of competition in the provision of public services. In order to do that, however, most member states have also felt it necessary to simultaneously split up and privatise many of the previously public service providers, moving the control over these fundamental services to private companies.[83] This liberalisation project is complemented with another move to relinquish public responsibility. Namely, while the Commission announces the importance and gravity of the environmental challenges that humanity faces, it at the same time shifts the responsibility to consumers to act on it.

Firstly, with regard to public services, the Commission states that it '*has made considerable efforts* **to accelerate the liberalisation of essential services of public utility***. The introduction of competition in these services will have a positive impact for consumers*'.[84] This liberalisation of public services should ensure both affordability (qua market) and quality (qua market, with regulation for the provision to the weakest): '*While continuing to press for liberalisation to* **increase efficiency and to reduce prices** *to the benefit of consumers, the Commission will be concerned to ensure that the quality of service is improved and enhanced particularly for groups of consumers who are in a weak position and therefore very dependent on such services*'.[85] While from today's perspective it is obvious that neither affordability nor quality of services will be automatically delivered by the sole fact of introducing competition,[86] in the mid-1990s the trust in the market mechanism was mostly unconditional.

Secondly, regarding the environment, the Commission notes, '*The political recognition that society faces a major challenge in adjusting its habits and behaviour to the degree that they are sustainable has developed globally*'.[87] The Commission also recognises a particular responsibility of the EU with its large market. Yet immediately it also suggests that it is the '*Consumers* [who] *can exercise a considerable pressure, by their choices, toward*

---

[83] Christoph Hermann and Koen Verhoest, 'Varieties and Variations of Public Service: Liberalisation and Privatisation in Europe', *PIQUE Policy Paper* 1 (2008): 1–12.
[84] Consumer Policy 1995, p. 7.   [85] Consumer Policy 1995, p. 8.
[86] Marija Bartl, 'The Affordability of Energy: How Much Protection for the Vulnerable Consumers?', *Journal of Consumer Policy* 33, no. 3 (2010): 225–45.
[87] Consumer Policy 1995, p. 10.

design, production and marketing of products and services with a reduced environmental impact'.[88] This important role of consumers must be facilitated by making sure that '*information is provided covering the relevant environmental and performance aspects, and the information given is neutral and reliable*'.[89] It is quite remarkable then that in the face of major collective challenges that will require a considerable degree of global cooperation and coordination, the proper way forward was to place this task in the hands of the smallest unit: the (properly informed) individual consumer.

Finally, when it comes to the conception of politics, the Commission is committed to strengthening the consumer "movement" in the EU. It will finance the consumer movement, particularly in the European South. '*Consequently, the need for the Commission to sustain and increase support is essential in order to ensure the short and medium term development of the consumer movement in these countries*'.[90] While this move to strengthen consumers' movement may appear as part of the collective imaginary, the document leaves some ambiguity in this regard as the justification for this move is mainly to ensure that the consumers' representatives can contribute to private rule-making processes – for instance, within the different standardisation bodies such as CEN and CENELEC.[91]

3.5 The Transient Hegemony of the Privatised Prosperity (1998–2012+)

3.5.1 1998: The Birth of Common Interest and the Death of Politics

Reading the 1998 Consumer Agenda makes for a very special experience. One cannot fail to notice a particular confidence, internal coherence, and even elegance of this text. This consumer agenda marks the consolidation of the fully privatised imaginary of prosperity in consumer policy. The imaginaries of the economy, government, politics, law, or the consumer behind this policy are weaved in a confident story of prosperity, where well-functioning markets and smart consumers drive us towards a better future.

Even the table of contents, before the text has started at all, makes clear that the great future awaits us in this new world:

---

[88] Consumer Policy 1995, p. 10. [89] Consumer Policy 1995, p. 10
[90] Consumer Policy 1995, p. 12. [91] Consumer Policy 1995, p. 12.

94   REIMAGINING CONSUMPTION

1. CONSUMER POLICY IN A CHANGING WORLD 1
2. THE CONSUMER POLICY ACTION PLAN 6
3. 'A MORE POWERFUL VOICE FOR THE CONSUMER THROUGHOUT THE EU' 8
   3.1. More effective consumer associations 8
   3.2. Effective dialogue between consumers and business 9
   3.3. Euro guichets- serving EU consumers better 10
   3.4. Better infomlation and education for consumers 10
4. 'A HIGH LEVEL OF HEALTH AND SAFETY FOR EU CONSUMERS' 11
   4.1. Science-based policy making 11
   4.2. Safer products 13
   4.3. Safer services 13
   4.4. Better enforcement, monitoring and response to emergencies 14
5. 'FULL RESPECT FOR THE ECONOMIC INTERESTS OF EU CONSUMERS.' 15
   5.1. Financial services and a single currency for consumers 15
   5.2. A more up-to-date regulatory framework. 16
   5.3. Better enforcement and monitoring 17
   5.4. Better integration of consumer economic interests in other EU policies 18

Image 3.1

The Commission knows exactly at this point how to give '*a more powerful voice*' to consumers across the EU, how to provide '*a high level of health and safety*', and how to ensure the '*full respect for the economic interests of EU consumers*'. If in the previous policies there was always some doubt, hesitation, or measures that went both ways (some towards privatising power and resources and others towards collectivising power and resources), in this policy there is no doubt left – regarding both the direction and means. It can only get better from here.

However, this new future is not without demands on consumers. Within this document, an articulate new image of the consumer emerges. According to the Commission, the growing role of consumer law has to be '*matched by a* **new maturity** *on the part of consumers and their representatives. If consumers are to play their role fully as equal stakeholders in society, they need to understand the inter-linkages between their interests and those of others*'.[92] But what does this new 'new maturity' and equality require? '*Sometimes the respective interests of consumers and other groups will be mutually reinforcing, sometimes they will not and trade-offs will have to be found.* **Consumers themselves can recognise and accept such trade-offs because they are not only consumers but taxpayers, employees and beneficiaries of public policies too.** *(. . .) EU consumer policy should therefore ensure that consumer interests are equitably reconciled with those of other stakeholders. This reconciliation of interests* **will usually be a positive-sum game**'.[93]

Political struggle and conflicting group interests recede. Instead, it is the rationality of consumers and their newly found maturity that allow them and their representatives to see that making trade-offs is part of their freshly gained responsibilities. This will ultimately result in a "positive-sum game". '*A closer, more cooperative relationship between consumers and business, acting as equal partners, is essential. The goal is a balanced partnership between successful businesses and satisfied consumers*'.[94] The birth of common interest and the death of political struggle in consumer policy.

This document also fully crystalises the conception of government as a neutral, technocratic arbiter, who helps to 'equitably reconcile' the interests of consumers with those of other stakeholders (notably businesses). If in the previous policies the EU assumed responsibility for making sure, for instance, that the products are safe and healthy, such a straightforward normative approach is off the table here. '*The aim is to promote objective, coherent decision-making in the difficult task of reconciling the consumer interest with those of other stakeholders. A more* **systematic approach to the analysis of the competing interests** *and the weight to be given to these will simplify the process of reaching risk management decisions and* **obviate the need to have the whole debate afresh whenever a new hazard arises**. *This will bring greater reassurance to both consumers and business*'.[95] Government does not provide guarantees of safety and health par tout anymore but embeds these guarantees in a technocratic decision-making process, where all interests at stake are

---

[92] European Commission, Consumer Policy Action Plan 1999–2001, COM(1998) 696 final, p. 1.
[93] Consumer Policy Action Plan 1999–2001, p. 4.
[94] Consumer Policy Action Plan 1999–2001, p. 4.
[95] Consumer Policy Action Plan 1999–2001, p. 11.

balanced with the help of evidence and science. Government is a neutral arbiter, while science, rather than democratic politics, is the source of normative guidance for balancing various interests.

When it comes to the imaginary of law, the Commission commits itself to *'flexible and responsive approaches to regulation'*.[96] This includes on the one hand the limits of protection, recognising that *'consumers have a responsibility to their own interests'*,[97] while at the same time recognising that consumers will still *'depend on public authorities to promote their health and safety on their behalf'*, (...) or to *'establish a fair regulatory framework for the business consumer relationship, before, during and after each transaction'*,[98] on the other. The need for intervention will, however, vary *'depending on the nature of the consumer, with a greater need for more vulnerable consumers'*.[99] Protection is therefore going to become a scarcer good in this legal imaginary. Consumers need to take responsibility for their interests, while protection is reserved mainly for vulnerable consumers with special needs, who seem to particularly lack in rationality or capacity to reap the benefits of the market.

When it comes to flexible and responsive regulation, the Commission starts from the premise that *'In increasingly dynamic and innovative markets, flexible approaches are key and an appropriate balance between regulatory and non-regulatory approaches needs to be found'*.[100] This has several components. First, *'Where appropriate, the Commission will aim to foster the more sophisticated dialogue that leads to **self-regulation** agreements between consumers and business, including the retail sector'*.[101] Second, the Commission commits itself to the promotion of international cooperation, including something as important as health and safety, within the framework of largely private international regulators (e.g. Codex Alimentarius[102]). Third, the Commission commits to the regular consultation of businesses and consumers in the course of the regulatory process – with at that point perhaps unforeseen consequences of enabling concentrated interests to dominate the agenda of the government.[103]

---

[96] Consumer Policy Action Plan, 1998, p. 6. [97] Consumer Policy Action Plan, 1998, p. 9.
[98] Consumer Policy Action Plan, 1998, p. 4. [99] Consumer Policy Action Plan, 1998, p. 7.
[100] Consumer Policy Action Plan, 1998, p. 15.
[101] Consumer Policy Action Plan, 1998, p. 9.
[102] Marija Bartl, 'Regulatory Convergence through the Back Door: TTIP's Regulatory Cooperation and the Future of Precaution in Europe', *German Law Journal* 18, no. 4 (1 July 2017): 969–92.
[103] T. Hüller and B. Kohler-Koch, 'Assessing the Democratic Value of Civil Society Engagement in the European Union', in: Beate Kohler-Koch, Dirk De Bièvre, William

The confidence, clarity, and coherence of this policy document, in comparison with its predecessors, are hard to miss. The conceptions of the economy, law, politics, government, and consumer have all transformed, one could say, into the opposites of the 1975 policy. Long passed is the world where consumers needed protection from the Communities. Innovative and dynamic businesses and cunning and responsible consumers are the drivers of prosperity in this imaginary. The prize is a well-functioning, competitive market, which is in the benefit of all.

3.5.2 2001: Competitive Consumer Law

Just three years later, the Commission published a 'green paper' on consumer policy – a forward-looking document that aims to consult stakeholders on the future shape of the EU consumer law and policy.[104] The background for this new consumer policy are two important political documents produced in the same year: the 'Lisbon Agenda',[105] which sets out to make the EU the most competitive knowledge economy in the world, and the 'White Paper on Governance',[106] which comes with ideas about the importance of light touch regulation, self-regulation, and co-regulation as a mode of governance. These two documents embrace a privatising imaginary of both politics and law and thus lend further support to the set of ideas articulated in the previous policy.

The Green Paper starts with a picture of the (political) economy: '*The internal market's main asset is that it has the largest pool of consumer demand in the world – and this asset is not being fully exploited. Enabling businesses, especially SMEs, to access this potential, as easily as domestic markets would be a **powerful stimulus to competitiveness**. (...)*'[107] Competitive markets, and competitiveness, become a central pursuit. The sacrifices, or the "trade-offs" as euphemistically named in the previous policy, are also becoming clearer here insofar as the EU consumer policy '***achieves as high as possible a level of consumer protection whilst also keeping costs to***

A. Maloney (Hrsg.): Opening EU-Governance to Civil Society. Gains and Challenges. 2008. Mannheim [CONNEX Report Series], 145–83.

[104] European Commission, Green Paper on the European Consumer Protection, COM(2001) 531 final.
[105] Lisbon European Council Conclusions, 23 and 24 March 2000, available at www.consilium.europa.eu/uedocs/cms_data/docs/pressdata/en/ec/00100-r1.en0.htm, last accessed 5 January 2024.
[106] European Commission, European Governance: A White Paper, COM(2001) 428 final.
[107] Green Paper on Consumer Protection 2001, p. 9.

business to a minimum.[108] If we are to keep our business globally competitive, we need to make sure that consumer protection does not cost too much.

The concern with competitiveness also translates into the normative leitbild of the consumer. '*It is the cross-border movement of goods and services that allows consumers to search out bargains and innovative products and services and thus ensures that they **optimise their consumption decisions**. This cross-border demand increases competitive pressure within the internal market and allows for **a more efficient and competitively priced supply** of goods and services*'.[109] The consumer is thus an individually calculating actor, who advances her own purposes, as well as the internal market, by engaging smartly in cross-border shopping. Distance selling and online sales are to become one of the most important vehicles for the making of the internal market for consumers.

The Green Paper also further institutionalises the previously outlined legal imaginary; this time, however, with the additional justification by the White Paper on Governance. The Commission continues to praise the role of self-regulation as a fundamental way of regulation: '*Many problems may not be suitable for regulatory action. **Self-regulation can achieve some consumer protection goals** (. . .). Effective self-regulation that contains clear voluntarily binding commitments towards consumers and which is properly enforced can **reduce the need for regulation or coregulation**'.*[110] Importantly, the Commission drops references to the dialogue between consumers and trader's associations in the preparation for self-regulation. It is now fully on traders to get this job done, paired only by more effective enforcement of such voluntary commitments. It is mainly in the field of enforcement in front of the courts where consumer associations retain an important role.

While it is unclear which problems cannot be solved by (public) regulation, it is clear that some powers are best exercised by private actors, and in particular by traders, who set the norms themselves. Regulation, where still necessary, needs to be '*as simple as possible and is sufficiently flexible to respond quickly to the market, and which involves stakeholders as much as possible*'[111] and importantly '*simplifying existing rules and, **where possible, deregulating** would also help reduce disproportionate burdens on business*'.[112]

---

[108] Green Paper on Consumer Protection 2001, p. 4.
[109] Green Paper on Consumer Protection 2001, p. 3.
[110] Green Paper on Consumer Protection 2001, p. 14.
[111] Green Paper on Consumer Protection 2001, p. 4.
[112] Green Paper on Consumer Protection 2001, p. 9.

Ultimately, the *'virtuous circle can only be achieved if the regulatory framework in place encourages consumers and businesses to engage in cross-border trade'*.[113]

3.5.3   2012: Out of the Crisis with Better Information

What seems like a ten-year gap from the previous Green Paper has been anything but calm. This period has been filled with a prolonged struggle over the initiatives that the Commission proposed in the wake of the previous consumer policies, namely, the full harmonisation of consumer law with a view to strengthen the "confidence" of consumers in cross-border shopping; the 'Optional Instrument' in the European contract law, in order to reduce obstacles in the internal market; and finally, the political fight about the ambit of the new 'Consumer Rights Directive'.

The Commission has failed, however, to fully realise any of the three projects – largely thanks to the opposition of some EU member states, who have resisted a significant competence transfer that the proposed measures implied.[114] These political dead-ends, together with the intervening great financial crisis, have exposed the limits of the Commission's neoliberal imaginary of prosperity.[115] In its 2012 policy, the Commission seems to be at a bit of a loss as to what it should make of these defeats.

The Commission clearly recognises the economic importance of consumers more so than previously: *'Consumer expenditure accounts for 56% of EU GDP and is essential to meeting the Europe 2020 objective of smart, inclusive and sustainable growth.* **Stimulating this demand can play a major role in bringing the EU out of the crisis**'.[116] If anything, in the wake of the

---

[113] Green Paper on Consumer Protection 2001, p. 3.
[114] Several scholars have discussed these attempts of the European Commission to make the EU consumer and general contract law internal market proof. Norbert Reich and Hans-Wolfgang Micklitz, 'Crónica de Una Muerte Anunciada: The Commission Proposal for a "Directive on Consumer Rights"', *Common Market Law Review* 46 (2009): 471–519. Stephen Weatherill, 'Competence Creep and Competence Control', *Yearbook of European Law* 23, no. 1 (1 January 2004): 1–55; Loos, 'Full Harmonisation as a Regulatory Concept and Its Consequences for the National Legal Orders'; Hans-W. Micklitz, 'A "Certain" Future for the Optional Instrument', in *A European Optional Contract Law: Policy Choices*, ed. by Sanne Jansen (De Gruyter, 2011), 181–94; Martijn W. Hesselink, 'Common Frame of Reference & Social Justice', *European Review of Contract Law* 4, no. 3 (2008): 248–69.
[115] Bartl, 'Internal Market Rationality, Private Law and the Direction of the Union'; Bartl, 'Internal Market Rationality: In the Way of Re-Imagining the Future', *European Law Journal* 24, no. 1 (2018): 99–115.
[116] European Commission, A European Consumer Agenda – Boosting confidence and growth, COM(2012) 225 final, section 1.

economic crisis, the objective of consumer policy becomes outright economic growth, or more precisely, *'sustainable and resource-efficient growth, whilst taking account of the needs of all consumers'*.[117]

However, there is little new in the EU's playbook to exploit this rediscovered potential of the Internal Market. The Commission sees its role in stimulating economic growth mainly by doing more of the same: *'building knowledge and capacity for more effective consumer participation in the market (...)* **empowered and confident consumers can drive forward the European economy**'.[118] The focus of governmental action remains to make consumers both confident and cunning. Once consumers are successfully included in the market, empowered by information, they can then themselves drive forward the European economy.

Also when it comes to the legal imaginary behind this consumer agenda, the Commission makes no new strides. The focus remains on the legal tools of market empowerment, choice, and information: *'Empowering consumers means providing a robust framework of principles and tools that enable them to drive a smart, sustainable and inclusive economy'. (...) 'Consumers should be empowered, assisted and encouraged to make sustainable and healthy choices which will lead to cost savings for themselves and for society as a whole'*.[119] To the extent that protection is considered at all, it is solely targeted at particularly vulnerable consumers – foremost within the context of financial services and digital economy. Interestingly, however, the general statement on vulnerable consumers and social exclusion are not translated into any concrete measures or steps.

Even more importantly, the Commission continues with its endorsement of self-regulation as central to the efforts of consumer policy, intending to encourage traders to *'move beyond mere compliance with legislation and* **to develop self-regulatory measures, as well as corporate social responsibility initiatives,** *thus enhancing their focus on customer service as a key competitiveness factor'*.[120] Fearing charges of over-regulation, in this rather resigned appeal to the traders, the Commission is hoping to convince private actors to take more obligations upon themselves in the light of their own economic interest – while delivering benefits to the EU as a matter of by-product.

---

[117] European Consumer Agenda 2012, section 1, p. 3.
[118] European Consumer Agenda 2012, p. 8.   [119] European Consumer Agenda 2012, p. 3.
[120] European Consumer Agenda 2012, p. 9.

3.6 Towards an Imaginary of Shared Prosperity after 2018?

3.6.1 *2018: First Cracks: What Is the Deal in the 'New Deal for Consumers'*

The decline of high neoliberalism in the previous EU consumer policy, even if without a sense of direction, is set forth in the 2018 New Deal for Consumers. The 2018 policy does not present a truly new path, where like in Roosevelt's New Deal public and collective institutions take more responsibility for the future prosperity of consumers and citizens. Instead, the ambitions are much smaller and perhaps mostly symbolic – in the title, language, and a couple of absences in the document. However, this does not make them unimportant in the long run.

If judged by its US predecessor,[121] the reference to 'New Deal' suggests that the Commission is aware that what is needed is a public intervention for the benefit of consumers – an intervention that would fit perhaps better with an imaginary of shared prosperity. However, the Commission itself immediately tampers expectations that may follow from such a big title: *'"New Deal for Consumers" builds on the existing consumer policy framework and* **takes it a step further** *by proposing modern rules fit for today's changing markets and business practices, stronger public and private enforcement tools and better redress opportunities'.*[122]

But the policy does still make some important, if small, departures from the previous imaginaries of consumption endorsed by the EU consumer policies. Firstly, the document places the environment at the forefront of its economic imaginary: a *'healthy consumer environment is a key factor for economic growth'*.[123] The environment is becoming more integral to consumer interest and will, in the next consumer policy, become grounds for justifying a departure from the short-term interest in price to a longer-term economic interest in a sustainable economy and liveable planet.[124]

In the Commission's view, however, this still does not really require a break from the previous information paradigm as the main locus of regulatory intervention. The Commission suggests that consumers are *'increasingly interested in sustainable products'*, and they *'need to be empowered to make informed purchasing choices and have easy access to products that are*

---

[121] Robert D. Putnam, *The Upswing: How America Came Together a Century Ago and How We Can Do It Again* (Simon & Schuster, 2020).
[122] European Commission, A New Deal for Consumers, COM(2018) 183 final, p. 3.
[123] A New Deal for Consumers 2018, p. 1. [124] See the following subsection.

*environmentally friendly'.*¹²⁵ It is thus still informed choices and rational consumers, who should drive forward sustainable growth in their free time.

Second, appearing thirty-three times in the text of this policy, the word 'protection' is prominently back on the agenda. This language of 'protection' is a significant mark of the welfare state imaginary of prosperity, which had for the most part disappeared in the previous decades, remaining at most linked to 'vulnerable consumers'. But the return of the language of protection in this document is not necessarily paired with any significant protective measures.

For instance, one important issue that the New Deal raises is the platform economy (Amazon, Airbnb, Uber, and the likes). The Commission here singles out as most relevant for consumers: '*Today, when consumers visit an online marketplace, they do not always know from whom they are buying (from a professional trader or another consumer). ... As a result, consumers may falsely think they are dealing with a professional trader (hence benefitting from consumer rights)*'.¹²⁶ But is the confusion about who the seller is truly the greatest problem for consumers – who are also '*taxpayers, employees and beneficiaries of public policies*'¹²⁷ – as the Commission reminded us in 1998?

The Commission will follow up on this plan with two measures that aim to reshape the digital market: the Digital Services Act and the Digital Markets Act. The first focuses on the obligations of due diligence of digital platforms for the content published on such platforms, taking a step away from relative lawlessness – but ultimately still letting digital platforms bear little liability or condoning the social media business model to make money out of ever more outraging content.¹²⁸ The Digital Markets Act in turn aims to deal with the market power of online platforms, with the designation of a group of 'gate keepers' that have to be mindful of not abusing their power – while being able to keep the power nonetheless.¹²⁹ Even if not strictly consumer law measures, these two interventions will certainly have an impact on the day-to-day life of consumers, fitting a slowly expanding understanding of consumer interest.

---

[125] European Commission, A New Deal for Consumers 2018, p. 15.
[126] A New Deal for Consumers 2018, p. 5.   [127] See Section 3.4.1.
[128] Regulation (EU) 2022/2065 on a Single Market For Digital Services and amending Directive 2000/31/EC (Digital Services Act).
[129] Regulation (EU) 2022/1925 on contestable and fair markets in the digital sector (Digital Markets Act).

3.6 TOWARDS AN IMAGINARY OF SHARED PROSPERITY 103

The third intervention prompted by the New Deal, which has received considerable academic attention,[130] is the proposal for the expansion of a system of collective redress. In particular, the Commission '*proposes a **modernised system of representative actions**, building on the existing Injunctions Directive. This system allows non-profit making qualified entities, such as consumer organisations or independent public bodies, to defend collective consumer interests in cases of mass harm. This will help individual consumers to secure their rights. It will be especially helpful for consumers who are deterred for various reasons from individual litigation*'.[131]

The Directive on Collective Redress[132] was adopted on 25 November 2020, and it repeals the 2009 Injunction Directive. The Directive expands the type of representative actions that 'qualified entities' (including consumer associations) can bring against infringements that harm 'collective interests of consumers', adding to previous actions for injunctions the actions for redress.[133]

The Directive understands that 'collective interests of consumers' means the general interest of consumers and, in particular, for the purposes of redress measures, the interests of a group of consumers.[134] It is the Annex, which specifies various EU legislative measures that can give rise to representative actions – and these include a rather broad range of consumer measures, medical advice, food safety, or financial services measures. They do not include, however, 'environmental law measures', with the Directive mentioning that it only 'takes account' of the Aarhus Convention.[135] The collective interests of consumers thus do not go so far as to include their environmental interests.

Perhaps most significant are the absences in the New Deal for Consumers. Namely, there is no reference to self-regulation, co-regulation, or private standardisation. In terms of legal imaginary, this is symbolically highly important. From 1981, private rulemaking has been

---

[130] See, for instance, a Special Issue 6, Volume 27, (pp. 1219–1436) of the European Review of Private Law, edited by Anna van Duin and Candida Leone.
[131] European Commission, A New Deal for Consumers 2018, p. 6.
[132] Directive (EU) 2020/1828 on representative actions for the protection of the collective interests of consumers.
[133] Candida Leone and Joanna M. L. Van Duin, 'The Real (New) Deal: Levelling the Odds for Consumer-Litigants: On the Need for a Modernization, Part II', *European Review of Private Law* 27, no. 6 (1 December 2019): 1227–50.
[134] Directive (EU) 2020/1828 on representative actions, art 3(3).
[135] Directive (EU) 2020/1828 on representative actions, Recital 75.

one of the standing imaginaries of how we should go about market regulation. Post-1998, it has been the businesses themselves that seemed to be the preferred way of governing the market in the eyes of the Commission. But in 2018, self-regulation, co-regulation, and standardisation were not mentioned a single time. To the extent that they still exist in consumer related matters – as we will see in Chapter 4 – this is not transparent from this document. Yet, on a symbolic level, it signals that the legal imaginary is changing.

3.6.2 2020: A New Consumer Agenda: A Next Step?

In January 2020, just before the outbreak of the Covid crisis, the European Commission published the European Green Deal (EGD) – an overarching political programme that at the time of writing this book was still having a large, and contested, influence on overall EU policy and action.[136] Surely, an attentive reader will not have missed the recent proliferation of the language of "deals" in the vocabulary of the European Commission. The Commission seems to realise that significant change is needed. However, while the previous New Deal for Consumers did not present an all too good deal for consumers, the EGD, and more relevantly for this chapter the New Consumer Agenda inspired by it, takes more serious steps towards reimagining prosperity.

Let us be clear; in the 2020 New Consumer Agenda, we are still far from an imaginary of shared prosperity in the EU; notable aspects of the privatised imaginary of prosperity still remain prevalent. When it comes to the legal imaginary, the information paradigm continues to be as prominent as ever,[137] as does the overwhelming focus on labelling,[138] while the economic imaginary is still dominated by the ideas of 'market failures'.[139] However, this document and the legal measures on its basis present an important step towards setting new parameters for thinking about political economy.

When it comes to problems that the Commission sets out, most of the great challenges of today – climate change and the biodiversity crisis, the

---

[136] European Commission, The European Green Deal, COM(2019) 640 final.
[137] European Commission, New Consumer Agenda: Strengthening Consumer Resilience for Sustainable Recovery, COM(2020) 696 final. 'Information' is mentioned 32 times in the document.
[138] European Commission, New Consumer Agenda, p. 8.
[139] European Commission, New Consumer Agenda, p. 12.

Covid pandemic, indebtedness, as well as digital transformations – are included in this document. What is more, they are presented at least in part as collective problems, which in turn require collective, legislative solutions.

For the first time, after decades of narrowing down what consumer policy deals with, we enter into a world where everything seems to be on the table and is interconnected (sustainability, surveillance capitalism, vulnerability and over-indebtedness, as well as geopolitics). *'The Agenda takes a **holistic approach** covering various Union policies that are of particular relevance for consumers. It reflects the need to take account of consumer protection requirements in the formulation and implementation of other policies and activities. complements other EU initiatives, such as the European Green Deal, the Circular Economy Action Plan and the Communication on Shaping Europe's digital future. It also supports relevant international frameworks, such as the United Nations' 2030 Agenda for Sustainable Development and the UN Convention on the Rights of Persons with Disabilities'.*[140]

Consumer interest has also expanded. Price and choice are not seen as the only relevant consumers' interests. Rather, all kinds of problems, concerns, and interests need to be accounted for, while proposed solutions involve interventionist legislative proposals – alongside "wise" consumption choices by consumers. This is a consumer policy that discusses the problems of *people* living in the EU – people who are also unavoidably consumers, but people nevertheless. In fact, when reading the document, one has a sense that the term consumer could be easily replaced with the term citizen, or resident, for the document to make even more sense.

In many respects, the new consumer agenda takes things out of the invisible hands of the market and puts them onto the table (if still not in the hands) of law and government. Sustainability, durability, and quality are less private goods to be delivered by market and competition, and more public goods to be delivered by legislation. In this document, the Commission commits – and later delivers as we see below – to legislative initiatives on Sustainable Products, 'right to repair', on prolonging statutory guarantees, combating early obsolesce, and greenwashing.[141] The Commission is thus also increasingly focused on the supply side of the market, lifting some of the responsibility for sustainable consumption from however "well-informed" consumers.

---

[140] European Commission, New Consumer Agenda, p. 1.
[141] European Commission, New Consumer Agenda, pp. 7 and 9.

While sustainability *information* still has a prominent role in this agenda, the Commission now aims to push for a more "painful" set of information sharing that is usually resisted by the business – such as the expected *durability* of products. Furthermore, the Commission at least mentions that more attention needs to go into '*promoting new consumption concepts and behaviours, such as the* **sharing economy**, *new business models allowing consumers* **to buy a service rather than a good**, *or support for* **repairs through community and social economy** *organisations actions (e.g. repair cafés) and for second-hand markets*'[142]

Two important legislative measures, at the moment of writing of the book both well advanced in the legislative process, have been delivered as indicated by the Agenda. The first measure concerns the 'Right to Repair' Directive.[143] This measure aims to prioritise repair over purchasing new products, in cases of products that do *not* fall under the legal guarantee. The Directive requests that for certain type of products – such as washing machines or televisions – the producer either provides for repair or at least makes products that are repairable.[144] When providing repair, the price is not capped, however – in order to foster competition in the SME repair sector that should both provide for good prices and reinvigorate employment.

The Right to Repair proposal has three important implications. First, both symbolically and practically it aims to prolong the life cycle of products, in order to improve their environmental footprint. Second, in terms of imaginaries of consumption, repair should be both attractive as an environmentally sustainable practice and as a cost-cutting measure for consumers – altogether lowering the consumption of new products. Third, and importantly, the Directive aims to restructure (if limitedly) the economy in the sense that it aims to create at least a partial shift from resource-intensive *manufacturing* to labour-intensive *services* of repair.

The other important legislative proposal is the 'Green Claims Directive',[145] which aims to empower consumers to make green choices by banning unsupported green claims from the market. While the language of

---

[142] European Commission, New Consumer Agenda, p. 8.
[143] European Commission, Proposal for a Directive of the European Parliament and of the Council on common rules promoting the repair of goods and amending Regulation (EU) 2017/2394, Directives (EU) 2019/771, and (EU) 2020/1828, COM(2023) 155 final.
[144] This links also to Ecodesign and the Sustainable Products Regulation (See Chapter 4).
[145] European Commission, Proposal for a Directive of the European Parliament and of the Council on substantiation and communication of explicit environmental claims (Green Claims Directive), COM(2023) 166 final.

the document is about empowering consumers via better information, the measure itself has a strong interventionist dimension. To make environmental claims, providers (except for micro enterprises) have to engage in a serious degree of knowledge collection and assessment, over all *life stages* of the product, different *types of environmental impact*, and finally across the whole supply chain.[146] The responsibility that lies on those making green claims is significant.

3.7 The Contours of the New Imaginary of Prosperity

As new policy and legal documents are gradually instituting changing understandings of the economy, law, politics, government, and society, they also prefigure the 'compossible' futures. I conclude thus this chapter by outlining what the most important discursive and normative building blocks for the new imaginary of prosperity are at the present, and where the EU can be said to *not* go far or quickly enough with an eye on ushering shared and sustainable prosperity.

First, both the most recent consumer policies and legislative proposals in their wake, while hardly far-reaching, still aim to foster a less wasteful, and more *caring, attitude towards both nature and people*. Care, as intimated by these legislative proposals, is not primarily an individual attitude. Rather, it is a social, or collective, achievement, in which people are assisted (or not) by their institutional environment. Thus, moving away from a throw-away culture, towards taking better care of the products we already have and use, requires institutional enablers such as the Right to Repair proposal. And even if one has to buy a new product, one should be able to trust that any alleged green claims are not only hot air.

Second, a prominent feature of the new emergent imaginary of consumption relies on a more *steered conception of the economy*. The New Deal for Consumers, the 2020 Consumer Agenda, as well as the various legislative proposals take many issues out of the invisible hands of the market and place them in the visible hands of government and law. Namely, all the legal measures mentioned earlier are far more 'interventionist' than we have seen in the previous decades, requiring more 'market shaping' (mandatory duties and requirements

---

[146] Green Claims Directive 2023, p. 19.

and (re)distributive elements) rather than focusing only on 'market optimisation' (i.e. information duties or the promotion of self-regulation).

Epistemologically and ontologically, this hints at a first step towards a more constructivist interpretation of the economy, where law and legal institutions are recognised as infrastructures that shape market (outcomes). The more one sees the economy as constructed, the more one realises that different legal and governance designs can bring about different distributive outcomes and environmental impacts. What is more, government (i.e. the EU in this case) must assume some degree of responsibility for such distributive and environmental outcomes.

However, the recent proposals still leave a considerable degree of responsibility for sustainable consumption to consumers.[147] Trusting that such a large social problem, which requires an enormous degree of coordination, can be mostly left to individual consumers makes clear that the privatising imaginaries of progress are still well and kicking. This is not without social consequences. Taking the market approach to environmental matters, which at the same time requires consumers not only to have good intentions but also deep pockets, will leave those who do not fit the bill disenfranchised – raising eventually citizens' opposition against the 'elite' environmental project.[148]

And still, third, a growing concern with the supply side of the market reveals that the Commission is realising that consumers need greater legislative support to deliver on that expectation. This includes, importantly, making public choices on the availability and characteristics of certain goods, services, innovations, and processes, and public responsibility for making sure that these goods and services are both socially and environmentally acceptable. Such responsibilities cannot be externalised entirely to the consciousness and wallets of individual consumers.

Fourth, the return of the language of 'protection', with a caring twist, is clearly discernible in the recent EU consumer policies. The protective obligations gradually encompass not only cognitive but also material limitations and constraints of consumers – or citizens – and aim to protect them against economic exploitation (the issues of contractual fairness and distribution),[149] environmental dangers (*enabling* caring attitudes towards

---

[147] V. Mak and E. Terryn, 'Circular Economy and Consumer Protection: The Consumer as a Citizen and the Limits of Empowerment through Consumer Law', *Journal of Consumer Policy* 43, no. 1 (2020): 227–48.

[148] Patrick Chamorel, 'Macron versus the Yellow Vests', *Journal of Democracy* 30, no. 4 (2019): 48–62.

[149] European Commission, New Consumer Agenda, p. 14.

goods, peoples, and services, as a vehicle for sustainability),[150] and surveillance (providing safe digital infrastructures).[151]

Fifth, already from 2018 but more prominently from 2020, we see the expansion of the concept of consumer and consumer interests. Consumers are not seen solely as economic actors who care only for low prices and their own comfort, but instead increasingly also for issues beyond the narrow self, including social matters and the environment – even if that means a higher price (e.g. green claims) or less comfort (e.g. taking steps towards repair). Also, the 'collective interest of consumers' that we see in the Directive on Collective Redress seems not to be only narrowly focused on economic interests but also goes further – even if stopping short of collective environmental claims.

Finally, when it comes to the conception of politics, references to "common interest" or "maturity" of consumers are absent from recent EU consumer policies and legislative proposals. The new imaginary of collective prosperity does not try to depoliticise consumer law and policy, including various conflicting distributive choices – only to see it return as growing inequality and exclusionary radicalism.[152] Instead, EU policy documents increasingly seem to be ready to both acknowledge the earlier narrowness of framing consumer issues and recognise various distributive conflicts inherent in this policy field, which require a public response.

But, given the degree of crises that we are facing, is the EU going far enough, quickly enough? There is certainly room for improvement. In fact, many of the more transformative ideas presented in the recent policy documents are often just shortly mentioned and left to "dry" when it comes to what is finally turned into legislative proposals. Two large omissions are, first, thinking about *rationalising* consumption via sharing – that is via public, shared, and communal consumption, and second, any reflection on the global distributive conflicts when it comes to consumption. Both are left unattended to. Let me end this chapter by mentioning a couple of such *compossible futures* that rather "naturally" follow from the policy documents mentioned.

First, the EU raises here and there several transformative ideas, without engaging with the question of how those may be publicly facilitated. For

---

[150] European Commission, New Consumer Agenda, pp. 7 and 8.
[151] European Commission, New Consumer Agenda, pp. 10 and 11.
[152] See Chapter 2; also Chantal Mouffe, *The Return of the Political*, vol. 8 (Verso Books, 2006); Mouffe, *Agonistics: Thinking the World Politically* (Verso Books, 2013).

instance, the 'product as a service', which is possibly a promising pathway to creating more sustainable design, improving durability, disposal, recyclability, and lowering material consumption, as well as transitioning the economy towards more labour-intensive services, is left without further engagement. Also, the question of 'shared economy', where some of the goods that we have previously consumed individually (such as cars) are shared, is not taken up – even if they, next to environmental objectives, may hold a promise to lower costs, countering thus the widespread 'cost of living crisis'. Without public facilitation, however, such developments will remain limited only to the richest European regions and cities (e.g. Amsterdam). At the same time, such experiments also require some hard thinking about the broader societal implications *before* being rolled out, including *who owns what* and *for what purpose*.

Second, the question of public services and public provision has not been mentioned by the EU consumer policies since 1995, when the Commission advocated liberalisation and privatisation. And yet, it is clear that making public services more widely accessible is an important means of delivering a high standard of living for many more Europeans, with lesser financial and environmental costs.[153] The EU needs to facilitate the provision of such services at the level of member states, including, for instance, by adjusting fiscal rules, as well as focusing on European provision. The conversation on 'European public goods' is a step in a good direction: the scope and ambition will be, however, decisive.

Third, one of the most important types of 'consumption' – housing – is not discussed by the Commission after the 2014 Mortgage Directive, which is more concerned with financial stability than the right to housing. In fact, if it was not for the Court of Justice and the Unfair Terms Directive, consumers would be even more exposed to grossly unjust contractual terms in relation to mortgage contracts, en masse thrown out of their houses with each new economic crisis.[154]

The EU could and should go further beyond unfair terms protection when it comes to contributing to access to housing, for instance, via its competences to regulate finance. One simple way may be to facilitate various forms of collaborative housing more actively, which are both environmentally (more shared spaces and fewer resources) and socially

---

[153] Tim Jackson, *Prosperity without Growth: Foundations for the Economy of Tomorrow* (Taylor & Francis, 2016).

[154] Chantal Mak, 'Gutiérrez Naranjo – On Limits in Law and Limits of Law', *Amsterdam Law School Research Paper*, no. 2017-38 (2017).

(loneliness, childcare, and elderly care) beneficial.[155] The attempts to create such sustainable forms of living often hit the financing wall, as they are considered by banks both more risky and more administratively intensive.[156] Making sure that such experiments are not made excessively difficult for those who want to pursue them may be crucial in ensuring both broad availability of housing and community, in the context of ageing populations.[157]

Last but not least, why do we see so little engagement with people abroad? The interdependence and the global nature of crises, including the environmental degradation driven by the excessive consumption of people in the Global North – without sharing many benefits with the Majority world – is poised to fuel those global crises only further. Any credible new imaginary of consumption has to take global perspective seriously, both in its environmental and distributive dimensions. Failing to do so has led some consumer scholars to ask whether the perspective of 'consumers' and 'consumer law and policy' is a good starting point for thinking about consumption at all.[158]

---

[155] Ghodsee, *Everyday Utopia*.
[156] Within the ERC-funded project N-EXTLAW (no. 852990), we have collected evidence suggesting that this is one of the major problems with the creation of more communal forms of housing.
[157] Ghodsee, *Everyday Utopia*.
[158] Martijn W. Hesselink, 'Alienation Commodification: A Critique of the Role of EU Consumer Law', *European Law Open* 2, no. 2 (2023): 405–23.

4 Designing Technology

4.1 Introduction

Technology has been transformative of life and ecosystems. The Industrial Revolution, digital revolution, globalisation, industrial food production, or the revolution in transport, are just some examples of new technologies prompting new ways of production and distribution, which in turn have had vast impacts on socio-economic conditions and natural ecosystems. Technology is also central to any imaginary of political economy - as it is intimately connected to how we understand progress and prosperity.[1]

When thinking about technology through the lens of imaginaries of prosperity, what matters is its governance: who makes technologies, to what purpose, for whose benefit, and at what cost. While descriptively, technology has been certainly transformative, prescriptively, that is *in what way*, it has been a matter of intense political and economic struggles. As businesses compete and strive for economic success, they aim to adopt, appropriate, develop, or implement various types of technologies quicker and better than their competitors.[2] Workers can benefit from technologies, as they can free them from difficult or menial work. Yet, more often than not, technologies have been 'labour productivity enhancing', thus aiming to replace workers or at least subject them to

---

[1] Carl Benedikt Frey, *The Technology Trap: Capital, Labor, and Power in the Age of Automation* (Princeton University Press, 2019); Simon Johnson and Daron Acemoglu, *Power and Progress: Our Thousand-Year Struggle Over Technology and Prosperity* (Hachette UK, 2023).

[2] I do not account in this chapter for the development of military technology, which is one of the most important sources of technological advance as well as between states competition. Often, however, that advance has been translated into economic advantages, thus feeding back into economic competition.

various types of disciplines, first and foremost in order to increase the return on capital invested.[3]

The task of governments in relation to technology is starkly "two-faced"[4]: the governments need to foster technological advance of their economies, in order to ensure future prosperity as well as geopolitical relevance. At the same time, technology can also be very disruptive from the governments' perspective – especially where it is aimed at increasing 'labour productivity' (replacing labour and increasing unemployment)[5] or having large environmental (chemicals, pesticides, and industrial agriculture)[6] or social consequences (social media or AI).[7]

Governments can have many different relations to technology – they can actively support its development, they can steer it, they can shield people from its impacts, or they can leave its governance to market. In the analytical framework of this book, the core question when it comes to technology is who – private, public or collective actors – controls technological futures. Who gets to decide what kind of technologies are developed? How are the benefits of those technologies distributed? And what kind of social, environmental, or political futures are we set up with?

The two imaginaries of prosperity have different responses to these questions. In the imaginaries of privatised prosperity, technological progress is understood as market driven, and private actors are seen as its leaders (whatever the reality[8]). The government in such an imaginary would be well advised not to intervene, or to intervene lightly, for instance, in a 'horizontal' way.[9] In the imaginaries of shared prosperity, in contrast, the questions of development of technologies, its public steering and shielding from technological impacts, will become much more central, as the distributive and distributed effects of technology become more politicised.[10]

---

[3] Ibid. Also Karl Aiginger and Dani Rodrik, 'Rebirth of Industrial Policy and an Agenda for the Twenty-First Century', *Journal of Industry, Competition and Trade* 20 (2020): 189–207.
[4] Or three-faced, if you also account for military technology, as mentioned in fn. 2.
[5] Aiginger and Rodrik, 'Rebirth of Industrial Policy and an Agenda for the Twenty-First Century'.
[6] Paul Harremoes et al., *The Precautionary Principle in the Twentieth Century: Late Lessons from Early Warnings* (Routledge, 2013).
[7] Jürgen Habermas, *A New Structural Transformation of the Public Sphere and Deliberative Politics* (John Wiley & Sons, 2023).
[8] Marianna Mazzucato, *The Entrepreneurial State: Debunking Public vs. Private Sector Myths*, 1st ed. (Anthem Press, 2013).
[9] Mario Pianta, 'An Industrial Policy for Europe', *Seoul Journal of Economics* 27 (2014): 277–305.
[10] Johnson and Acemoglu, *Power and Progress*.

In this chapter then, I will take as a "case-study" one increasingly significant element of the EU's technological governance: ecodesign. The reasons to look into ecodesign are at least twofold. First, ecodesign presents a success story in the governmental steering of technological development in the EU. Remaining for the most part at the sideline of public discussion, ecodesign has fundamentally impacted the daily life of all Europeans, making everyday products (vacuum cleaners, lamps, or washing machines) more energy efficient and longer lasting. Second, the framework that we see put in place today will create important background conditions for any impending *compossible technological futures*.[11] It sets the grounds for the conversation on how technology relates to sustainable economy; what kind of technological advances are necessary; what is the relation between production, distribution, and consumption of technologies; what are the limits to these interventions; and importantly, what are their distributive consequences. These questions will become ever more salient as we pursue sustainable futures, from digital economy to energy transition, from possible transport mix to sustainable food provision.

In what follows, I will track the changing imaginaries of political economy on the background of the changes in the ecodesign framework. After shortly outlining the development of the ecodesign framework from its inception until the present day, I concentrate on the transformation of imaginaries of economy, politics, government, and law post-2005. Empirically, this chapter is based on a systematic survey of the ecodesign legislation, proposals, and ecodesign workplans, as well as various 'circular economy' staff documents and communications, which have directly shaped the implementation of the ecodesign framework.[12]

4.2 Embedding the Product

4.2.1 Ecodesign Framework

Almost fifty years after the very first ecodesign measures, the most recent Commission's Proposal for a Sustainable Products Regulation, well advanced in the legislative process at the time of writing, expands

---

[11] Ngai-Ling Sum and Bob Jessop, *Towards a Cultural Political Economy : Putting Culture in Its Place in Political Economy* (Edward Elgar Publishing, 2013).

[12] This chapter also includes references to the two (negative and conditionally positive) positions of the 'Regulatory Scrutiny Board' on the 2022 Proposal for a Sustainable Product Regulation. See Commission, Communication Regulatory Scrutiny Board Opinion, Sustainable Products Initiative, SEC(2022) 165.

the 'ecodesign approach' to any products that carry substantial environmental impact, ranging from textiles to electronics and plastics.[13] This is a significant expansion of the scope that can reshape not only how we go about making technologies but also how we think in that regard about the relationship between public and private, the state and the market. But let us start from the more modest beginnings.

The first ecodesign legislation dates back to the 1970s when, in the wake of the oil crisis (!), the European institutions introduced the first mandatory rules on energy efficiency, complemented with the first labelling directive,[14] in order to reduce *'the rate of growth of internal consumption by measures for using energy rationally and economically without jeopardizing social and economic growth objectives,* stressing that *any improvement in the rational use of energy is generally beneficial to the environment'*.[15] These first measures, however, still only required the member states (MSs) to develop and set the minimum performance standards within their national markets.

The new wave of regulations in the 1990s – including refrigerators and gaseous boilers,[16] as well as a new labelling directive for household appliances[17] – Europeanised the field, in line with the Single European Act and the White Paper for the Competition of the Internal Market. Thus, in order to *'promote measures aimed at the progressive establishment of the internal market in the period up to 31 December 1992'*, as well as to account for the need of the *'Community* [to] *take proper account of potential climatic change linked to the greenhouse effect'*, the EU would from then onwards set itself the minimum performance standards as it concerns

---

[13] European Commission, Proposal for a Regulation of the European Parliament and of the Council establishing a framework for setting ecodesign requirements for sustainable products and repealing Directive 2009/125/EC, COM(2022) 142 final, art. 1.
[14] Robin Barkhausen, Antoine Durand, and Katharina Fick, 'Review and Analysis of Ecodesign Directive Implementing Measures: Product Regulations Shifting from Energy Efficiency towards a Circular Economy', *Sustainability* 14, no. 16 (2022): 103-18.
[15] Council Recommendation of 25 October 1977 on the rational use of energy in industrial undertakings (77/713/EEC), p. 1.
[16] The EU first introduced the energy-saving requirements on heating systems, the production of hot water, and the insulation of heat and domestic hot-water distribution (Council Directive 1978/170/EEC [5]), followed by hot-water boilers fired with liquid or gaseous fuels (Council Directive 1992/42/EEC of 21 May 1992) and household refrigerating appliances (Council Directive 96/57/EC of 3 September 1996).
[17] Council Directive 92/75/EEC of 22 September 1992 on the indication by labelling and standard product information of the consumption of energy and other resources by household appliances.

energy consumption for product groups and require MSs to ensure the free movement of goods that comply with such standards.[18]

In the 2000s, several important shifts in the thinking about ecodesign took place. In 2001, in the European Green Paper on Integrated Product Policies, the Commission proposed a 'life-cycle' thinking about product design,[19] which requires as a later Working Plan clarifies *'improving the environmental performance of products throughout their life cycle (raw material selection and use; manufacturing; packaging, transport and distribution; installation and maintenance; use; and end-of-life) by systematically integrating environmental aspects at the earliest stage of product design'*.[20] This life-cycle approach will be adopted in the new 2005 ecodesign framework directive.[21]

The 2005 Directive marks another shift. The EU will move from drafting independent product-specific directives on ecodesign requirements to a framework directive,[22] which sets out the process for the regulation of ecodesign, while leaving the development of rules for particular product groups to the level of implementing legislation, in the co-regulation framework.[23] What is more, with the amended 2009 directive, the scope of the framework directive also further expands, with a focus shifting from energy-*using* products[24] to a broader category of energy-*related* products – thus giving the EU competence to regulate also products such as tyres.[25] The framework directive has been supplemented with a new Directive 2010/30/EU establishing a framework for energy labelling of energy-related products.[26] By the end of the 2000s, we see also the first implementing measures on the basis of the 2005 directive[27]

---

[18] Council Directive 92/42/EEC of 21 May 1992 on efficiency requirements for new hot-water boilers fired with liquid or gaseous fuels, art. 4.
[19] European Commission, Green paper on Integrated Product Policy, COM(2001) 0068 final. See also Section 4.4.2.
[20] European Commission, Establishment of the Working Plan for 2009–2011 under the Ecodesign Directive, COM(2008) 660 final, p. 2.
[21] Directive 2005/32/EC of the European Parliament and of the Council of 6 July 2005 establishing a framework for the setting of ecodesign requirements for energy-using products and amending Council Directive 92/42/EEC.
[22] Ecodesign Directive 2005/32/EC.   [23] Ecodesign Directive 2005/32/EC, art. 15.
[24] Ecodesign Directive 2005/32/EC, art. 1(1).   [25] Ecodesign Directive 2009/125/EC, art. 1.
[26] Directive 2010/30/EU of the European Parliament and of the Council of 19 May 2010 on the indication by labelling and standard product information of the consumption of energy and other resources by energy-related products.
[27] Commission Regulation (EC) No. 107/2009 of 4 February 2009 implementing Directive 2005/32/EC of the European Parliament and of the Council with regard to ecodesign requirements for simple set-top boxes.

as well as a first working plan outlining the action for the upcoming years.[28]

4.2.2 Embedding the Product in Time (Life-Cycle) and Society (Circular Economy)

While the 2005 directive had already incorporated reference to 'life-cycle', it took a while before the idea to minimise the environmental impact across the life span of products got a foothold in the ecodesign thinking. Thus, the 2005 directive stated that when developing the standards, the Commission *'should consider the life cycle of the product and all its significant environmental aspects, inter alia, energy efficiency'*.[29] However, the 'life-cycle' was not a political priority, instead *'greenhouse gas mitigation through increased energy efficiency should be considered a priority environmental goal pending the adoption of a working plan'*.[30] The reasons for this initial disinterest were several, including the incapacity of methodologies chosen to actually assess environmental impact other than energy efficiency, as well as (more prosaically) the overestimation of the environmental impacts of energy efficiency by the consultants working on the file, or potentially the fact that it was DG Energy and Enterprise that was in charge of Ecodesign.[31]

It took until the 2015 Circular Economy Action Plan, followed by the 2016 Ecodesign Working Plan, before it became clear that energy efficiency could not be the sole, or even the main focus of ecodesign – that is, if the ecodesign is to achieve its environmental objectives. There was, according to the Commission, *'an increasing need, and political priority, to improve resource efficiency in the EU"*.[32] The resource efficiency acquires circular reading (i.e. reduce, reuse, and recycle),[33] with the Commission suggesting that what is required is *'Extending product lifetime, Ability to re-use components or recycle materials from products at end-of-life, Use of re-used components and/or recycled materials in products'*.[34]

---

[28] Ecodesign Working Plan 2009–2011. [29] Ecodesign Directive 2005/32/EC, art. 15(4)(a).
[30] Ecodesign Directive 2005/32/EC, Recital 12.
[31] Anaïs Michel, 'Premature Obsolescence: In Search of an Improved Legal Framework, KU Leuven Thesis, 2022, pp. 122 and 123.
[32] European Commission, Ecodesign Working Plan 2016–2019, COM(2016) 0773 final, p. 2.
[33] Kris Hartley, Ralf van Santen, and Julian Kirchherr, 'Policies for Transitioning towards a Circular Economy: Expectations from the European Union (EU)', *Resources, Conservation and Recycling* 155 (2020): 1–10.
[34] Ecodesign Working Plan 2016–2019, p. 9.

By 2016, only one regulated 'product group' had been designed around a whole range of circular economy standards. The 2009 and 2012 lighting regulations have focused especially on durability, minimum lifetime, warranty and limiting 'planned obsolesce'[35] – perhaps one of the most remarkable commercial interventions to limit the life span of products otherwise perfectly able to function longer. The lighting regulations remained, however, an exception even post-2016, as mandatory durability requirements were not, with a limited exception of vacuum cleaners,[36] too widely imposed on other product groups in the following years.

Post-2016, we have, however, seen first the increase in circular economy *informational* requirements (for example on recycled content), as correlated with the increase in the number of regulated product groups.[37] Only with the 2019 generation of implementing measures (updates for electronic displays, televisions, computers, and computer servers, info on battery loading cycles, etc.) do we also see a broader increase in more demanding, or steering, circular economy requirements.[38] Today the possible implications are best seen in their, at present, most advanced incarnation: the Battery Regulation.[39]

The 2019 European Green Deal has blazed new life into the circular economy orientation of the ecodesign framework. In the 2020 Circular Economy Action Plan (CEAP), it is argued that *'there is currently no*

---

[35] Commission Regulation (EC) No. 244/2009 of 18 March 2009 implementing Directive 2005/32/EC of the European Parliament and of the Council with regard to ecodesign requirements for non-directional household lamps; Commission Regulation (EC) No. 245/2009 of 18 March 2009 implementing Directive 2005/32/EC of the European Parliament and of the Council with regard to ecodesign requirements for fluorescent lamps without integrated ballast, for high-intensity discharge lamps, and for ballasts and luminaires able to operate such lamps, and repealing Directive 2000/55/EC of the European Parliament and of the Council; Commission Regulation (EU) No. 1194/2012 of 12 December 2012 implementing Directive 2009/125/EC of the European Parliament and of the Council with regard to ecodesign requirements for directional lamps, light-emitting diode lamps, and related equipment.

[36] The Commission will propose new rules for vacuum cleaners; the Consultation has ended and the new rules are expected in the second half of 2023; see https://ec.europa.eu/info/law/better-regulation/have-your-say/initiatives/12832-Energy-efficiency-ecodesign-requirements-for-vacuum-cleaners-review-_en.

[37] Barkhausen et al., 'Review and Analysis of Ecodesign Directive Implementing Measures', p. 15.

[38] Ibid., p. 16.

[39] Regulation (EU) 2023/1542 of the European Parliament and of the Council of 12 July 2023 concerning batteries and waste batteries, amending Directive 2008/98/EC and Regulation (EU) 2019/1020 and repealing Directive 2006/66/EC.

comprehensive set of requirements to ensure that all products placed on the Union market become increasingly sustainable and stand the test of circularity'.[40] '*As a result, products are being replaced frequently, involving significant energy and resource use in order to produce and distribute new products and dispose of old ones*'.[41] What is called for, then – and to a degree delivered by the Commission in 2022 – is a new Ecodesign framework, which would significantly expand both the scope of the previous directive, going beyond 'energy *related* products' to all products that have a significant environmental footprint, and more genuine application of the circular economy principles (reparability, durability, upgradability, and recyclability), including the stronger mandatory rules for producers and distributors.[42]

The new 2022 Regulation proposal aims to embed the circular economy commitments more prominently. '*Directive 2009/125/EC has been generally successful in fostering the energy efficiency and some circularity aspects of energy-related products, and its approach has the potential to progressively address the sustainability of all products. To deliver on Green Deal commitments, this approach should be extended to other product groups and systematically address key aspects for increasing the environmental sustainability of products with binding requirements*'.[43] To do so, the new regulation aims not only to expand the scope of the directive in terms of product groups – to include other important consumer goods such as textiles[44] – but also stresses that this will come with new 'mandatory requirements' for producers and distributors '*to improve product durability, reusability, upgradability and reparability, improve possibilities for refurbishment and maintenance, address the presence of hazardous chemicals in products, increase their energy and resource efficiency, reduce their expected generation of waste materials and increase recycled content in products, while ensuring their performance and safety, enabling remanufacturing and high-quality recycling and reducing carbon and environmental footprints*'.[45] The more steering law seems to be in the making.

Over time, we have seen the expansion of what the product means in the context of ecodesign in two distinct ways. First, and more obviously, the scope of the EU legislation has been gradually expanding, to include

---

[40] European Commission, a New Circular Economy Action Plan for a cleaner and more competitive Europe, COM(2020) 98 final, section 2.1.
[41] Sustainable Products Regulation Proposal 2022, Recital 2, p. 16.
[42] Sustainable Products Regulation Proposal 2022.
[43] Sustainable Products Regulation Proposal 2022, Recital 1, p. 16.
[44] Sustainable Products Regulation Proposal 2022, p. 4.
[45] Sustainable Products Regulation Proposal 2022, Recital 5, p. 17.

eventually any product groups with large environmental footprint, with the last 2022 Regulation.[46] In the second sense, ecodesign as a matter of circular economy aims to '[connect] *the design of a product to the larger situation of materials extraction, production, transportation, use and disposal and attempts to minimize environmental impacts across the entire life-cycle*'.[47] Focusing on the 'life-cycle' of products is thus to pay attention to relations of production, distribution, consumption, and disposal of products – embedding the product in its social and natural context.

This expansion of what product is, the embedding of the product so to say, is a similar tendency to what we have observed also in Chapter 3 on consumption, and we will see later in the chapter on corporation – expanding or thickening the *objects* of regulation, beyond their narrow privatised "selves". Yet, this socialisation has hit some limits, perhaps a bit too early in the context of ecodesign.

Despite the considerations in the 2020 Circular Economy Action Plan, the Commission's 2022 Proposal for Framework Regulation does not consider, unlike the targeted Battery Regulation, some of the more effective measures that would make life-cycle an integral part of production, such as 'extended producer responsibility', or the 'end of life responsibility' of producers – even if the producers may be hereby both better incentivised to account for life-cycle in the production and later best placed to ensure the effective recycling and the final disposal of the product.[48]

Overall, however, the gradual shift from energy efficiency to 'resource efficiency', and later to a more ambitious understanding of 'circular economy',[49] presents an important change in terms of political economy of technology. To the extent that the focus remains on energy efficiency, or even narrowly understood resource efficiency, such a focus has the capacity to make the goods ultimately cheaper – fostering in turn greater consumption.[50] The focus on circular economy points already to a different model of circulation, which counts with the reduction of consumption

---

[46] Sustainable Products Regulation Proposal 2022, art. 5.
[47] Kate Fletcher, 'Environmentally Responsible Design in Textiles', in *EcoTextile'98 - Sustainable Development*, ed. A. R. Horrocks (Woodhead Publishing, 1999): 271–8 as cited by Renate Hübner, 'Ecodesign: Reach, Limits and Challenges 20 Years of Ecodesign – Time for a Critical Reflection', *Forum Ware International* 1 (2012): 25–38, p. 27.
[48] Michel, Premature Obsolescence.
[49] Barkhausen et al., 'Review and Analysis of Ecodesign Directive Implementing Measures', p. 6.
[50] Anja Marie Bundgaard, Mette Alberg Mosgaard, and Arne Remmen, 'From Energy Efficiency towards Resource Efficiency within the Ecodesign Directive', *Journal of Cleaner Production* 144 (2017): 358–74.

and the replacement of products with services such as repair. This presents cracks in the understanding of prosperity as economic growth.

4.3 Steering Growth

When it comes to the imaginaries of the economy, we see an increasingly complex relationship between ecodesign framework and the objective of economic growth. If in 2005 and 2009, ecodesign was still seen as a cheap way of protecting nature, given that the *'significant potential for improvement in terms of the environmental impact of these product groups will not entail excessive costs'*,[51] in 2015 we see a shift to underline the "growth potential" potential of ecodesign and circular economy themselves: *'The circular economy will **boost the EU's competitiveness** by protecting businesses against scarcity of resources and volatile prices, helping to create new business opportunities and innovative, more efficient ways of producing and consuming. It will create local jobs at all skills levels and opportunities for social integration and cohesion. At the same time, it will **save energy and help avoid the irreversible damages** caused by using up resources at a rate that exceeds the Earth's capacity to renew them in terms of climate and biodiversity, air, soil and water pollution'*.[52]

The first Circular Economy Action Plan (CEAP) thus makes a very strong *business case* for circular economy, as it is expected to stimulate sustainable activity in key sectors, provide new business opportunities, unlock the growth and job potential of the circular economy, foster innovation, and generate new and sustainable competitive advantages for Europe.[53] Similar enthusiasm for the "growth potential" potential of circular economy is also present in the 2016 Ecodesign Working Plan, where the Commission states that the *'Ecodesign, complemented by energy labelling rules, supports the Commission's overarching priority to strengthen Europe's competitiveness and boost job creation and economic growth; it ensures a level playing field in the internal market, drives investment and innovation in a sustainable manner, and saves money for consumers while reducing CO2 emissions'*.[54]

The 2020 Circular Economy Action Plan backtracks somewhat from the traditional language of growth and competitiveness, to use "regenerative growth" as a leitmotiv, while stressing the environmental *urgency* of transition and the negative sides of (over)consumption of resources:

---

[51] Ecodesign Directive 2009/125/EC, art. 15(2)(c).
[52] European Commission, Closing the loop – An EU action plan for the Circular Economy, COM(2015) 0614 final, p. 2. All emphases in the quotes, in this and the following chapters, were added by the author of this book.
[53] Circular Economy Action Plan 2015.   [54] Ecodesign Working Plan 2016–2019, p. 2.

'the EU needs to accelerate the transition towards a **regenerative growth model** that gives back to the planet more than it takes, advance towards keeping its resource consumption within planetary boundaries, and therefore strive to **reduce its consumption footprint** and double its circular material use rate in the coming decade'.[55]

One of the central ways in which the Commission sees that the potential of circular economy can be harnessed is via its link to digital economy, seen as a medium creating possibilities for innovative business models based on '*closer relationship with customers, mass customisation,* **the sharing and collaborative economy,** *and* **powered by digital technologies,** *such as the internet of things, big data, blockchain and artificial intelligence,* [which] *will not only accelerate circularity but also the dematerialisation of our economy and make Europe less dependent on primary materials*'.[56]

The 2022 Regulation proposal is based fully on a "green growth" paradigm (rather than a "regenerative growth") model, aiming at '*decoupling of economic development from natural resource use and reduction of material dependencies*, all the while *supporting economic growth, job creation and social inclusion*'.[57] The Regulation is strongly motivated by innovation potential, where the early movers will have advantages later, as '*producers that use more sustainable production and transparent supply chains are expected to gain EU market share and increase their competitiveness over producers that use less sustainable methods*'.[58]

Now, while green growth and the attempts at decoupling are pointedly criticised for not being able to revert us from ecological catastrophe on time,[59] what we should still appreciate is the (potential of the) underlying shift in the imaginary of the economy. The shift is not only that the growth is supposed to be *green* but, more fundamentally within the framework of this book, that the growth has to be *steered*. This growth thus in principle does not require removing regulation or freeing the hands of private actors. Rather it requires *more* governmental steering, and *more* tightening of the hands of private actors, so that we can see both *more* and *better* growth and innovation. Thus, while the transition to

---

[55] Circular Economy Action Plan 2015, p. 2.
[56] Circular Economy Action Plan 2020, p. 2.
[57] Sustainable Products Regulation Proposal 2022, p. 1.
[58] Sustainable Products Regulation Proposal 2022, p. 8.
[59] Alevgul H. Sorman, 'Deceitful Decoupling: Misconceptions of a Persistent Myth', in *The Barcelona School of Ecological Economics and Political Ecology*, ed. Sergio Villamayor-Tomas and Roldan Muradian, vol. 8, *Studies in Ecological Economics* (Springer International Publishing, 2023), 165–77.

"green growth" may not go far enough, quickly enough, a different way of thinking and talking about economy and growth is a fundamental precondition for developing a more credible new imaginary of shared and sustainable prosperity.[60]

4.4 Beyond Win-Win

By and large, the picture presented in the previous paragraphs may seem to suggest that the imaginary of politics behind ecodesign continues to be of a "win-win" kind that we know from the times of neoliberalism. But that is not the full story: a careful reading of the underlying documents makes clear that there are some clear distributive trade-offs between different groups – consumers, businesses, SMEs, or workers – and later documents are also increasingly ready to both acknowledge the distributive conflicts and make a choice for that or other 'winner'. Thus, we also see emerging a new imaginary of politics, which moves beyond the neoliberal "win-win" story, making distributive conflicts both visible and potentially open to further politicisation.

4.4.1 *Distributive Trade-Offs 1: Consumers*

Both the 2005 and 2009 framework directives promised environmental benefits[61] without many downsides for consumers: *'There shall be no significant negative impact on the functionality of the product, from the perspective of the user; (b) health, safety and the environment shall not be adversely affected; (c) there shall be no significant negative impact on consumers in particular as regards the affordability and the life cycle cost of the product'*.[62]

If anything, consumer's interests seemed aligned (energy efficiency), and consumers were seen as allies who would contribute to ecodesign objectives by exercising their freedom of choice in the market to choose more energy-efficient products. Thus *'while ecodesign progressively bans the least-efficient appliances from the market, energy labelling guides consumers towards the most energy efficient appliances leading to concrete economic benefits to the consumer over the life cycle of the product'*.[63] By *'encouraging and*

---

[60] Tim Jackson, *Prosperity without Growth: Foundations for the Economy of Tomorrow* (Taylor & Francis, 2016).
[61] Ecodesign Working Plan 2009–2011. At this stage, it is assumed that the significant potential for improvement in terms of the environmental impact of these product groups will not entail excessive costs.
[62] Ecodesign Directive 2009/125/EC, art. 15(5)(b) and (c).
[63] Ecodesign Working Plan 2012–2014, p. 1.

empowering consumers to buy the most efficient products based on useful information (through energy labelling) [...] it reduces the energy consumption of consumers and businesses, and thereby their energy and utilities bills'.[64]

An important change in the imaginary of consumption, however, takes place in the background. Once the Commission's story becomes more than just the 'energy efficiency' that should fill consumers' pockets, and a move to circular economy principles becomes necessary, consumption patterns will also need to change. This means that consumers should want and consume somewhat different things than they have so far. The consumers are encouraged to shop also for second-hand and refurbished products, both as a sign of rationality and taste for quality. '***Second-hand products** can represent an affordable, high-quality alternative **for low quality new products**'*.[65] For consumers, the 2020 Circular Economy Action Plan suggests that circular economy will provide '*high-quality, functional and safe products, which are efficient and affordable, last longer and are designed for reuse, repair, and high-quality recycling*'.[66] Importantly, such second-hand and refurbished products are already incorporated in the "cost structure" of the 2022 Regulation Proposal, changing thus considerably the 'cost-benefit analysis' when it comes to 'consumer welfare': '*Thus there shall be no significant negative impact on consumers in terms of the affordability of relevant products, also **taking into account access to second-hand products, durability and the life cycle cost of products**'*.[67]

This is an important shift away from the neoliberal imaginary of consumers and consumption. If online shopping was the core message twenty years ago, as both rational and market-improving, today the situation is different. On the one hand, at least the worst effects of e-commerce (such as the major destruction of unsold goods) have to be controlled.[68] On the other hand, the Commission seems to envisage a slower kind of consumption. Consuming second-hand or refurbished goods is not fully standardised consumption, available in large quantities online and offline. Rather, such consumption will more often than not require us to go to a shop or, in the case of refurbished goods, encourage

---

[64] Ecodesign Working Plan 2016–2019, p. 2.
[65] European Commission Staff Working Document, Sustainable Products in a Circular Economy – Towards an EU Product Policy Framework contributing to the Circular Economy, SWD(2019) 91 final, p. 19.
[66] Circular Economy Action Plan 2020, p. 2.
[67] Sustainable Products Regulation Proposal 2022, art. 5(5)(c).
[68] Sustainable Products Regulation Proposal 2022, art. 1.

bringing in one's old device next to buying a new refurbished device, etc. The same goes for repair, which both takes time and care.

4.4.2 Distributive Trade-Offs 2: Businesses

The starting point for both the 2005 and 2009 framework directives is low cost. '*At this stage, it is assumed that the significant potential for improvement in terms of the environmental impact of these product groups will not entail excessive costs*'.[69] The 2009 Directive promises that '*there shall be no significant negative impact on industry's competitiveness; in principle, the setting of an ecodesign requirement shall not have the consequence of imposing proprietary technology on manufacturers; and no excessive administrative burden shall be imposed on manufacturers*'.[70]

The overwhelming concern with the costs – be it placed on industry, or on competitiveness – is becoming less prominent in recent years. While the Commission's 2022 Proposal accepts that '[o]*verall, this means* **costs for economic actors involved in product manufacturing are likely to increase, with some costs passed on to consumers**'',[71] the gains are to be made mainly on economic growth potential as '*producers that use more sustainable production and transparent supply chains are expected to gain EU market share and increase their competitiveness over producers that use less sustainable methods*'.[72]

Where the concern for the economic actors remains at its strongest is in the concern for stable regulation and standards. '*Industry needs harmonised requirements applicable across the board, efficient means to comply with them, proper enforcement, reinforced market surveillance and customs controls based on a risk analysis*'.[73] What is more, it is about protecting our economic operators against those who do not abide by the same standards, as it is a '**level playing field** *for businesses operating on the internal market*'.[74] Thus, it is not the costs per se, but the degree of governmental guarantee of a "level playing field" for European producers that matters to the Commission.

It is not the case that competitiveness based on price is not important, but the bar of concern is much higher than a decade ago. Only

---

[69] Ecodesign Working Plan 2009–2011, p. 5.
[70] Ecodesign Directive 2009/125/EC, art. 15.
[71] European Commission, Executive Summary of The Impact Assessment, Accompanying Sustainable Products Regulation 2022, SWD(2022) 83 final, p. 2.
[72] Sustainable Products Regulation Proposal 2022, p. 8.
[73] Sustainable Products Regulation Proposal 2022, p. 2.
[74] Sustainable Products Regulation Proposal 2022, p. 5.

'*disproportionate negative impact on the competitiveness of economic actors*' really counts, and even that is qualified as applying '*at least of SMEs*'.[75] With the circular economy becoming an important growth/industrial strategy, in the face of the sluggish growth (of productivity) in the EU over the past decade, the investment in *regulation-led* innovation is seen as a strategy that gives first mover advantages.

The disinterest in costs is also (critically) observed by the Regulatory Scrutiny Board, the Commission's (de)regulation watchdog.[76] The RSB has been made particularly nervous about this proposal, demanding in its second 'positive with reservations' opinion, '*Considering the difficulty of estimating the costs and benefits of what will likely be a costly measure, the methodology should be more explicit as to **what would be "acceptable" cost increases**. It should clarify whether there is an expected time horizon for durability savings to offset increased product prices resulting from the sustainability requirements*'.[77]

As there are broadly shared concerns that the regulation-led innovation may be to the disadvantage of small- and medium-sized businesses,[78] the 2022 Regulation proposal aims to provide some cushioning. The measures that are encouraged include training and financial support, as well as one-stop shops or similar institutional mechanisms to aid the SMEs.[79] Generally, the impact assessment predicts a positive impact: '*including from a shift of activity from the processing of primary towards secondary raw materials and from production of products to maintenance, reuse, refurbishment, repair and second-hand sales, which is expected to benefit SMEs significantly because they are more active in these sectors*'.[80] This conclusion in the impact assessment is not an obvious one though: earlier documents suggest, for instance, that in the repair sector there is a '*tendency towards a higher centralisation of the sector, with large repairers gaining a higher share of the market and small independent repairers being either absorbed by larger repair*

---

[75] Sustainable Products Regulation Proposal 2022, art. 5(5)(c) and (d).
[76] Regulatory Scrutiny Board is the main protagonist in the later chapter on corporation. More information can be found here: https://commission.europa.eu/law/law-making-process/regulatory-scrutiny-board_en.
[77] European Commission Regulatory Scrutiny Board, 'Opinion: Sustainable Products Initiative', SEC(2022) 165, p. 2.
[78] Sustainable Products Regulation Proposal 2022, art. 5(5)(d).
[79] Sustainable Products Regulation Proposal 2022, art. 19.
[80] Executive Summary of the Impact Assessment, Accompanying the Sustainable Products Regulation Proposal 2022, p. 2.

services or withdrawing from the sector'.[81] Yet this concern with the concentration does not feature in the 2022 Regulation proposal.

4.4.3 Distributive Trade-Offs 3: Workers

Of all economic actors, workers get the least attention in the Ecodesign framework. In the 2005 and 2009 directives, there is no mention of workers or work whatsoever. The CEAP of 2020 is the only document, among the studied, that has something to say about work and workers. Namely, that *'circularity can be expected to have a positive net effect on job creation provided that workers acquire the skills required by the green transition'.*[82] The strategy of the CEAP to achieve such skills acquisition is twofold. On the one hand using the *'potential of the social economy, which is a pioneer in job creation linked to the circular economy'*, which, on the other hand, *'will be further leveraged by the mutual benefits of supporting the green transition and strengthening social inclusion, notably under the Action Plan to implement the European Pillar of Social Right'.*[83]

The 2022 Regulation proposal does not pick up on the aspects of work or the aspects of social economy. The only reference to the 'social aspects' is their relegation to other uncertain legislative proposals: *'due to the adoption of the Commission Proposal for a Directive on Corporate Sustainable Due Diligence during the preparation of this initiative, it was deemed appropriate to exclude requirements on social aspects from the scope of this legislative proposal'.*[84] The relevance of the due diligence proposal is also quite unclear, as that is mostly meant to require very large companies to monitor their operations outside of the EU – where EU and MS public law obligations do not reach. Moreover, this proposal sets rather minimal substantive standards on corporations, thus hardly being an ambitious target within the borders of the EU. One explanation for this exclusion is some sort of gesture to the Regulatory Scrutiny Board, which has singled out these two proposals (Due Diligence Directive and new Sustainable Products Regulation) for particularly unsympathetic treatment.

The omission of the social economy from the Regulation proposal is also remarkable. As the social economy is in several places considered crucial for innovation in the area of circular economy, it is unclear why the

---

[81] European Commission, Staff Working Document, Sustainable Products in a Circular Economy – Towards an EU Product Policy Framework Contributing to the Circular Economy, SWD(2019) 92 final, p. 18.
[82] Circular Economy Action Plan 2020, p. 15.
[83] Circular Economy Action Plan 2020, p. 15.
[84] Sustainable Products Regulation Proposal 2022, p. 8.

Commission is not more interested in tapping into its potential. Not only are social enterprises and Bcorps some of the most innovative entities in relation to circular production[85], but if circular economy is also to provide indeed more 'local jobs at all skills levels', that ideally should *not* lead to the concentration in, for instance, repair sectors as the Commission has already observed. Drawing on the old and the new social economy (i.e. repair shops and public workshops on the one hand and innovative social enterprises on the other) may be a promising way forward.

4.5 Shoring up Publicness

From its inception, the Ecodesign framework could be considered a particularly 'interventionist' type of legislation, inasmuch as it entrusts public authorities – rather than private actors and "market forces", – with the leading role in setting performance standards for at least one segment of 'energy-related products'. In comparison with many other fields of market regulation, around the mid-2000s, this presented a notable sign of trust in the competence of government on the one hand and the lack of trust in the market mechanism on the other.

With every new iteration of legislative measures and plans, the trust in this public leadership has increased. The reason is that overall, ecodesign has booked large success for both energy savings and consumers' purse – in spite of persistent concerns about the efficacy of market surveillance.[86] Thus in 2016, the expectation was that '*By 2020 this framework is estimated to deliver energy savings of around 175 Mtoe per year in primary energy, more than the annual primary energy consumption of Italy. For consumers, this translates into €490 savings per household per year on energy bills. [...] As such, it also contributes to energy security by reducing the import of energy into the EU by the equivalent of 1.3 billion barrels of oil each year and by reducing CO2 emissions by 320 million tonnes annually*'.[87] In the Working Package 2022, the Commission confirms that large savings of energy took place, arguing that '*the cumulative effect of EU rules on ecodesign and energy labelling in 2020 reduced EU primary energy demand by 7 % or

---

[85] Opinion of the European Economic and Social Committee on Communication from the Commission to the European Parliament, the Council, the European Economic and Social Committee and the Committee of the Regions – Building an economy that works for people: an action plan for the social economy, COM(2021) 778 final, p. 38.
[86] Sustainable Products Regulation Proposal 2022.
[87] Ecodesign Working Plan 2016–2019, p. 2.

1 037 TWh/year (ca. 170 Mt CO2 equivalent GHG reduction), including some 16 bcm of gas'.[88]

How did the EU achieve those goals? Already the 2005/2009 directives set the basic elements of the ecodesign framework. In the legislative procedure,[89] every 'implementing measure' that will come to regulate an entire product group (such as washing machines or TVs) has to be accompanied by an 'impact assessment'. This impact assessment has to account for both environmental aspects and more narrowly economic aspects, including cost-benefit analysis and the impact on the competitiveness of the EU businesses. Importantly, however, the legislator suggests that the uncertainty about non-environmental impacts should not stand in the way of regulating. The implementing measures should be developed in consultation with the relevant stakeholders: to this effect, the Commission was also to set up a specific body named the 'Consultation Forum', which would bring together a balanced group of stakeholders. This body is tasked with contributing to defining and reviewing implementing measures, examining the effectiveness of the established market surveillance mechanisms, and assessing voluntary agreements and other self-regulation measures.

When it comes to the obligations of producers or distributors, before they place a product from within a regulated product group on the European market, they have to certify the 'product's conformity' with the ecodesign requirements. The certification is undertaken by a 'notified body': in principle, a private company, but with ever more requirements placed on its operation in order to make sure that it is not a *consultancy* for compliance but instead fulfils the public function.[90] Once the product has been certified, it could be affixed with a **CE conformity marking** and put on the market.

---

[88] European Commission, Ecodesign and Energy Labelling Working Plan 2022–2024, 2022/C 182/01, section 2.

[89] Ecodesign Directive 2009/125/EC, art. 15(4):
(a) **the life cycle of the product and all its significant environmental aspects, inter alia, energy efficiency**. The adoption of ecodesign requirements on the significant environmental aspects of a product **shall not be unduly delayed by uncertainties** regarding the other aspects;
(b) carry out **an assessment**, which shall consider the impact on the environment, consumers and manufacturers, including SMEs, in terms of **competitiveness** – including in relation to markets outside the Community – innovation, market access and costs and benefits;
(c) take into account **existing national environmental legislation** that Member States consider relevant;
(d) carry out **appropriate consultation with stakeholders**.

[90] Sustainable Products Regulation Proposal 2022, Recital 75, p. 35.

The 2022 revision of the ecodesign framework with the New Regulation proposal does not bring vast changes in governance structure, or to the powers of the Commission. The changes that were made concerned the reclassification of the measures as delegated (rather than implementing) acts, a procedure that gives a greater normative force to the measures, as well as more voice to both Parliament and the Council, that can object to the measures within a certain timeframe. The aforementioned Consultation Forum also has been kept by the new Proposal, if renamed as the Ecodesign Forum.

What the Regulation proposal does, however, is to further specify the roles and responsibilities of all actors involved in order to safeguard the public nature of the process. This concerns additional conditions placed on both private and public actors in the process, including those who control the conformity, the obligations of the online platforms to survey the products they offer, or by requiring that sufficient financial resources are placed at the disposal of the relevant authorities at the EU or the MS level. Let me take each one in turn.

First, the Regulation requires that the private actors engaged in the conformity assessment, the so-called notified bodies, have to remain autonomous and not outsource certain tasks regarding the conformity assessment of products and other activities internal to the notified body, to other organisations.[91] Even more importantly, *'Prior to taking a final decision on whether a product can be granted a conformity certificate, the economic operator that wishes to place that product on the market should be allowed to* **supplement the relevant documentation once only.** *[...] as that would mean that the service provided resembles a consulting service and could in practice dilute the* **public interest nature of notified bodies' tasks**'.[92] Importantly, the incentive structures for notified bodies also need to be aligned with the public interest purpose of these bodies, as '*the* **remuneration of the top-level management and assessment personnel** *of a conformity assessment body shall not depend on the number of assessments carried out or their results*'.[93]

Second, the Regulation also aims to place surveillance and cooperation obligations on online platforms, '*Given their important role in intermediating the sale of products between economic operators and customers, online marketplaces should take responsibility for addressing the sale of products that do not*

---

[91] Sustainable Products Regulation Proposal 2022, Recital 82, p. 37.
[92] Sustainable Products Regulation Proposal 2022, Recital 82, p. 37.
[93] Sustainable Products Regulation Proposal 2022, art. 45(8).

comply with ecodesign requirements and should cooperate with market surveillance authorities'.[94] Not only are the online platforms responsible for cooperation and surveillance but they are also obliged to enable market surveillance authorities to scrape their interfaces for non-compliant products or to remove illegal content if *ordered* by the market surveillance authority.[95]

Third, the Regulation aims to improve the material capacity of national governments to make this policy efficacious. To that purpose, the Regulation adds provisions on green procurement, which postulate that the Commission may stipulate an obligatory amount of green public procurement from within the regulated product group.[96] The Regulation also encourages member states to make use of fiscal measures to reward the best-performing companies, by, for instance, introducing eco-vouchers and green taxation. The incentives would have to be targeted at products in the two highest classes of sustainability performance: '*Then Member States decide to make use of incentives to reward the best-performing products among those for which classes of performance have been set by delegated acts pursuant to this Regulation, they should do so by targeting those incentives at the highest two populated classes of performance*'.[97] Altogether, such targeted governmental support for *chosen* products and *chosen* services suggests a shift from a regulating market framework to directly making choices in the market. A nod thus to the following industrial policy chapter.

Fourth, and final, the Regulation also aims to ensure that the authorities, as well as conformity assessment bodies (!), have sufficient resources to do their job well. The Commission is clearly indicating resolve to '*significantly **step up resources** allocated to implement ecodesign policy as part of a more ambitious sustainable product policy*'.[98] The Regulation, however, goes even further than that and requires that MSs also have '*sufficient number of competent personnel and sufficient funding at their disposal for the proper performance of their tasks*'.[99] Where the states appear to not have enough competent personnel, it will be on the

---

[94] Sustainable Products Regulation Proposal 2022, Recital 58, p. 32.
[95] Sustainable Products Regulation Proposal 2022, art. 29.
[96] Sustainable Products Regulation Proposal 2022, art. 58.
[97] Sustainable Products Regulation Proposal 2022, Recital 86, p. 38.
[98] Ecodesign and Energy Labelling Working Plan 2022–2024, p. 10.
[99] Sustainable Products Regulation Proposal 2022, Recital 74, p. 36.

Commission to set a full-time equivalent that should be at the disposal of the notifying authorities.[100]

Overall, two trends can be discerned. On the one hand, the Commission wants to make sure that government has the capacity to govern – not only at the EU level but also at the national level, as both the certification and enforcement need a boost. On the other hand, where private actors are called to act as notified bodies, they need to do so along public (public-interest regarding as well as competent and well staffed) rather than private (profit-making) lines. Thus, a certain degree of "publicisation" of private certification bodies ought to take place.

4.6 Hardening Law

From its inception, ecodesign has relied more or less heavily on law as a means of governance. The first Ecodesign directives were very specific and narrow; they have been 'hard law' in their scope of application. From 2005, however, the EU changes the strategy and moves away from a product-specific approach to an 'Ecodesign framework', where the directive sets the objectives and procedures for developing ecodesign implementing measures, while leaving the specific measures themselves to be developed in the process of co-regulation between the Commission, industry, scientists, and other relevant stakeholders. As the Commission itself observes, this approach fits neatly with the 'new approach to technical regulation'.[101]

4.6.1 Rise and Fall of Self-Regulation

The starting point for both the 2005 and 2009 directives has been that legislation serves a subsidiarity role, as *'priority should be given to alternative courses of action such as **self-regulation** by the industry where such action is likely to deliver the policy objectives faster or in a less costly manner than mandatory requirements'*.[102] Yet, if the perception was that market forces were not *'evolving in the right direction, or at an acceptable speed'*,[103] the EU authorities could intervene with common specifications.

---

[100] Sustainable Products Regulation Proposal 2022, Recital 74, p. 36.
[101] European Commission Notice, The 'Blue Guide' on the implementation of EU products rules, C/2016/1958 (2016).
[102] Ecodesign Directive 2009/125/EC, Recital 18.
[103] Ecodesign Directive 2009/125/EC, Recital 18.

Both 2005 and 2009 directives aim to provide procedurally a more robust understanding of what self-regulation needs to look like, taking on board a widespread critique of the lack of inclusivity of self-regulatory measures. Namely, self-regulatory processes must secure *'openness of participation, added value, representativeness, quantified and staged objectives, involvement of civil society, monitoring and reporting, cost-effectiveness of administering a self-regulatory initiative and sustainability'*.[104]

Where the industry indeed develops self-regulatory 'voluntary agreements', a slightly different model applies to those measures than to the norms and standards developed under the public arm of the Ecodesign framework. Namely, the self-regulation was not expected to remove the worst-performing products from the market – as is the case with mandatory public rules. Rather it was expected to motivate innovation and the improvement of performance of a growing portion of the products on the market. Thus, a certain amount of products (30 per cent, 50 per cent, 80 per cent, etc.) had to be placed on the market that aligned with the voluntarily set ecodesign standards – while leaving the worst-performing products still in the market.[105]

The voluntary agreements, in the rare cases when they were concluded,[106] suffered from some limitations. Thus, Bundgaard et al. argue that *'In the voluntary agreement covering imaging equipment, durability requirements were not included; even though the preparatory study showed that the short lifespan of inkjet printers resulted in a high impact from the manufacturing phase'*.[107] This, the authors suggest, has been due to the fact that incorporating durability standards would have reduced sales.[108]

The 2022 Regulation proposal presents a break in this (over)reliance on self-regulation. Rather than being a *preferred* (as in cheaper and more effective) form of regulation, self-regulation is presented now only as a *valid alternative* – if and only if a number of old and new conditions are met. These include requirements as to what a self-regulation measure should contain, what the industry should submit as evidence to the Commission, and the procedure for the Commission to recognise the

---

[104] Ecodesign Directive 2009/125/EC, Recital 20.
[105] Bundgaard et al., 'From Energy Efficiency towards Resource Efficiency within the Ecodesign Directive', p. 371.
[106] Overall, the voluntary agreements present only a fraction in the overall regulation of the thirty-one product groups, as of now.
[107] Bundgaard et al., 'From Energy Efficiency towards Resource Efficiency within the Ecodesign Directive', p. 371.
[108] Ibid.

self-regulation measure as a valid alternative to a delegated act. At any point, the Commission can also require the signatories to submit a revised and updated measure or, if existing and proposed self-regulatory measures do not align with public objectives, decide to regulate the issue itself.[109]

4.6.2 Toward a More Mandatory Law

The recent Regulation proposal stresses, instead, mandatory rules as a path to circularity. This is necessary as circularity's core principles – reduce, reuse, and recycle[110] – are not shared by all stakeholders. When it comes to *reducing* consumption, mainly by extending product lifetime, it has usually been the industry that has worked against it.[111] The lack of durability requirements in the 'voluntary ecodesign agreements', which serve as the alternatives to mandatory rules within the framework of the 2009 directive, is a particular sign at hand.[112] *Reuse* is still culturally a difficult sell, so long as consumers want novelty and are steered to want novelty above all else.[113] Finally, when it comes to *recycle,* neither consumers nor companies are 'natural allies'. While consumers have little economic incentives to choose recycled goods, for companies recycling remains a far more expensive alternative to date. Mandatory rules on durability, reuse and recycled content, and recyclability of products, next to information on recycled content, become thus a necessary ingredient if one is to steer the economy in a different direction.

And that is also what the Commission seems to have established from the 2020 CEAP as the shift towards circular economy would require several additional measures, and powers, on the side of the public authorities. The CEAP suggests that such measures should go beyond the existing Ecodesign requirements to include also measures against premature obsolescence, a ban on the destruction of unsold but durable goods, 'end of life responsibility' and the concept of 'product-as-a-service'. The latter two have not found their way into the 2022 Regulation

---

[109] Sustainable Products Regulation Proposal 2022, Recital 76, p. 36.
[110] Barkhausen et al., 'Review and Analysis of Ecodesign Directive Implementing Measures', p. 7.
[111] Bundgaard et al., 'From Energy Efficiency towards Resource Efficiency within the Ecodesign Directive', p. 370.
[112] Barkhausen et al., 'Review and Analysis of Ecodesign Directive Implementing Measures', p. 20.
[113] For a good overview of the psychology of advertising, see Bob M. Fennis and Wolfgang Stroebe, *The Psychology of Advertising* (Psychology Press, 2015).

Proposal: it is not inconceivable that this was due to the intervention of the Regulatory Scrutiny Board.[114]

The 2022 Sustainable Products Regulation proposal presents a tendency towards *hardening* law in the ecodesign framework, on several levels. First, the Regulation begins with the shift from a (framework) directive to a (framework) regulation. Regulation need not be implemented by MSs and thus improves legal certainty for businesses – at the expanse of not only MS discretion but also experimentation with different ways of regulating at the national level.[115]

Second, in order to *'deliver on Green Deal commitments, this approach [ecodesign] should be extended to other product groups and systematically address key aspects for increasing the environmental sustainability of products with **binding requirements**'*.[116] Thus harder, mandatory law is necessary, on two levels: *performance requirements* (such as durability or recycled content) and *information requirements* (product passport or substances of concern) that would enable consumers to compare, repair, or dispose of the product.[117]

The Regulation also introduces the requirements that products come equipped with the so-called product passports. Product passports are the true child of the circular economy movement, as 'waste is material without an identity'.[118] Product passports should contain information that would enable over time increased recyclability, repairability, refurbishment, etc. The question remains what kind of information the EU rules will require – this is still to be specified by delegated acts, stipulating what information such passports need to comprise for specific product groups, how such information should be stored, and who should have access to what part of that information.[119] Product passports nevertheless create basic pre-conditions for improving circularity.

---

[114] Regulatory Scrutiny Board, 'Opinion: Sustainable Products Initiative', SEC(2022) 165.
[115] Evelyne Terryn and Estelle Valentine Irambona, 'Duurzame Consumptie En Maximum Harmonisatie: Water En Vuur?', *SSRN* (2023), https://papers.ssrn.com/sol3/papers.cfm?abstract_id=4376907, last accessed 5 January 2024.
[116] Sustainable Products Regulation Proposal 2022, Recital 10, p. 19.
[117] Davide Polverini, 'Regulating the Circular Economy within the Ecodesign Directive: Progress so Far, Methodological Challenges and Outlook', *Sustainable Production and Consumption* 27 (2021): 1113–23.
[118] A philosophy, and a business strategy, of a Dutch architect and innovator Thomas Rau. For the whole vision, see Thomas Rau and Sabine Oberhuber, *Material Matters: Developing Business for a Circular Economy* (Taylor & Francis, 2022).
[119] Sustainable Products Regulation Proposal 2022, Recital 32, p. 26.

One of the more important substantive measures that were mentioned in the CEAP and the Regulation includes the (qualified) prohibition on the destruction of unsold goods.[120] The practice of the destruction of unsold goods became widespread with the rise of online commerce.[121] While the full breadth of this practice is still unclear – as companies keep this information mostly secret – one report suggests that in the EU we are talking about billions in value and that companies such as Amazon have been engaged in the destruction of unsold goods across EU countries.[122] The reasons for the destruction range from concerns with brands to the costs of more sustainable disposal.[123] To counter the waste of resources, companies (except for SMEs under certain conditions) will be required to publish relevant information as it concerns discarded products and how those products had been dealt with, on a publicly accessible website.[124] The Commission would then be further empowered to ban the destruction of products that have a significant environmental impact.[125]

Clearly, despite being a Regulation, it remains a framework regulation, which means that many difficult choices will come in the implementation phase. It is still worth noting, however, that the Regulation places durability first in the list of ecodesign requirements.[126] Such a prominent place is at least a nod towards a different imaginary of production and consumption. The omission of the Regulation to engage with the 'extended producer responsibility' or the 'product as service' as suggested by the 2020 CEAP is regrettable, in as much as such a step would bring *sustainability by design* one step closer.

---

[120] Sustainable Products Regulation Proposal 2022, art. 20.
[121] Pourya Pourhejazy, 'Destruction Decisions for Managing Excess Inventory in E-Commerce Logistics', *Sustainability* 12 (2020), p. 20.
[122] Ökopol for the European Environmental Bureau, 'Policy Brief on Prohibiting the Destruction of Unsold Goods' (2021), https://eeb.org/wp-content/uploads/2021/10/Prohibiting-the-destruction-of-unsold-goods-Policy-brief-2021.pdf, last accessed 5 January 2024.
[123] Ariele Elia, 'Fashion's Destruction of Unsold Goods: Responsible Solutions for an Environmentally Conscious Future', *Fordham Intellectual Property, Media and Entertainment Law Journal* 30, no. 2 (2020): 539–91.
[124] Sustainable Products Regulation Proposal 2022, Recital 47, p. 30.
[125] Sustainable Products Regulation Proposal 2022, Recital 48, p. 30.
[126] Sustainable Products Regulation Proposal 2022, art. 1. The list is not in alphabetical order!

4.7 The Contours of the New Imaginary of Prosperity

I argue above that the ecodesign framework is gradually institutionalising a different understanding of economy, law, politics, government, and technology, setting the ground for different 'compossible' technological futures. Let me thus conclude this chapter by outlining what the most important discursive and normative building blocks of such a new imaginary of technology and prosperity are as well as what may be (more or less) glaring omissions.

Ecodesign plays excellently into the EU's strengths. Inspired by a 'new approach to technical regulation', the EU has over time managed to improve a wide range of consumer products, without much ado, to the benefit of both consumers and environment. Over time, it became clear that governmental intervention needed to go beyond energy efficiency and be expanded to a greater range of product groups – if the environmental objectives were to be achieved. The expansion of the requirements regarding products' circularity (i.e. durability, recyclability, repair, and reuse) has at the same time shown that a more *strategic* relation to "economic growth" is necessary and immanent.

The framework makes clear that technological innovation is not entirely a market matter. Instead, as we have learned above, to be more socially useful (e.g. durable and serve many customers), resilient as well as truly innovative, innovation often needs public steering. Such public steering is here entrusted with public institutions and increasingly mandatory law.[127] Where private bodies are involved in certification, this is acceptable to the extent that such action carries a high degree of regard for the public nature of decision-making.[128] While over time, the co-regulation remains important, public authorities drew more responsibility towards themselves as to what rules and expectations are to be delivered by the products and technologies behind them. It is only then that innovation holds '*large potential in terms of* **sustainability in the broadest sense**, *benefiting* **people, planet and prosperity**'.[129]

What the ecodesign framework so far does not do is to further develop some of the more transformative ideas that have been aired by the Commission. First, as mentioned earlier, more transformative policies

---

[127] Sustainable Products Regulation Proposal 2022, p. 4.
[128] Sustainable Products Regulation Proposal 2022, p. 35.
[129] European Commission, Staff Working Document, Sustainable Products in a Circular Economy – Towards an EU Product Policy Framework Contributing to the Circular Economy, SWD(2019) 92 final, p. 3.

such as 'product as service' as well as 'end of life responsibility' are not developed further by the policymakers. With regard to the product as service, and 'shared economy', the ongoing spread of this (socially and environmentally promising) practice should be shaped via public regulation, as it at the same time raises serious questions of concentration of ownership and widespread dependency on the one hand[130] and regional distribution on the other.[131] With regard to the end-of-life responsibility, this potentially powerful circular economy technique is so far sparsely used – with one exception, namely the Battery Regulation, which includes a series of circular economy requirements such as durability, recycled content, and the collection of used batteries, as well as mandatory due diligence for the many rare materials (cobalt, nickel, lithium, etc.) used in batteries. The regulation will go into effect in 2025.[132]

Second, the ecodesign framework also does not engage seriously with the distributive effects of technologies vis-à-vis labour, hoping rather than ensuring that innovation is labour enhancing and produces more quality jobs rather than fewer and/or bad ones. The framework also leaves the impact on the third countries largely unaddressed: the reference to the CSDDD proposal as a means to deal with 'social aspects' seems to be a way to avoid rather than tackle this question.

Third, despite the recognition of the importance of social economy for advancing the circularity agenda, social economy aspects remain unmapped even if they (typified by social purpose, limited profit distributions, and participatory governance of organisations[133]) may be a crucial vehicle for making sure that the promises of technology and innovation are more equitably shared. Ultimately, how the benefits of technological innovation will be distributed will to a large degree depend on who owns technologies and to what purpose. A conversation that only has to start.

---

[130] Feja Lesniewska and Katrien Steenmans, *Circular Economy and the Law: Bringing Justice into the Frame* (Taylor & Francis, 2023).
[131] Shared cars as needed in peripheral towns as in Amsterdam, for instance.
[132] Battery Regulation 2023, Recital 30.
[133] See here: https://social-economy-gateway.ec.europa.eu/about-social-economy_en.

5 Reinventing Industrial Policy

5.1 Introduction

When French President Macron spoke in Amsterdam in April 2023, he put industrial policy at the centre of the European future,[1] affirming its belonging to the core of the European Union's (EU) imaginaries of prosperity. After years of privatisation of (political) responsibility and faltering action, it turns out that Europe needs an actual industrial policy. For at least three reasons. To start, EU policymakers have been increasingly confronted with the fact that one cannot rely entirely on manufacturing partners, and thus a greater stress on 'strategic autonomy' is needed.[2] Also, the growing de-industrialisation means not only losing *capacity* but also losing *knowledge* in how to make things we need: this makes the EU vulnerable to all types of geopolitical shocks.[3] Finally, with the war in Ukraine and the pending energy crisis, we need to develop clean technology urgently, giving an implicit permission for governments to 'pick winners' in order to steer development in the desired direction. *'This decade will be decisive for the world to limit the rise in global temperatures and to take the necessary steps towards net-zero. The stakes are high and the challenges complex – but there is a once in a generation*

---

[1] Mike Corder and Sylvie Corbet, *Domestic Unrest Interrupts Macron's European Future Speech* (The Associated Press, 2023), https://apnews.com/article/france-netherlands-macron-rutte-europe-c338d160f99a47830f6d90ce2c21600d, last accessed 8 January 2024.
[2] European Commission, Europe's Moment: Repair and Prepare for the Next Generation, COM(2020) 456 final, p. 13; European Commission, A New Industrial Strategy for Europe, COM(2020) 102 final, p. 13.
[3] Regulation (EU) 2023/1781 of the European Parliament and of the Council of 13 September 2023 establishing a framework of measures for strengthening Europe's semiconductor ecosystem and amending Regulation (EU) 2021/694 (Chips Act), Recital 21.

opportunity to use this imperative to act as a catalyst to invest in the clean energy economy and industry of the net-zero age'.[4]

Industry, or public support for it, is not a novel matter. Public support for industry has been provided in many different ways over the past centuries. In Europe, when industrial manufacturing proliferated in the nineteenth century, the "public support" for the new manufacturing was twofold: on the one hand, states have (if in different ways) ensured migration of people from villages to towns and cities, in order to provide a workforce.[5] On the other hand, the lack of any real environmental standards or labour protections provided a sort of public subsidy to manufacturing.[6] The economic growth, as the economic inequality, that ensued in countries such as the UK, Belgium, and later also in Germany and France, was considerable.[7]

This 'laissez-faire industrial policy' has been replaced in Europe after WW2, with a set of active measures that were intended to support particular sectors, industries, and technologies. This 'vertical industrial policy' involved everything from state-owned enterprises, especially in the case of natural monopolies, to public procurement and subsidies to particular industries, such as steel or cement. In the 1950s and 1960s, public support in European Communities went mainly to heavy industry, while in the 1970s, it expanded to electronics, aircraft, and biotechnology.[8]

From the 1980s onwards, with the rise of neoliberal thought, the recipes of this welfare state industrial policy were said not to work any longer.[9] The EU member states (MSs) thus increasingly moved to the so-called horizontal measures,[10] such as generalised tax incentives for Research & Development or the purchase of machinery and/or specific products (cars),[11] as a means to foster a "good investment climate" rather than any specific sectors. The EU itself pushed for the liberalisation of public

---

[4] European Commission, A Green Deal Industrial Plan for the Net-Zero Age, COM(2023) 62 final, p. 1.
[5] Karl Polanyi, *The Great Transformation: The Political and Economic Origins of Our Time* (Beacon Press, 1944).
[6] Ibid.
[7] Carl Benedikt Frey, *The Technology Trap: Capital, Labor, and Power in the Age of Automation* (Princeton University Press, 2019).
[8] Mario Pianta, 'An Industrial Policy for Europe', *Seoul Journal of Economics* 27, no. 23 (2014): 277–305, p. 278.
[9] Ibid., p. 280.
[10] Laissez-faire 'all goes' approach can be arguably also seen as a 'horizontal' industrial policy.
[11] Pianta, 'An Industrial Policy for Europe'.

services on the one hand and constrained state aid on the other, making alternative pathways for its MSs less readily available.[12]

Shortly after the onset of the 2008 crisis, the EU launched its first present-day attempts to develop EU industrial policy. Yet, as we will see in later sections, at the start these efforts were still strongly conditioned by neoliberal conceptions of development and prosperity. This will change partially with the European Green Deal (EGD), which has entertained large aspirations on both economic and environmental fronts. The realisation of these objectives remains, however, constrained by the EU's own limited competences and limited resources, while giving the unconstrained green light to MSs' own industrial policy investment threatens to put the internal market and regional development in danger, as there is a vast difference among the MSs as to how much state aid they can provide.[13]

What is more, in the most recent instalments of the series 'NET ZERO' industrial policy, the EU has relapsed back into a "publicly-financed market approach".[14] Driven by concerns of lagging behind the competitors (US and China), in its newly found narrative of competitiveness, the EU seems to ready itself to condone large subsidies and tax breaks to clean tech industry production, even at the expense of internal market concerns[15] and without any conditionality worth its name concerning companies' social and environmental standards, or increased public voice and sharing in the benefits (rather than only costs) of technological advance.

The whole question of industrial policy is also a contested one: what kind of 'green technology' and 'clean economy' Europeans want and can realistically get? There has been little democratic discussion about this question: do we really need all those electric SUVs, given their environmental impact and the level of extraction needed to produce them? Can "money" (e.g. taxing CO_2 emissions) mediate all distributive choices – or is more needed? Is the financing of carbon storage, the core climate fantasy of big oil, indeed the best way to invest public money? Shall we perhaps invest instead in technologies that can deliver excellent and affordable public transport? Not only are these conversations not being

---

[12] Ibid.   [13] Repair and Prepare for the Next Generation 2020, p. 3.
[14] Gabor calls this 'de-risking'; see Gabor, 'The (European) Derisking State'.
[15] John Springford and Sander Tordoir, *Europe Can Withstand American and Chinese Subsidies for Green Tech* (European Centre for Policy Research, 2023).

had in Brussels or nationally, but also the new set of EU austerity measures may directly undermine the possibility of public solutions even being realistically contemplated.[16]

In this chapter then, I aim to explore the changing imaginaries of prosperity in the EU's industrial law and policy. I focus on the present-day industrial policies of the European Commission starting with the 2010 Industrial Policy[17] and including a more recent avalanche of legislative proposals and measures (Chips Act,[18] Batteries Act,[19] Critical Minerals Act,[20] and Net Zero Industry Act[21]), the changes in the General Exception,[22] and the Temporary Crisis and Transition Framework.[23] I will mainly be interested in how the EU has been repositioning itself in response to changing economic and political circumstances, on the background of the changing geopolitical situation and shifting scientific knowledge. Importantly, rather than focusing on particular technologies or sectors, I will discuss the leading themes in industrial policy such as industrial strategy, competitiveness, financing, or taxation, as they express the changing imaginaries of economy, law, politics, government, and ultimately also of our relation to nature.

---

[16] Público, 'Brussels asks Spain for a Tax Adjustment and Urges It to Withdraw Energy Aid' (2023), www.publico.es/economia/bruselas-pide-espana-ajuste-fiscal-y-le-insta-retirar-ayudas-energeticas.html#md=modulo-portada-bloque:4col-t5;mm=mobile-verybig, last accessed 8 January 2024.

[17] European Commission, an Integrated Industrial Policy for the Globalisation Era Putting Competitiveness and Sustainability at Centre Stage, COM(2010) 614 final.

[18] Chips Act 2023.

[19] Regulation (EU) 2023/1542 of the European Parliament and of the Council of 12 July 2023 concerning batteries and waste batteries, amending Directive 2008/98/EC and Regulation (EU) 2019/1020 and repealing Directive 2006/66/EC.

[20] European Commission, Proposal for a Regulation of the European Parliament and of the Council establishing a framework for ensuring a secure and sustainable supply of critical raw materials and amending Regulations (EU) 168/2013, (EU) 2018/858, 2018/1724, and (EU) 2019/102, COM(2023) 160.

[21] European Commission, Proposal for a Regulation of the European Parliament and of the Council on establishing a framework of measures for strengthening Europe's net-zero technology product manufacturing ecosystem (Net Zero Industry Act), COM(2023) 161.

[22] Regulation (EU) 2023/1315 of 23 June 2023 amending Regulation (EU) No 651/2014 declaring certain categories of aid compatible with the internal market in application of Articles 107 and 108 of the Treaty and Regulation (EU) 2022/2473 declaring certain categories of aid to undertakings active in the production, processing and marketing of fishery and aquaculture products compatible with the internal market in application of Articles 107 and 108 of the Treaty, C/2023/4278.

[23] European Commission, Amendment to the Temporary Crisis and Transition Framework for State Aid measures to support the economy following the aggression against Ukraine by Russia, COM(2023) 1188.

5.2 Greening Growth

5.2.1 EU Industrial Strategy

We start our story in 2010, when the European Commission, after a longer pause, again produced a communication on 'industrial policy'. In this period, the EU is plagued not only by the ongoing economic crisis, asymmetric recovery, low growth, low demand, and low productivity but also by widespread deindustrialisation due to the outsourcing of manufacturing to third countries.[24] The disregard for industrial policy was both the outcome of the neoliberal concern with the *'government failure if it becomes too involved in industrial policy by "picking winners"'*[25] and the assumption that as an advanced economy, the EU is far more about providing (financial and technological) services than manufacturing goods.[26] In the 2010 communication, thus the Commission reasserted the importance of manufacturing for the health of the economy in general: *'An ambitious strategy framework for a new industrial competitiveness policy must put the competitiveness and sustainability of European industry at centre stage'*.[27]

While the 2010 industrial policy reasserts the importance of manufacturing and industrial production, it resembles the welfare state vertical industrial policy only by its name.[28] The 2010 policy remains firmly committed to horizontal policies, stressing the centrality of general infrastructural conditions, or "business environment", for industrial development, including liberalisation of public services, as it is the *'Competition, the efficiency of public and private services, and infrastructure* [that] *are important determinants of industrial competitiveness in Member States. In many Member States, increasing competition in the network industries remains a challenge'*.[29] What it seems to want to add to what is already in place is, first, its concern with greater alignment between various policies (e.g. competition and trade) relevant for industrial development and, second, the preoccupation with innovation, that is turning

---

[24] Pianta, 'An Industrial Policy for Europe', p. 280.
[25] Mariana Mazzucato, Rainer Kattel, and Josh Ryan-Collins, 'Challenge-Driven Innovation Policy: Towards a New Policy Toolkit', *Journal of Industry, Competition and Trade* 20, no. 2 (2020): 421–37, p. 424.
[26] New Industrial Strategy for Europe 2020, p. 3.
[27] European Commission, An Integrated Industrial Policy for the Globalisation Era Putting Competitiveness and Sustainability at Centre Stage, COM(2010) 614 final, p. 4.
[28] Pianta, 'An Industrial Policy for Europe', p. 288.   [29] Industrial Policy 2010, p. 10.

(academic) knowledge into marketable products as *'Europe is not good enough at turning its excellence in ideas into marketable goods and services'*.[30]

The following 2014 Industrial Renaissance policy[31] makes a very careful shift towards steering in the direction of technological and industrial development, mostly via the 'regional turn'. Thus the idea behind the 'Smart specialisations' programme has been that the regions themselves would bring together industry, knowledge institutions, public institutions, investors, and more to develop particular regional industrial 'specialisations', co-financed by the European Structural and Investment Funds.[32] These specialisations should have in principle contributed to six rather broad strategic areas (advanced manufacturing, key enabling technologies, clean vehicles and transport, bio-based products, construction and raw materials, and smart grids) identified already in the 2012 industrial policy.[33]

While Smart Specialisation were intended to further both industrialisation and regional economic convergence, Wigger argues that they have enjoyed a limited success.[34] Not only did they not lead to a new wave of industrialisation, but they have also possibly only increased divergence between the regions. While the advanced regions were developing plans for advanced technologies and getting large co-financing from the EU, the regions lagging behind, with worse infrastructure, less knowledge institutions, and less capital, could only stick with their traditional (non-advanced) production sectors, usually focused on food or tourism.[35]

Even if the importance of green and circular approaches has already been declared in the 2010 policy, and remarkably *less* stressed in the 2014 policy,[36] it is only with the Green European Deal that *green* as well as *social* – that is the transition must be inclusive and just – became a

---

[30] Industrial Policy 2010, p. 12.
[31] European Commission, for a European Industrial Renaissance, COM(2014) 14 final.
[32] Pianta, 'An Industrial Policy for Europe', p. 289.
[33] European Commission, a Stronger European Industry for Growth and Economic Recovery, Industrial Policy Communication Update, COM(2012) 582 final.
[34] Angela Wigger, 'The New EU Industrial Policy and Deepening Structural Asymmetries: Smart Specialisation Not So Smart', *JCMS: Journal of Common Market Studies* 61, no. 1 (2023): 20–37.
[35] Ibid., p. 28.
[36] The reasons are discussed below, as the 2014 policy seems to have been possibly quite narrowly following the ERT (Business association), ERT, 'EU industrial renaissance, ERT agenda for action 2014–2019' (2014).

somewhat more central orientation for industrial policy.[37] The 2020 industrial policy starts by saying that the EU '*cannot afford to simply adapt – it must now become the accelerator and enabler of change and innovation. Our industrial policy must help make this ambition a reality*'.[38] It thus embraces quite outspokenly the circular economy model, on economic, environmental, and importantly moral grounds: '*To do this, we must move away from the age-old model of taking from the ground to make products, which we then use and throw away. We need to revolutionise the way we design, make, use and get rid of things by incentivising our industry. This more circular approach will ensure a cleaner and more competitive industry by reducing environmental impacts, alleviating competition for scarce resources and reducing production costs.* **The business case is as strong as the environmental and moral imperative**. *Applying circular economy principles in all sectors and industries has potential to create 700,000 new jobs across the EU by 2030, many of which in SMEs*'.[39]

The Next Generation EU (NGEU), while not strictly an industrial policy but a recovery plan to deal with the Covid crisis, however, adds (some) money where the EU's mouth is. The recovery funds (with the anticipated height of some 750 billion from the EU in loans and grants) should be directed towards the 'twin transition – digital and green', on the basis of projects developed by MSs. At the same time, unlike the previous 2008 crisis, the NGEU tries to make solidarity – between states, regions, groups, and citizens – the guiding principle: '*In our Union, a euro invested in one country is a euro invested for all. A collective and cohesive recovery that accelerates the twin green and digital transitions will only strengthen Europe's competitiveness, resilience and position as a global player. This is why solidarity, cohesion and convergence must drive Europe's recovery. No person, no region, no Member State should be left behind*'.[40] In 2021, the Commission published an update on the 2020 industrial policy to account for the additional priorities due to the Covid crisis.[41]

Perhaps the 'busiest' year in the field of industrial policy was 2023: the year of writing this chapter. Several important documents were put forth. First, the Commission publishes in March 2023 the Net Zero Plan,[42] provoked by the concerns about the US Inflation Reduction Act

---

[37] European Commission, The European Green Deal, COM(2019) 640 final.
[38] Industrial Strategy 2020, p. 1.
[39] Industrial Strategy 2020, p. 9. All emphases in the quotes, in this and the following chapter, were added by the author of this book.
[40] Repair and Prepare for the Next Generation 2020, p. 1.
[41] European Commission, Updating the 2020 New Industrial Strategy: Building a Stronger Single Market for Europe's Recovery, COM(2021) 350 final.
[42] Net Zero Plan 2023.

and characterised by a somewhat more bellicose stance due to the growing concern about China and the ongoing Russian aggression in Ukraine. The Plan has been accompanied by the Proposal for a Net Zero Industrial Act[43] and the Proposal for Critical Raw Materials Act (preceded by the Critical Raw Material Strategy[44]). Later in the same year, two other legislative measures are approved: in September 2023, the Chips Act,[45] and in July 2023, the Battery Regulation[46] (which is also an Ecodesign instrument).

In what follows, I will set out the most important elements of the 'Green Deal Industrial Plan for Net Zero Age' (hereafter 'Net Zero Plan'), with references to legislative measures on its basis, in order to decipher the last turn in the EU's thinking about industrial policy. The first prong of Net Zero Plan concerns the 'predictable and simplified regulatory framework'. The implementation is to take place via key aspects of the Net Zero Industry Act, which provides a framework to foster clean technologies such as batteries, windmills, pumps, and solar panels. The Net Zero Industry Act divides technologies in line with their "readiness" to contribute to net zero targets in 2030 and beyond[47] and aims to give those more ready the greatest amount of advantages in the permission process.[48] The Act introduces a 'one-stop-shop' for the facilitation of the permissions processes,[49] 'regulatory sandboxes' for more disruptive innovation and testing of clean tech,[50] and it aims to foster public and private demand, by designating criteria for public procurement, concessions, incentives, etc.[51]

To be able to produce clean technology, the Net Zero Plan relies on the Critical Minerals Action Plan,[52] implemented finally via the Proposal for the Critical Raw Materials Act.[53] The most important element of the Act

---

[43] Net Zero Industry Act Proposal 2023.
[44] European Commission, Proposal for a Regulation of the European Parliament and of the Council establishing a framework for ensuring a secure and sustainable supply of critical raw materials and amending Regulations (EU) 168/2013, (EU) 2018/858, 2018/1724, and (EU) 2019/102, COM(2023) 160.
[45] Chips Act 2023.   [46] Battery Regulation 2023.
[47] Net Zero Industry Act Proposal 2023, p. 15.
[48] Net Zero Industry Act Proposal 2023, p. 23.
[49] Net Zero Industry Act Proposal 2023, art. 4.
[50] Net Zero Industry Act Proposal 2023, art. 26.
[51] Net Zero Industry Act Proposal 2023, p. 6.
[52] European Commission, Critical Raw Materials Resilience: Charting a Path towards Greater Security and Sustainability, COM(2020) 474.
[53] Critical Raw Materials Act Proposal 2023.

includes the support for 'strategic projects', in both extraction and recycling, that can take place both within and outside the EU.[54] The Act also provides for 'one-stop-shops' to speed up and simplify administrative procedures for such projects, creates a framework for 'strategic partnerships' with third countries and facilitates 'joint purchasing' of raw materials.[55] The partnerships should go first and foremost to countries that ensure better respect for social, human rights, and environmental standards, and enable a meaningful engagement with local communities.[56]

A second prong of the Net Zero Plan concerns access to finance. As the new wave of industrial policy is a response to the US's Inflation Reduction Act, the EU wants to level the playing field for European firms. The most important financing instruments mentioned in the Plan are the NGEU, which have already made 250 billion available for clean tech. Further, Horizon Europe dedicates 40 billion to clean technologies and cohesion policies have made available another 100 billion, including the Just Transition Fund. Importantly, the Commission laments that to date most of *'these EU funding sources have largely benefitted research and innovation and deployment of renewable energy and related infrastructures, rather than targeting manufacturing capacity in the sector'*.[57] The EU funding should, instead, increasingly find its way to manufacturing – an aspect that many less developed regions in Europe will likely welcome, should they ever become the space where clean tech is produced.

When it comes to MSs funding, the EU extends and expands the use of state aid in order to allow MSs to grant aid towards Net Zero projects, within the framework of the Temporary Crisis and Transition Framework[58] and the revision of the General State Aid exception.[59] The aid may be set out as a percentage of overall investment costs for clean tech (hydrogen, energy efficiency, or electrification projects) and 'enhanced support schemes' for strategic net zero technologies (including controversial technologies such as carbon capture and storage and electric vehicles) that should match the aid received by competitors abroad or the aid offered by a third country. The aid can also be provided as tax benefits.

---

[54] Critical Raw Materials Act Proposal 2023, chapter 3, s. 1.
[55] Critical Raw Materials Act Proposal 2023, chapter 6, art. 33. The first one was concluded with Morocco.
[56] Critical Raw Materials Act Proposal 2023, chapter 5.   [57] Net Zero Plan 2023, p. 8.
[58] Temporary Crisis and Transition Framework 2023, section 2.8.
[59] General Block Exemption Regulation Amendment 2023, Article 36(b).

Both instruments try to thread a difficult path of both mustering public financing for clean tech projects on the one hand and the danger that increased aid, which only some MSs are able to give, will lead to further divergence between the MSs. This also means that funding cannot come only from the MSs – not least because that would potentially cause a rise of disparities across the internal market. In order to limit this threat, the EU intends to expand the REPowerEU funding and issue guidance on how to best use the Recovery and Resilience plan in the context of the NGEU to further clean tech. This should also include funding to create one-stop-shops for permits, tax breaks, and skills training. The EU hopes to support investment through several additional schemes and institutions, including InvestEU, the European Investment Bank, the EBRD, and the Innovation Fund as well as 'Important Projects of Common European Interest' (IPCEI) with many billions.[60] Perhaps most importantly, in the midterm, the EU proposes a 'European Sovereignty Fund' that should increase its financing capacity, based on EU borrowing and own funds via taxation. While the European Parliament, in reaction to the Net Zero Plan, has called on the Commission to be more ambitious in expanding its taxation capacity (including financial transactions tax and VAT changes as well as the income from ETS and carbon border mechanism),[61] there seems to not be enough support from the side of MSs for this new financing instrument. Thus, for the 2024 budget, the Commission has proposed the 'precursor' to the Sovereignty Fund, the 'Strategic Technologies for Europe Platform', that should better coordinate the existing funding, and with an additional 10 billion euro, Von der Leyen hopes to reach some 160 billion euro in private investment in the upcoming years.[62]

The third prong of the Plan relates to enhancing skills. The Net Zero Industry Act proposes 'Net Zero Academies'[63] that would make sure that enough of a workforce will be educated with necessary skills.

---

[60] Importantly, two out of five projects today are the controversial hydrogen projects, which are more often than not seen as wasteful projects driven by big oil and aiming to skim more public funding – to boost their already vast fossil energy profits in the wake of war in Ukraine.

[61] European Parliament, Report on own resources: a new start for EU finances, a new start for Europe (2022/2172(INI)).

[62] European Commission, 'EU budget: Commission Proposes Strategic Technologies for Europe Platform (STEP) to Support European leadership on Critical Technologies', https://ec.europa.eu/commission/presscorner/detail/en/ip_23_3364, last accessed 9 January 2024.

[63] Net Zero Industry Act Proposal 2023, Art. 23.

While the Commission is hereby committed to provide incentives for creating such academies, it is unclear who is going to carry the brunt of the work and pay the costs. Industries themselves, including the industries that enjoy public support, are not mentioned in this section in one way or another; it seems that this is likely to be left to public educational institutions. This is quite unlike the US Inflation Reduction Act, which relies on financial incentives and conditionalities for the recipients of public funding in order to provide apprenticeships in the industry.[64]

The fourth element of the Net Zero Plan concerns resilient supply chains. While the Plan remains vague, two important Regulations have been proposed in 2023. The Chips Act takes a more institutional approach to fostering this important sector, which has proven very sensitive to supply chain risks. The Act provides for the creation of specific testing and manufacturing facilities (integrated manufacturing facilities and founding facilities) as well as forms of institutional cooperation (Chips Joint Undertaking, and national Competence Centres). The Act also creates a specific legal form – the European Chips Infrastructure Consortium – that should have easier access to public funding. All types of cooperation need to bring together at least three MSs or their actors to engage in manufacturing and project coordination to receive all kinds of benefits as a special public interest entities. Further, the Act also puts forth Common Purchasing framework for periods of crisis and introduces some degree of conditionality for industries that have received public funds, namely to produce and supply certain output as a matter of priority, trumping both their private and public law obligations.[65] The other important instrument is the Batteries Regulation, which introduces a whole set of due diligence obligations with regard to battery supply chains, including some relating to diversification and resilience.[66]

More generally, when it comes to "making trade work for clean transition",[67] the EU continues to rely on trade openness, supporting the WTO, and concluding more FTAs. In the Net Zero Plan, the Commission does not engage with the structure of those trade agreements, which have thus far fallen short of sustainability objectives,

---

[64] Inflation Reduction Act of 2022, Pub. L. No. 117–169, 136 Stat. 1818.
[65] Chips Act 2023, art. 26. [66] Battery Regulation 2023, art. 48.
[67] Net Zero Plan 2023, p. 17.

relegating sustainability to special chapters – and leaving the rest for business as usual.

The EU also singles out in this document its special relation to Africa, *'The EU has developed Sustainable Investment Facilitation Agreements (SIFA) in particular with partners in Africa, in order to make it easier to attract and expand investments while integrating environment and labour right commitments. Climate and energy is a key area for partnerships under Global Gateway, the EU's contribution to narrowing the global investment gap worldwide. Moreover, the EU will support developing countries in their efforts to adapt and comply with the EU's autonomous sustainability requirements'.*[68] As I discuss in the last section, how far these objectives are truly oriented towards benefiting Africa remains questionable. The EU still seems to prioritise its own commercial interests, as the Action Plan on Critical Raw Materials makes clear, that is to *'ensure undistorted trade and investment in raw materials in a manner that supports the EU's commercial interests'*.[69]

5.2.2 Making Europe 'Competitive' via Green Growth

Competitiveness is perhaps one of the most notable elements in the economic imaginary of neoliberal capitalism.[70] One is not to be surprised thus that this is also one of the most frequently used words in the EU industrial policy. So, what makes an industry (or even more complex, a country) competitive? There are many grounds on which one can compete, especially in the context of industrial policy: on advanced technologies, high skills base, good infrastructure, and good institutions as well as cheap energy and raw materials, cheap labour, cheap credit, fertile land, etc. Or, most likely, some combination of the above.

The extractive and distributive stakes between various pathways to "competitiveness" clearly differ. Competing via technologies seems to be the most desirable mode of advancing one's competitiveness, having benefited the Western economies over the past centuries. Technologies can be however labour *enabling*, making it easier for workers to do their jobs, or labour *replacing*, thus not only privileging capital but also, as Dani Rodrik argues, making economic growth a must – if people are not to get poorer.[71]

---

[68] Net Zero Plan 2023, p. 18.   [69] Critical Raw Materials Plan 2020, p. 15.
[70] Paul Krugman, 'Competitiveness: A Dangerous Obsession', *Foreign Affairs* 73, no. 2 (1994): 28–44.
[71] Karl Aiginger and Dani Rodrik, 'Rebirth of Industrial Policy and an Agenda for the Twenty-First Century', *Journal of Industry, Competition and Trade* 20 (2020):189–207, p. 201.

In contrast, when it comes to the "developing countries" over the past decades, cheap labour and low labour and environmental standards was the main road to competitiveness. More generally, Global South countries are the source of what Moore calls cheap natures – be it labour or other "natural resources" – which have often been extracted from these countries and peoples, with most benefit accruing to multinational corporations and local elites and most of the cost left for the local populations.[72] Today, many also fear a new 'green extractivism', especially in the North African context, as new sustainable sources of energy threaten to 'eat up' much of indigenous land, water, and other resources, in order to deliver on European energy needs.[73]

In the EU, post-2008 crisis, deregulation and the flexibilisation of labour remained one of the favourite receipts to improve competitiveness, as internal deregulation often seemed the only possible solution in the monetary union without fiscal solidarity.[74] The EU's industrial policy, in both 2010 and later in 2014, amplified that trend. Namely, these policies still focus on neoliberal favourite 'horizontal measures', that is in principle improving overall economic, social, and infrastructural preconditions for economic *competitiveness*. These however, Wigger argues, had the objective of the improvement of labour productivity in a very specific sense of *'unit labour costs, a ratio between productivity and total labour compensation indicating whether labour costs rise in line with productivity gains'*.[75]

The 2010 Communication on industrial policy suggests that *'It is essential to increase productivity in manufacturing industry and associated services to underpin the recovery of growth and jobs, restore health and sustainability to the EU economy and help sustain our social model'*.[76] To do so, the Commission advises governments to modernise and increase the flexibility of workforces, as *'workers need support to manage these processes*

---

[72] Jason W. Moore, *Capitalism in the Web of Life: Ecology and the Accumulation of Capital* (Verso Books, 2015).
[73] Natacha Bruna, 'A Climate-Smart World and the Rise of Green Extractivism', *The Journal of Peasant Studies* 49, no. 4 (7 June 2022): 839–64.
[74] M. Keune and M. Jepsen, *Not Balanced and Hardly New: The European Commission's Quest for Flexicurity* (ETUI-REHS, 2007).
[75] Angela Wigger, 'The New EU Industrial Policy: Authoritarian Neoliberal Structural Adjustment and the Case for Alternatives', *Globalizations* 16, no. 3 (2019): 353–69, p. 356; see also European Commission, Industrial Policy: Reinforcing competitiveness, COM (2011) 642 final: compared with its major competitors, the EU relative unit labour costs improved by 12 per cent since 2008, mainly due to the exchange rate effect.
[76] Industrial Policy 2010, p. 3.

successfully through flexicurity in lifelong learning' and *'support reallocation of labour, within the framework of a flexicurity system'.*[77]

By 2014, the Commission lamented that competitiveness had not been improved. If anything, EU competitiveness has decreased: *'Europe has traditionally ranked well as a place for business and industrial production, but is now losing competitiveness as compared to other regions in the world'.*[78] The lack of competitiveness is attributed by the Commission to two things: *'Administrative burdens and regulatory complexity are being eliminated too slowly and unevenly and some labour markets are not flexible enough'.*[79] In order to ensure fewer regulatory burdens, as well as to make labour more flexible (and thus less costly), the Commission undertook monitoring the *'competitiveness performance and business environment on a regular basis, notably through the European Semester process and the Member States' Competitiveness Report under Article 173 of the TFEU'.*[80]

To illustrate the concern with decreasing competitiveness in the 2014 Industrial Renaissance policy, the Commission references the fact that there were fewer EU countries in the top twenty of the World Bank's Doing Business Index in 2014 than in 2008. This index, recently discontinued because of shady methodology as well as the WB selling their consultancy services to countries willing to improve their index,[81] has been foremost criticised because of its inbuilt preference for labour market deregulation, based on the conviction that the *'laws created to help workers often hurt them'.*[82]

Corporate Europe Observatory (CEO) reports that the reason for this particular shape of the 2014 European 'Industrial Renaissance policy', and its concern with labour deregulation, may be related to the influence that the European Roundtable of Industrialists and BusinessEurope have exercised on the Commission's industrial imaginaries.[83] CEO refers, there, to the Barosso's speech at the annual conference of BusinessEurope's: *'For that, your recommendations that I will certainly read,*

---

[77] Industrial Policy 2010, pp. 15 and 21.   [78] Industrial Renaissance Plan 2014, p. 7.
[79] Industrial Renaissance Plan 2014, p. 7.   [80] Industrial Renaissance Plan 2014, p. 7.
[81] Independent Evaluation Group, *Doing Business, an Independent Evaluation: Taking the Measure of the World Bank-IFC Doing Business Indicators* (World Bank, 2008), p. 8.
[82] This will start slowly shifting in 2016; see Simon Deakin, 'The Contribution of Labour Law to Economic Development and Growth', WP 478 (2016).
[83] Corporate Europe Observatory, 'The "Permanent Liaison": How ERT and BusinessEurope Set the Agenda for the EU Summit' (2014), https://corporateeurope.org/en/lobbycracy/2014/03/permanent-liaison-how-ert-and-businesseurope-set-agenda-eu-summit, last accessed 9 January 2024.

but that I have heard, are very much in line with our preoccupations, are certainly in the right direction. Now the real key issue is implementation. (...) What we need now (...) is to focus on delivery, on implementation, so that we can have a stronger industry for a stronger Europe'.[84]

The understanding of competitiveness as concerned with labour productivity in the specific sense of labour flexibility/cheapness will remain mostly intact until the late 2010s, enforced via European Semester.[85] The winds start to change after great political shifts and turmoil, including Brexit, Trump, Modi, Bolsonaro, and the general rise of the so-called populist politics. This turmoil seems to demand some more engagement with the underlying causes of discontent. Rampaging inequality, and gradually also environmental degradation, will slowly arrive on the political agenda,[86] with even the World Bank making a turn on its advice to undo labour protections in 2016.[87] The 'return of the big state', to evoke the Economist, will become a reality from the next big economic shock – the Covid crisis.[88]

The EU is also due to respond to the challenges of this period – and it responds with the EGD, a new "growth strategy" that purports to take both the environmental and social crisis seriously. The EGD, with the ambition to deliver a carbon-neutral Europe by 2050, was a promise of the current European Commission President von der Leyen for support (foremost of the Greens) in the European Parliament.[89] As an important signal of the seriousness of her commitment, von der Leyen has also appointed her losing social-democratic opponent, Frans Timmermans, as the vice president of the Commission for climate.

---

[84] European Commission, 'Speech by President Barroso at BusinessEurope Day: Industry Matters' (2014), p. 6, https://corporateeurope.org/sites/default/files/speech-14-64_en_barroso_businesseurope_day.pdf, last accessed 9 January 2023.

[85] Paul Copeland and Mary Daly, 'The European Semester and EU Social Policy', *JCMS: Journal of Common Market Studies* 56, no. 5 (2018): 1001–18; Mark Dawson, 'New Governance and the Displacement of Social Europe: The Case of the European Semester', *European Constitutional Law Review* 14, no. 1 (2018): 191–209; . For a more positive reading, see Jonathan Zeitlin and Bart Vanhercke, 'Socializing the European Semester: EU Social and Economic Policy Co-ordination in Crisis and Beyond', *Journal of European Public Policy* 25, no. 2 (2018): 149–74.

[86] Not least within the European Green Deal 2019.

[87] Deakin, 'The Contribution of Labour Law to Economic Development and Growth'.

[88] The Economist, 'The virus means the big state is back' (2020), www.economist.com/britain/2020/03/21/the-virus-means-the-big-state-is-back, last accessed 9 January 2024.

[89] France 24, 'European Commission Hopeful Von der Leyen Faces Sceptical Parliament' (2019), www.france24.com/en/20190716-europe-european-commission-president-hopeful-ursula-von-der-leyen-struggles-win-support, last accessed 9 January 2024.

The EGD presents a first attempt to shift the EU away from the prevailing neoliberal imaginaries of economy in the EU, with "labour cheapness" at its core. The EGD aims to present a *'new growth strategy that aims to transform the EU into a fair and prosperous society, with a modern, resource-efficient and competitive economy where there are no net emissions of greenhouse gases in 2050 and where economic growth is decoupled from resource use'*.[90]

The EGD marks a shift from the obsession with competitiveness, the word mentioned only three times in the EGD – in comparison with fifty-six times in the 2014 Industrial Renaissance policy and eighty-two times in the 2010 policy. Furthermore, if the 2014 Industrial Renaissance doubled down on using the European Semester to enforce competitiveness through cutting labour costs,[91] the language of the EGD aims instead *'to refocus the European Semester process of macroeconomic coordination to integrate the United Nations' sustainable development goals, to put sustainability and the well-being of citizens at the centre of economic policy, and the sustainable development goals at the heart of the EU's policymaking and action'*.[92]

When it comes to the industrial policy more specifically, the EGD envisages as its future competitive advantage *'the development of lead markets for climate neutral and circular products, in the EU and beyond'*.[93] In the 2020 industrial policy, which further articulates the EGD in relation to industry, the EU supplants the language of competitiveness for that of entrepreneurship. Thus *'Our new industrial strategy is* **entrepreneurial** *in spirit and in action'*,[94] And *'In the* **entrepreneurial spirit** *of this strategy, EU institutions, Member States, regions, industry and all other relevant players should work together to create lead markets in clean technologies and ensure our industry is a global frontrunner'*.[95] The focus on entrepreneurship continues: *'In the* **entrepreneurial spirit** *of this industrial strategy, Europe must pool its strengths to do collectively what no one can do alone'*.[96] And *'In the co-design and* **entrepreneurial spirit** *of this strategy, this should be supported through Public Private Partnerships to help industry develop the technologies to meet their goals, as has successfully been done in industrial alliances'*.[97]

---

[90] European Green Deal 2019, p. 2.
[91] Wigger, 'The New EU Industrial Policy'. Zeitlin and Vanhercke instead argue that we have seen the socialisation of implementation of the European Semester between 2011 and 2016; see Jonathan Zeitlin and Bart Vanhercke, 'Socializing the European Semester? Economic Governance and Social Policy Coordination in Europe 2020', Watson Institute for International Studies Research Paper No. 2014–17, 2014.
[92] European Green Deal 2019, p. 3. [93] European Green Deal 2019, p. 7.
[94] Industrial Policy 2020, p. 1. [95] Industrial Policy 2020, p. 3.
[96] Industrial Policy 2020, p. 4. [97] Industrial Policy 2020, p. 10.

Clearly, those who have been reading contributions to the field of industrial policy in recent years may recognise the influence of the London-based economist Mariana Mazzucato on this policy. The language of the 'entrepreneurial state' and the 'public-private partnerships' as well as the recognition of the centrality of the state in steering groundbreaking innovations are signposts of this London-based economist.[98]

But competitiveness is not gone entirely. As a concept, it appears relatively limitedly in the 2020 policy, but to the extent it appears, its meaning changes. It is less concerned with cutting labour costs and presents instead a conception of economy steered towards the *'circular approach* [that] *will ensure a cleaner and more competitive industry by reducing environmental impacts, alleviating competition for scarce resources and reducing production costs'*.[99] Thus, if the costs are to be cut, those are the costs on resources and energy.

The meaning of competitiveness changes again in 2023. In the Net Zero Plan, competitiveness is back in the game – not only does it appear more frequently (it appears eighteen times in the document), but it is understood in yet another typical sense of "international competitiveness" – vis-à-vis other countries that are trying to develop clean technology.[100] *'The EU has also shown how the green transition can strengthen competitiveness. (...) Our net-zero ecosystem was worth over EUR 100 billion in 2021, doubling in value since 2020'*.[101]

What is needed according to the Net Zero Plan is to foster *'three key proposals for industrial competitiveness, rooted in the need for reform'*.[102] First, competitiveness requires the increase of industrial capacity in several sectors (like batteries, hydrogen, and carbon storage[103]). Second, competitiveness requires access to critical raw materials, sourced diversly and retained within the circular economy. Third, competitiveness requires the supply of renewable, and cheap, energy.[104] Importantly,

---

[98] Mariana Mazzucato, *The Entrepreneurial State: Debunking Public vs. Private Sector Myths*; 1st ed. (Anthem Press, 2013); Mazzucato, *Mission Economy: A Moonshot Guide to Changing Capitalism* (Penguin UK, 2021).
[99] Industrial Policy 2020, p. 9.   [100] Net Zero Plan 2023, p. 4.
[101] Net Zero Plan 2023, p. 1.   [102] Net Zero Plan 2023, p. 3.
[103] Some of these technologies are controversial. See Frida Kieninger, '"Clean Hydrogen" Is the Fossil-Fuel Industry in Disguise', EU Observer (2023), https://euobserver.com/opinion/156899, last accessed 9 January 2024; Inga Davis, 'The Greenwashing Scam behind EU's "Grey" Hydrogen', EU Observer (2023), https://euobserver.com/opinion/157518, last accessed 9 January 2024.
[104] Net Zero Industry Act Proposal 2023, p. 6.

the understanding of competitiveness does not (so far) fall back to cutting labour costs. Rather, *'Greater competitiveness must go hand in hand with well-paid quality jobs and investment in human capital'*.[105] Except for 'academies', however, neither the Net Zero Plan nor the Net Zero Industry Act adds much on how public support and investment should more directly contribute to "well paid jobs" or "the investment in human capital".

5.3 Law as Burden

EU industrial policies stress abundantly the importance of law and regulation: *'Legislation must be predictable and proportionate and provide the legal certainty required for longer-term investments'*.[106] In 2010, this proportionality and predictability seems to be put in question especially by environmental regulation: *'since legislation in the past naturally focussed on tackling primary objectives (such as ensuring Single Market regulation, meeting environmental objectives etc.), potential spillovers on industrial competitiveness and in particular the cumulative impact of legislation was not always fully evaluated'*.[107]

In order to ensure that *'Environmental and industrial policies must go hand in hand'*[108] and that *'environmental regulation can act as a beneficial lever for innovation and industrial development, rather than as an impediment'*,[109] the European Commission has committed to taking another step in what today is known as the 'Better Regulation' agenda. Namely, it committed in 2010 to introducing two new disciplines. First, *'"fitness checks" will assess whether the regulatory framework for a policy area is fit for purpose and, if not, what should be improved'*.[110] Second, *'"ex post evaluation" of the effects of legislation on competitiveness. The systematic evaluations of legislation must become an integral part of smart regulation'*.[111]

This focus on better regulation – understood here as predictability, proportionality, and competitiveness-friendliness – is not new in the EU at the time that the 2010 industrial policy was published. The 'better regulation' agenda dates to the beginning of the 2000s: the period that we have identified as "mature neoliberalism" in the chapter on consumption. At this time, a concern with "regulatory simplification" driven by demands of the industry and challenges in the WTO

---

[105] Net Zero Industry Act Proposal 2023, p. 2.   [106] Industrial Policy 2010, p. 20.
[107] Industrial Policy 2010, p. 6.   [108] Industrial Policy 2010, p. 20.
[109] Industrial Policy 2010, p. 20.   [110] Industrial Policy 2010, p. 6.
[111] Industrial Policy 2010, p. 5.

tribunals,[112] combined with some admiration of American regulatory culture,[113] will see the Prodi Commission issue a first Better Regulation package in 2002,[114] on the basis of the White Paper on Governance.[115] The package banked on impact assessments, consultations, transparency, and simplification of the regulatory framework as a way to improve both the quality and democratic standing of EU regulations.

The subsequent Barosso Commissions (2004–2014) have made "cutting red tape" and "promoting competitiveness" the two main regulatory objectives. The deregulatory agenda was to be further reinforced by introducing common methodologies, which place US-like cost-benefit analysis more central in EU policymaking, as well as installing an Impact Assessment Board to assess the quality of impact assessments. The 'ex-post' assessments, which are mentioned in the 2010 industrial policy, are part of that package. This agenda has been both criticised, mainly for its possible negative implications on the precautionary principle[116], and fought by some DGs in the Commission who saw it as undervaluing the importance of regulations, in the interest of competitiveness (ie. business interests).[117]

The 2014 industrial policy tables, *'Top 10 regulatory burdens (as perceived by business organisations and stakeholders) will simplify EU legislation and reduce regulatory burden on businesses. Competitiveness Proofing has been fully integrated into the Commission's impact assessments for all major proposals with significant effects on competitiveness'*.[118] This cutting of regulatory burdens was, also an early concernin relation to the burdens imposed on oil-refining sector, where the fitness check was to be undertaken as one of the first and *'finalised in 2014. In the future, the Commission will gradually undertake comprehensive reviews of the competitiveness and regulatory*

---

[112] Warren H. Maruyama, 'A New Pillar of the WTO: Sound Science', *International Lawyer* 32, no. 3 (1998): 651–77.

[113] Anne C. M. Meuwese, *EU–US Horizontal Regulatory Cooperation: Mutual Recognition of Impact Assessment?*, in *Transatlantic Regulatory Cooperation: The Shifting Roles of the EU, the US and California*, ed. David Vogel and Johan F. M. Swinnen (Edward Elgar Publishing, 2011).

[114] European Commission, Action plan 'Simplifying and improving the regulatory environment' COM(2002) 0278 final.

[115] European Commission, European Governance: Better lawmaking, COM(2002) 275 final.

[116] Marija Bartl, 'Regulatory Convergence through the Back Door: TTIP's Regulatory Cooperation and the Future of Precaution in Europe', *German Law Journal* 18, no. 4 (2017): 969–92.

[117] Ragnar E. Lofstedt, 'The 'Plateau-ing' of the European Better Regulation Agenda: An Analysis of Activities Carried Out by the Barroso Commission 1', *Journal of Risk Research, Taylor & Francis Journals* 10, no. 4 (June 2007): 423–447.

[118] Industrial Renaissance Plan 2014, p. 8.

frameworks in each of the main industrial value chains, using fitness checks and cumulative cost assessments'.[119]

Juncker's Commission will enact another Better Regulation package in 2015.[120] The package continues in the spirit of cutting regulatory burdens, expanding the methodological guidance, including giving more prominence to welfare economics' quantitative cost-benefit analysis, and, perhaps most importantly, turning the advisory Impact Assessment Board into a decision making 'Regulatory Scrutiny Board', which is to issue binding opinions on the quality of impact assessments. Populated mainly by economists and public administration scholars, this Board has been one of the greatest opponents of more transformative proposals,[121] all the while only rubberstamping that which seemed not to step out of the neoliberal mainstream.[122]

This institutional and methodological "strengthening" of the Better Regulation agenda seems to have been one of the ways in which the EU attempted to gratify its trading partners, the US and Canada in particular, with whom the negotiation of the free trade agreements had started around the same time. It was via these new regulatory disciplines that shared language is found for "regulatory convergence" and "regulatory cooperation".[123] As the Industrial Renaissance policy also makes clear, in the modern free trade agreements *'the primary focus will be on "behind-the-borders" obstacles to trade and investment. Raising the level of transparency and regulatory convergence will significantly enhance overseas opportunities for EU companies and help reduce the costs of accessing markets'*.[124] Given that American and Canadian counterparts were ardent challengers of the EU's precautionary principle in the WTO context,[125] exactly on the account that the EU has not been sufficiently rigorous with its methodologies for identifying and removing regulatory burdens, the

---

[119] Industrial Renaissance Plan 2014, p. 8.
[120] European Commission, Better Regulation for Better Results – An EU agenda, COM(2015) 0215 final.
[121] As we have discussed in the previous chapter on ecodesign and will return back to in Chapter 6 on corporation.
[122] Corporate Europe Observatory, 'Corporate Sustainability Due Diligence File, "Better Regulation," and the Regulatory Scrutiny Board' (2022), https://corporateeurope.org/sites/default/files/2022-11/Commission%20complaint%20CSDD%2015.7.2022%20FINAL.pdf, last accessed 9 January 2024.
[123] Bartl, 'Regulatory Convergence through the Back Door'.
[124] Industrial Renaissance Plan 2014, p. 21.
[125] Rupert Read and Tim O'Riordan, 'The Precautionary Principle under Fire', *Environment: Science and Policy for Sustainable Development* 59, no. 5 (2017): 4–15.

precautionary principle had to be somewhat set aside to support trade cooperation in this period.[126]

Another all-time favourite in the repertoire of the "cutting-regulatory-burdens" is the alleged protection of SMEs, as *'Inflexible administrative and regulatory environments, rigidities in some labour markets and weak integration in the internal market'* need to be tackled, since the *'regulatory and administrative costs can impact SMEs up to ten times more than larger companies'*.[127] The "think small first" principle, which the Commission announced in the 2014 Industrial Renaissance, sits uneasily, however, with the fact that the first regulatory fitness checks were done in industries that were hardly populated by SMEs – such as the aforementioned oil-refining industry.

The focus on cutting public regulatory burdens in the EU was complemented with a strong commitment to (private) standardisation. Thus, *'In the regulatory domain, a particularly urgent need is for globally compatible rules and standards for newly emerging tradable goods, services and technologies'*.[128] The EU has an important role to play in *'promoting international standards and regulatory cooperation, building on the EU's role as a de facto standard setter and to take a leading role in reinforcing the international standardisation system'*.[129] While markets need rules, the competitive gains are higher if those are drafted by the industry itself.

After the EGD, the deregulatory narratives somewhat cede. In 2020, the Commission, instead, suggests that the EU needs to lead *'by example complying with the highest social, labour and environmental standards, allowing Europe to project its values'*.[130] Not only values but also the differences between the power of various market actors need to be addressed. *'In the SME Strategy, the Commission emphasised the need to enhance fairness in B2B relations to support SMEs which due to asymmetries in bargaining power with larger organisations face an increased risk of being subject to unfair business practices and conditions both online and offline'*.[131] The mention of the concern with power between private parties is an important nod to the welfare-state imaginary of shared prosperity.

---

[126] Similarly, a "complicated relationship" has also been between trade and the EU's flagship privacy concerns; see Kristina Irion, Svetlana Yakovleva, and Marija Bartl, 'Trade and Privacy: Complicated Bedfellows?', *How to Achieve Data Protection-Proof Free Trade Agreements* (13 July 2016). Available at SSRN: https://ssrn.com/abstract=2877166 or http://dx.doi.org/10.2139/ssrn.2877166.
[127] Industrial Renaissance Plan 2014, p. 17. [128] Industrial Policy 2010, p. 17.
[129] Industrial Policy 2010, p. 21. [130] New Industrial Strategy 2020, p. 2.
[131] New Industrial Strategy 2020, p. 9.

With almost the same breath, however, the Commission suggests that it needs to maintain *'increased attention to regulatory burden under the Commission's revised approach to Better Regulation'*.[132] It is in particular a controversial, and US-inspired, "one in, one out" approach that has become the badge of honor of the Von Der Leyen Commission: *'by introducing a "one in, one out" approach adapted to the policymaking in the EU, it strengthens the attention of policymakers for the implications and costs of applying legislation, especially for SMEs'*.[133] This will come back also in 2023, as the *'additional "competitiveness check" on all new regulation to ensure that all potential competitiveness impacts are addressed and unnecessary burdens avoided'*.[134]

The Net Zero Plan, and the accompanying legislation, arrives with a set of legal tools that aim to foster innovation. First, under the auspices of the Commission, it will work to *'establish regulatory sandboxes to allow for rapid experimentation and disruptive innovation to test new technologies'*.[135] These regulatory carve outs, so far applicable mainly to fintech, are now to be extended to clean tech under the Net Zero Industrial Act for the technology less ready for innovation. Second, the Commission will also work to *'reduce the length and enhance the predictability of permitting processes by defining specific time limits for different stages of permitting, and significantly reinforce Member States' administrative capacity, e.g. by introducing a "one-stop-shop" – a sole point of contact for investors and industrial stakeholders during the entire administrative process'*.[136] We can find one-stop-shops in all relevant legislations, including the Net Zero Industrial Act and the Chips Act as well as for the strategic projects under the Critical Raw Materials Act.[137] Third, under the Chips Act, the Commission even creates a special legal form – the European Chips Infrastructure Consortium – which is an entity, with legal personality, designed in order to foster cross-border development of capacity.[138]

5.4 Resourceful Government

When neoliberalism became the dominant imaginary of political economy, it changed how we think about government in terms of its capacity.

---

[132] New Industrial Strategy 2020, p. 9.   [133] New Industrial Strategy 2020, p. 9.
[134] Net Zero Plan 2023, p. 3.   [135] Net Zero Plan 2023, p. 5.
[136] Net Zero Plan 2023, p. 5.
[137] Net Zero Industry Act Proposal 2023; Chips Act 2023; Critical Raw Materials Act Proposal 2023.
[138] Chips Act 2023, art. 7.

5.4 RESOURCEFUL GOVERNMENT

Given government's large inadequacies and knowledge problems, government was supposed to govern less, to do less and to own less – leaving as much as possible to the market. In turn, government that needs to do less also needs fewer capabilities, and thus we have seen a gradual dismantling of the capacity of governments (national and European) to govern – including their legislative and policy as well as financial and institutional capacities and resources.[139] Such incompetent government, however, does not fit with any stronger conception of industrial policy.

At the outset of its 2010 industrial policy wave, Europe was mainly concerned with improving the competitiveness of European industry, by fostering general conditions for industrial development. To this effect, *'closer co-operation with Member States and monitoring the success and competitiveness performance of policies at the European and Member State level'*[140] were called for in order to make the industrial policy successful. More specifically, the purpose of government on both levels was to improve industrial competitiveness via reducing burdens of regulation and labour (costs). This approach has only been made more prominent by the Industrial Renaissance policy in 2014, which comes with a concept of "Growth-Friendly Public Administration",[141] with a particular understanding of what "best practices" in public administration should stand for.

Only with the EGD, the EU's 2019 'growth strategy', do we see a growing concern for the capacity of governments and resources put behind this public agenda – including taxation. Taxation, like industrial policy itself, has been shied away from by the EU, both because of its very limited competences and its ideological misfit with "competitiveness" narratives. The EGD, even if it relies predominantly on private investment, argues that *'Ensuring that taxation is aligned with climate objectives is also essential'*.[142] The Commission additionally stresses the importance of national budgets. *'National budgets play a key role in the transition. (...) At the national level, the European Green Deal will create the context for broad-based tax reforms, removing subsidies for fossil fuels, shifting the tax burden from labour to pollution, and taking into account social considerations'*.[143]

---

[139] Mariana Mazzucato and Rosie Collington, *The Big Con: How the Consulting Industry Weakens Our Businesses, Infantilizes Our Governments and Warps Our Economies* (Penguin Press, 2023).
[140] Industrial Policy 2010, p. 31.   [141] Industrial Renaissance Plan 2014, p. 8.
[142] European Green Deal 2019, p. 5.   [143] European Green Deal 2019, p. 17.

While the EGD has tabled a more general discussion, the 2020 Industrial Policy, as well as the NGEU (discussed below), tries to reinvigorate a more specific tax debate about the consolidated corporate tax base: *'Enhancing tax harmonisation would help remove one of the main obstacles faced by business when operating cross-border, notably by making a common consolidated corporate tax base a reality'*.[144] The later 2021 industrial policy announces a new approach, via *'the upcoming Communication on "Business Taxation for the 21st century"* [which] *will set out concrete plans to support both objectives, including concrete measures for SMEs'*.[145] Currently, the EU is pursuing several piecemeal measures, as much of its more ambitious attempts have been stranded. Perhaps the most important of those is the Minimum Corporate Tax directive,[146] building on the OECD agreement. Pundits remain concerned, however, that it's both too little and too leaky.[147]

The question of taxing capacity is a fundamental one, not least in the context of green transition. Yet tax competition has instead placed serious limits on the income of states and limited their democratic agency.[148] These constraints are a particularly salient problem in the EU, where the EU internal market rules present infrastructure that enables tax competition among the MSs themselves – while at the same time European Treaties make serious attempts to make tax harmonisation close to impossible thanks to the unanimity rules.[149] Thus even if after post-2008 crisis it has become increasingly clear to the Commission that the tax competition in the EU has a plethora of negative consequences, competitive fiscal federalism remains a reality in the EU.[150]

So how is the EU going to finance the transition, which will admittedly *'require massive public investment and increased efforts to direct private capital towards climate and environmental action, while avoiding lock-in into*

---

[144] New Industrial Strategy 2020, p. 5. [145] New Industrial Strategy Update 2021, p. 10.
[146] Council Directive (EU) 2022/2523 of 14 December 2022 on ensuring a global minimum level of taxation for multinational enterprise groups and large-scale domestic groups in the Union.
[147] Thomas Tørsløv, Ludvig Wier, and Gabriel Zucman, 'The Missing Profits of Nations', *The Review of Economic Studies* 90, no. 3 (2023): 1499–534.
[148] Ibid.
[149] Consolidated Version of the Treaty on the Functioning of the European Union, Part Three – Union Policies and Internal Actions, Title VII – Common Rules On Competition, Taxation And Approximation of Laws, chapter 2 – Tax Provisions, arts. 110–3.
[150] Jussi Jaakkola, 'Taming the Leviathan or Dismantling Democratic Government? Evolving Political Ideas on Spontaneous Income Tax Integration in the European Union', *European Law Open* 2, no. 3 (2023): 575–615.

unsustainable practice'?[151] Only a year after the EGD, which relied heavily on private investment as a response to this question,[152] the EU introduces a large funding package in response to the COVID-19 crisis: NGEU.

The details behind the NGEU are important, as they allow us to see how the EU can raise money as well as how a more solidary focused EU industrial approach could look like. The NGEU is the first occasion when states are engaging in significant common borrowing, *'by temporarily lifting the own resources ceiling to 2% of EU Gross National Income. This will allow the Commission to use its very strong credit rating to borrow €750 billion on the financial markets for Next Generation EU'.*[153]

Unlike the recovery programmes after the 2008 crisis, the NGEU is a joint financing instrument, revolving around solidarity and fairness, as *'Left to individual countries alone, the recovery would likely be incomplete, uneven and unfair'.*[154] In terms of the distribution of funds, the special needs of the country were considered, and thus some countries, such as Italy or Croatia, have received far bigger packages than stronger economies: in the case of Croatia, the package (grants and loans) is 27 per cent of its GDP.[155] The funds were to be used to finance the EU's twin transition, digital and green, and included a commitment that public investment must respect the green oath to '*do no harm*'. Importantly, given its green objectives, the Recovery and Resilience plans that countries develop in order to tap into the funding are referenced regularly as a stream of funding in the upcoming industrial policies, including, importantly the Net Zero Industrial Act.

In order to repay the borrowed funds, the Commission will rely on the EU's future budgets (up to 2046), with several new financial streams coming into play, including the Emissions Trading Scheme, the Carbon Border Adjustment Mechanism, financial transaction tax, a new digital

---

[151] European Green Deal 2019, p. 2.
[152] EuroMemo Group, 'EuroMemorandum 2020', www.euromemo.eu/euromemorandum/euromemorandum_2020/index.html, last accessed 9 January 2024.
[153] Repair and Prepare for the Next Generation 2020, p. 4.
[154] Repair and Prepare for the Next Generation 2020, p. 3; moreover, in the Net Zero Plan the Commission announces that it will put forth a proposal for the European Sovereignty Fund, in order to create a new instrument to counter the asymmetrical development among the EU MSs.
[155] European Commission – Press release, 'NextGenerationEU: European Commission Endorses Positive Preliminary Assessment of Croatia's Request for €700 Million Disbursement under the Recovery and Resilience Facility' (2022), https://ec.europa.eu/commission/presscorner/detail/en/ip_22_6654, last accessed 10 January 2024.

tax, VAT on non-recycled plastics, or similar.[156] The Net Zero Plan clarifies indeed that the Emissions Trading Scheme as well as the Carbon Border Adjustment Mechanism incomes will be used for green industrial policy.

In reaction to the Net Zero Plan, the European Parliament has called on the Commission to be more ambitious in proposing new resources, as *'new own resources are a key enabler for the Union to implement its policy priorities'*[157] and it is necessary to *'avoid new EU priorities being financed to the detriment of existing EU programmes and policies'*.[158] More specifically, the European Parliament *'urges the Commission and the Member States involved in the negotiations on the enhanced cooperation to do their utmost to reach an agreement on the **financial transaction tax** before the end of June 2023; asks, in addition, the Commission to be even more ambitious and come forward with proposals for new genuine own resources'*.[159] In that regard, the European Parliament also strongly supports the proposal for the European Sovereignty Fund, mentioned earlier, and says that it should not be financed at the expense of cohesion funds that have already been committed to.[160]

But the capacity of the government goes beyond just the question of financial resources. It requires competent public officials, well-organised institutions and systems, professionalism, and commitment to the rule of law. The 2020 industrial policy picks up one specific aspect of public competence that aligns with its "entrepreneurial spirit": *'that as we step up investment in disruptive and breakthrough research and innovation, we must accept failure along the way. This helps us to learn, adapt and, if necessary, reset our way of doing things to allow us to move forward. We must shift our mind-set from risk averse to failure tolerant'*.[161]

What the policy does not pick up is the question of *public benefit, voice, and ownership* in publicly supported and financed ventures. While the policy seems inspired by Mazzucato's approach, not even the inoffensively sounding "portfolio approach" to investments has made its way into the document: that is, funding broadly, but participating both in success and failure, so that successes can finance future investment.[162] The continuous deference to markets can also be seen from the fact that

---

[156] Repair and Prepare for the Next Generation 2020, p. 4.
[157] European Parliament resolution of 16 February 2023 on an EU strategy to boost industrial competitiveness, trade, and quality jobs (2023/2513(RSP)), p. 7.
[158] Ibid. [159] Ibid. [160] Ibid. [161] New Industrial Strategy Update 2021, p. 10.
[162] Mazzucato, *Mission Economy*.

the EU's industrial policy does not impose practically any conditionalities – with a small exception from the Chips Act, which provides for obligatory supplies in times of crisis[163] – remaining thus firmly within the neoliberal approach of socialising the risks and privatising the benefits.

5.5 The Contours of the New Imaginary of Prosperity: or *Im Westen nichts Neues?*

Is there any trace left of a move to a different imaginary of political economy when it comes to the EU's industrial policy? If the EGD is a green growth strategy that should '*transform the EU into a fair and prosperous society, with a modern, resource-efficient and competitive economy where there are no net emissions of greenhouse gases in 2050 and where economic growth is decoupled from resource use*',[164] what kind of political economy does it need? If '*The transition can only succeed if it is conducted in a fair and inclusive way*',[165] how are green, social, and democratic elements brought together in the imaginary that is being shaped here? And, even more in line with the spirit of this book, are there any nods to a more radical departure from the neoliberal toolkit?

We have seen three important shifts in the economic imaginaries behind industrial policy. First, we could observe a shift away from pursuing "everything goes growth" to pursuing "green growth', complicating thus the story of growth altogether. Second, in order to have that green growth, more *public steering* of the economy is necessary – markets will not get us there on their own. In terms of division of labour, that steering should increasingly happen at the EU level, with financing remaining a problem. Third, future "competitiveness" should build on advanced technologies, rather than on cheapening labour – even if the relation of new technologies towards sharing with labour remains unarticulated.

Legal and institutional imaginaries behind industrial policies have also seen a certain development. We have observed the proliferation of 'one-stop-shops' carried through most legislative acts, suggesting that one way to support sectors is to create effective institutional support. The Chips Act is by far the most interesting piece of legislation: having gone through a longer period of preparation, it has large institutional

---

[163] Chips Act 2023, art. 23.   [164] European Green Deal 2019, p. 2.
[165] European Green Deal 2019, p. 16.

ambitions, aiming to create a European 'Chips Joint Undertaking', a kind of 'DARPA' or 'Cybersyn', in this European "moon-shot mission".[166] It also creates a new legal entity, 'European Chips Infrastructure Consortium', as a special-purpose vehicle for large-scale investment and cooperation in the industry. This all happens at the background of the government, or public, steering the economy in desirable directions, complemented by the EU's attempt to muster more funding in order to accomplish this.

Where the EU does not make a step forward is in its conception of politics. Put together in haste, it seems that the EU will enable both national and European funding to flow to various industries, without a broader political discussion as to what priorities the transition should pursue. It matters, however, whether the EU invests significant public funds into hydrogen or carbon capture, electric vehicles or public transport, geoheating pumps, or the isolation of houses. While hydrogen and carbon capture seem to present a public financing stream to the fossil fuel industry, despite their overwhelming profits historically and most importantly in recent years, subsidies to electric vehicles may benefit the car industry – but perhaps at the expense of developing more broadly available public transport, or immiseration of third countries providing critical materials. Whatever the trade-offs are, more public debate around the choices would be fundamental to ensure *'fair and inclusive transition'*.[167]

Overall, the EU industrial policy has seen a couple of paths not taken, or even reversals, on issues where a more transformative approach was nodded to. Consider the 2020 attempt to push the EU to become Mazzucato's "entrepreneurial state". Or the recognition – without actual public support – for social economy. Let me briefly outline a few missed opportunities to institute the imaginary of shared prosperity more deeply.

First, the industrial policy remains in the old scheme of privatising profits while socialising risk. There is little to no mention of any conditionality as it concerns the use of public money, including the consequences this has for the distribution of profits on the one hand and any "above the standard" social and environmental performance on the other. For instance, the US Inflation Reduction Act, despite its difficult path towards adoption and the costs that it took the current administration,[168] introduces some elements that can make progress more shared. For instance, it makes the size of tax credits and subsidies

---

[166] Mazzucato, *Mission Economy*. [167] European Green Deal 2019, p. 16.
[168] Conditionality in the US Inflation Reduction Plan has been paid for by cutting the democratic promise of universal free childcare in the US.

dependent on the *'prevailing wage and registered apprenticeship requirements'*, that is on the higher wage usually paid by the public sector and set by the secretary of labour,[169] or it limits the distributions of public funds to shareholders via dividends of share buybacks.[170]

Also the European Parliament observes this peculiar tendency and *'[c]alls on the Commission and the Member States **to make EU funding conditional** on relevant requirements linked to public policy objectives, in particular social, environmental and financial requirements, and respect EU labour rights, standards and improved working conditions, which should be fulfilled by beneficiaries for as long as they receive public support, while ensuring fair and open competition, a level playing field between our companies, and respect for the fundamental principles on which our single market is based'*.[171] The Net Zero Plan, however, still seems to subscribe to "trickle down economics" when it comes to what happens among private actors: but what historical experience is there to suggest that public money will trickle down into 'well-paid quality jobs' that the Commission promises?

Second, the EU's industrial policy seems to be quite one-sidedly sensitive when it comes to international economic relations. *'Where the public footprint in private markets is outsized, distortions create an unlevelled playing field and unfair competition emerges. A particular concern exists in respect of non-market economies. The EU wants to lead a robust response to address these trends'*.[172] But what about the private footprint that creates distortions, an unlevel playing field, and leads to unfair competition? Multinational corporations, of which some European, have had a large negative footprint in global markets, and in particular on the economic conditions in the Global South.[173] But it goes further. Scholars working on the implications of green transition have warned against the tendencies of "green extractivism" that are already exacerbating land grabbing, worsening water availability, and thus also food security, indebting countries with costly infrastructures, while providing little to no jobs

---

[169] Inflation Reduction Act 2022, Subtitle D, Part 1(f).
[170] In a recent paper, Mazzucato and Rodrik articulate the types of conditionalities that we have seen across the globe, as well as some of their benefits. See Mariana Mazzucato and Dani Rodrik, 'Industrial Policy with Conditionalities: A Taxonomy and Sample Cases', Working paper WP 2023/07, Institute for Innovation and Public Purpose, 2023.
[171] European Parliament resolution, EU strategy to boost industrial competitiveness, trade, and quality jobs, p. 7.
[172] Net Zero Plan 2023, p. 2.
[173] Florian Wettstein, 'The History of Business and Human Rights and Its Relationship with Corporate Social Responsibility', in *Research Handbook on Human Rights and Business*, ed. Surya Deva and David Birchall (Edward Elgar Publishing, 2020), 23–45.

for local populations.[174] In the context of the disproportionate impact of the climate crisis on those developing countries, including the migration pressures, this seems like a dangerous strategy to take.

The Critical Minerals Action Plan only underscores the extractive logics of EU industrial policy as *'undistorted trade and investment in raw materials in a manner that supports the EU's commercial interests'*.[175] The Critical Raw Materials Act gives very few indications on the terms of 'strategic partnerships', or the degree of sharing of benefits of economic cooperation.[176] The EU funding instrument, Global Gateway, also seems to miss the mark in many countries,[177] while the EU shows little commitment to deal with the urgent question of debt that is decimating both the social and environmental chances of developing countries.[178]

Third, one important road *not* taken towards greater sharing internally and externally, is the still lacking support for social economy. Even if mentioned in several contexts – it is also where it ends. For instance, the 2011 industrial report argues that *'Developing social entrepreneurship, social businesses and the social economy is another important tool for strengthening the competitiveness and the sustainability of the European industry. The social economy employs over 11 million people in the EU, accounting for 6% of total employment and approximately one in four businesses founded in Europe is a social enterprise. This figure rises to one in three in Belgium, Finland and France. These companies are often highly productive and competitive, due to the very high level of personal commitment on the part of their employees and the better working conditions that they provide'*.[179] The 2014 Industrial Renaissance policy promises *'the new rules on European Venture Capital Funds and European Social Entrepreneurship Funds create a special EU passport for fund managers investing in start-up SMEs and social businesses'*,[180] while the NGEU suggests that a *'strong social economy can offer unique opportunities to help*

---

[174] Bruna, 'A Climate-Smart World and the Rise of Green Extractivism'.
[175] Critical Raw Materials Plan 2020, p. 15.
[176] Critical Raw Materials Act Proposal 2023.
[177] Joint Communication to the European Parliament, the Council, the European Economic and Social Committee, the Committee of the Regions and the European Investment Bank: The Global Gateway, JOIN(2021) 30 final.
[178] Ulrich Volz et al., 'Addressing the Debt Crisis in the Global South: Debt Relief for Sustainable Recoveries', Other (SOAS WP, 2022), www.think7.org/publication/addressing-the-debt-crisis-in-the-global-south-debt-relief-for-sustainable-recoveries/, last accessed 10 January 2024.
[179] European Commission Staff Working Paper, Member State Competitiveness Performance and Policies (2011 report), SEC(2011) 1187 final, p. 8.
[180] Industrial Renaissance Plan 2014, p. 12.

5.5 CONTOURS OF NEW IMAGINARY OF PROSPERITY 169

most vulnerable to return to the labour market'.[181] The 2020 CEAP underscores 'The potential of the social economy, which is a pioneer in job creation linked to the circular economy, will be further leveraged'.[182] But at some other time and place.

Equally, a more realistic and solidarity approach to SMEs in legal relations has not been seriously advanced in the policy. In the 2020 industrial policy, the Commission reminds that 'In the SME Strategy, the Commission emphasised the need to enhance fairness in B2B relations to support SMEs which due to asymmetries in bargaining power with larger organisations face an increased risk of being subject to unfair business practices and conditions both online and offline'.[183] However, while a more realistic, relational approach to contracting would present a better application of the "think small first" principle in industrial policy, it does not return in the legislative measures.

To conclude. The 2023 Net Zero Plan and the legislative measures in its wake are techno-optimist in the tritest sense. Once technology is there, everything else will follow: 'The starting point for the Plan is the need to massively increase the technological development, manufacturing production and installation of net-zero products and energy supply in the next decade, and the value added of an EU-wide approach to meet this challenge together'.[184] In this technological race, there is no time for deliberation about priorities or public voice and benefit.

Yet the question remains: to be first at what? Who is shaping the choices about collective investment? For instance, the question of green (and other coloured) hydrogen is a strongly divisive issue, as the question of its feasibility and distributive effects ranks high.[185] Also, who will ultimately profit from those investments? The Net Zero Plan unapologetically embraces and aims to publicly finance all kinds of clean tech – that may neither be that clean, nor fairly shared in terms of their benefits.

Clearly, the EU is doing more than many MSs in terms of greening the economy, as the Commission has fewer constraints in terms of short political cycles or social media frenzy. Yet, at the same time, the choices

---

[181] Repair and Prepare for the Next Generation 2020, p. 10.
[182] Circular Economy Action Plan 2020, p, 15.
[183] New Industrial Strategy Update 2021, p. 9.   [184] Net Zero Plan 2023, p. 3.
[185] Kieninger, '"Clean Hydrogen" Is the Fossil-Fuel Industry in Disguise'; Camilla Hodgson, 'Banks and Oil Groups Place Bets on Carbon Capture Schemes', Financial Times (2023), www.ft.com/content/7aa77038-62b6-4761-9ce3-1e0647ffb607?shareType=nongift, last accessed 10 January 2024; America Hernandez and Simon Van Dorpe, 'EU Goes Big on Hydrogen as Gas Crunch Looms', Politico (2022), www.politico.eu/article/industrial-hydrogen-state-aid-technology/, last accessed 10 January 2024.

that the EU makes have to be *right* choices, not least because much depends on its capacity to deliver shared prosperity. The EU must search for ways of making those choices in a democratically more robust way, without relying predominantly on knowledge supplied by fossil industry or car producers.[186] The Conference on Europe presented one way in which Europe could get in touch with reflective positions of the European citizens: such a conference may also be needed for the EU to develop a more democratically robust industrial policy, which could provide a credible hope for a liveable future - of people with practical education, of all age cohorts, including those living in European rural or peripheral regions, all the while not forgetting our growing debt toward Global South.

---

[186] Davis, 'The Greenwashing Scam behind EU's "Grey" Hydrogen'.

6 Transforming the Corporation[1]

6.1 Introduction

When we think of economy and prosperity, the role of corporation – be it positive, negative, or ambiguous[2] – will top the list. Most see corporations as organisations, sometimes huge, that sell goods and services we need or like. Corporations have been fundamental for foremost consumer-facing innovation (washingmachines, TVs, computers and smartphones), but they have also been a major cause of environmental and social problems (pollution or worker exploitation). Today, it is the profitability for shareholders that identifies a successful corporation – often expressed as their value on the stock exchange (for public corporations) or the lifestyle they enable to their "owners" (i.e. shareholders) for private corporations.

This privatised understanding of corporation is, however, a relatively recent one. In fact, seeing corporation as a private entity that pursues profit for its "owners" is far closer to Mise's understanding of the "enterprenuer" than a historic definition of corporation: enterpreneuer as: the self-interested capital investor and risk taker,[3] who invests their (hard won) capital into productive activity, delivering socially useful things under conditions of uncertainty, in order to reap the profits of such commercial activity.[4] For most of history, corporations (starting

---

[1] This chapter draws on the previously published article by Marija Bartl, 'Towards the Imaginary of Collective Prosperity in the European Union (EU): Reorienting the Corporation', *European Law Open* 1, no. 4 (2022): 957–86.
[2] People in Nigeria think differently about corporations than people in the NL, and workers in Bangladesh see these organisations differently than the retail shareholders in Germany.
[3] William Magnuson, *For Profit: A History of Corporations* (Hachette UK, 2022).
[4] Peter G. Klein, *The Capitalist & The Entrepreneur* (Ludwig von Mises Institute, 2010).

from ancient ones as well as early modern ones such as various Indian companies) were seen as *collective* undertakings, which were granted charters to operate because of some common good they took up to deliver.[5] For a long time then, incorporation was a matter of public choice and collective interest.[6]

This is all about to change at the end of the nineteenth/beginning of the twentieth century, when the first privatising imaginaries of prosperity became dominant. The corporation was privatised via two institutional routes: on the one hand, we see the shift away from the concession to incorporation by simple registration, with the implication that any private purpose was seen as sufficient.[7] On the other hand, the widespread institutionalisation of 'limited liability' set grounds for modern capitalism.[8] We can understand this moment as the first *privatisation* of corporation – that is the institution of corporation as a mere *extension* of the individual entrepreneur operating for his own self-interest – rather than a collective entity oriented towards shared goals.[9]

The social excesses of the first round of privatisation were quick to become apparent. Be it cartelisation, financial speculation, or labour exploitation, there was a resounding call for change – coming not only from the labour movement. Thus in this period, we see changes in competition law, financial law, and company law put in place in order to reign in the privatised corporation.[10] After the horrors of WWII, we can speak of the wholesale shift in the imaginary of corporation, with a growing "suspicion of profit"[11] and high taxation of both income and corporate profits, as well as a demand for social responsibility of the business and directors.[12] This new imaginary of corporation was comfortably dominant until the 1970s, when Milton Friedman gave the first powerful expression to the discontents.

Friedman saw the commitment to 'social responsibility' by both business and policy leaders as counterproductive: '*The businessmen believe that*

---

[5] Magnuson, *For Profit*.
[6] Giuseppe Dari-Mattiacci et al., 'The Emergence of the Corporate Form', *The Journal of Law, Economics, and Organization* 33, no. 2 (2017): 193–236.
[7] Private vice, public virtue.
[8] Dari-Mattiacci et al., 'The Emergence of the Corporate Form'; Paddy Ireland, 'Corporate Schizophrenia: The Corporation as a Separate Legal Person and an Object of Property', University of Bristol Working Paper (2016).
[9] Magnuson, *For Profit*.   [10] Magnuson, *For Profit*.
[11] Milton Friedman, 'The Social Responsibility of Business Is to Increase Its Profits', New York Times (1970), p. 5.
[12] Thomas Piketty, *Capital and Ideology* (Harvard University Press, 2020).

they are defending free enterprise when they declaim that business is not concerned "merely" with profit but also with promoting desirable "social" ends; that business has a "social conscience" and takes seriously its responsibilities for providing employment, eliminating discrimination, avoiding pollution and whatever else may be the catchwords of the contemporary crop of reformers'. Yet, the advocacy of corporate social responsibility was, according to Friedman, '*preaching pure and unadulterated socialism*'.[13]

Given the diversity between corporate structures in Europe, it took several decades before Friedmanite positions became more popular,[14] and Europe – like most of the world – partook in the trend of strengthening shareholder rights and instituting practically (if not legally) the "shareholder primacy" model.[15] This second privatisation of corporation was less a matter of company law[16] and more a question of a broader set of neoliberal policy prescriptions, which aimed to commodify and marketise most of the economy, opening them to private ownership, competition, and financial capital.[17] The most prominent element among all these policies was the liberalisation of financial markets, which will become the main vehicle for the institution of the shareholder primacy model across the world.[18]

As with the previous privatisation, this second privatisation of corporation came paired with the narrowing of interests and purposes that the corporation was supposed to serve, creating the "self" in the "self-interested" that ultimately eschewed everything but share prices.[19] Corporate scholars have reminded us time and time again that the "shareholder value" paradigm has never been institutionalised via company law.[20]

---

[13] Friedman, 'The Social Responsibility of Business Is to Increase Its Profits', p 1.
[14] Thomas J. AndréJr., 'Cultural Hegemony: The Exportation of Anglo-Saxon Corporate Governance Ideologies to Germany', *Tulane Law Review* 73, no. 1 (1998), 69–171.
[15] Mathias M. Siems, Siems, Mathias M. 'Shareholder Protection around the World ('Leximetric II')'. *Centre for Business Research, University of Cambridge Working Paper*, No. 359 (December 2007).
[16] Mariana Pargendler, 'The Corporate Governance Obsession', *Journal of Corporation Law* 42 (2016): 359–402.
[17] Tim Bartley, 'Transnational Corporations and Global Governance', *Annual Review of Sociology* 44, no. 1 (2018): 145–65.
[18] Katharina Pistor, *The Code of Capital: How the Law Creates Wealth and Inequality* (Princeton University Press, 2019).
[19] Jean-Philippe Robé, *Property, Power and Politics: Why We Need to Rethink the World Power System* (Policy Press, 2020).
[20] Beate Sjåfjell et al., 'Shareholder Primacy: The Main Barrier to Sustainable Companies', in *Company Law and Sustainability: Legal Barriers and Opportunities*, ed. Beate Sjåfjell and Benjamin J. Richardson (Cambridge University Press, 2015).

On a narrow reading, there is nothing in corporate law itself, at least in Europe, that forces corporations to take such a narrow understanding of corporate interest.[21] And yet, the combination of several distinct institutional mechanisms, such as financialisation, quarterly reporting, and management remuneration, has made shareholder value a social norm.[22] Corporate law scholars have, however, also played their role in institutionalising this paradigm; the enthusiasm with which they have devoted their research to exploring how to align the interests of shareholders and managers – even in Europe where it was slightly less poignant – has made shareholder primacy the dominant discourse in the field of corporate law for a long time.[23]

Today, there is a growing social consensus, in Europe and elsewhere, that we need to change how economies operate – at least if we are intent on preserving a liveable planet. The negative social and environmental consequences of economic activity are vast,[24] while the economic benefits seem to accrue rather asymmetrically – exacerbating thus a plethora of social and political problems.[25] While the European Green Deal (EGD) aims to present a comprehensive plan to shift economic activity towards sustainability via a number of policy areas, from transport to food, if we truly want to change how the economy operates, we cannot go around the design of the main actor that drives the current model – the corporation.

In this chapter then, I will discuss how the European institutions attempted to change the way in which corporations are structured and operate. Overall, there are two paths for transforming corporation. On the one hand, one can aim to limit the negative effects of corporate activity, by improving certain aspects of the administrative capacity of corporations, to monitor and remove negative impacts – via instruments such as due diligence – paired with some degree of administrative and/or civil liability. On the other hand, one can go after the fundamentals, that is by engaging with more fundamental aspects of corporate governance

---

[21] Ibid. Of course, if one adopted a broader reading of the corporate law that sees corporate governance codes as part of corporate law, this position would change dramatically.
[22] Sjåfjell et al., 'Shareholder Primacy'.
[23] Jaap W. Winter, 'Dehumanisation of the Large Corporation' (SSRN, 10 January 2020).
[24] Hoesung Lee et al., 'IPCC, 2023: Climate Change 2023: Synthesis Report, Summary for Policymakers. Contribution of Working Groups I, II and III to the Sixth Assessment Report of the Intergovernmental Panel on Climate Change [Core Writing Team, H. Lee and J. Romero (eds.)]. IPCC, Geneva, Switzerland', 2023.
[25] Thomas Piketty, *Capital in the Twenty-First Century* (Harvard University Press, 2014).

and ownership, as these condition the exercise of power and the distribution of surplus of economic cooperation. This chapter describes the EU's attempt to adopt what we can call a mixed approach, trying to address both administrative capacity and a few elements of the "fundamentals". After the pushback by its own internal body, the Regulatory Scrutiny Board (RSB), the Commission has retreated from its more transformative plans, focusing mostly on limiting corporations' negative impacts. The ultimate shape of the legislation is, however, still up for grabs, as both the Parliament and the Council have their own positions. In the last section then, I pick up on the possibilities still open for engaging with the fundamentals of corporate activity differently – by publicly facilitating those enterprises and organisations that have different fundamentals (ownership and governance), with a view to at least increase the pluralism of the corporate ecosystem.

6.1.1 'Corporate Governance File'

The "modern" story of the reigning in the corporation, especially in the countries of the Global South, starts in the 1970s. The attempt of the Global South to institutionalise a 'New International Economic Order' required the regulation of multinational corporations (MNCs), including their fundamentals, as one of its priorities. But as these efforts faltered, for a variety of reasons,[26] also the question of the regulation of MNCs has vanished from the radar. This was the case until the 1990s, when we see the birth of the so-called "business and human rights movement".[27]

The business and human rights movement has booked several successes over the course of the past decades, with the introduction of several international soft law instruments such as the UN Principles[28]

---

[26] Antony Anghie, *Imperialism, Sovereignty and the Making of International Law*, vol. 37 (Cambridge University Press, 2007); Mohammed Bedjaoui, 'Towards a New International Economic Order', 1979; Quinn Slobodian, *Globalists: The End of Empire and the Birth of Neoliberalism* (Harvard University Press, 2020).

[27] Florian Wettstein, 'The History of Business and Human Rights and Its Relationship with Corporate Social Responsibility', in *Research Handbook on Human Rights and Business*, ed. Surya Deva and David Birchall (Edward Elgar Publishing Limited, 2020), 23–45.

[28] United Nations Human Rights Office of the High Commissioner, 'Guiding Principles on Business and Human Rights: Implementing the United Nations "Protect, Respect and Remedy" Framework' (United Nations, 2011), www.ohchr.org/sites/default/files/Documents/Publications/GuidingPrinciplesBusinessHR_EN.pdf, last accessed 10 January 2024.

and the OECD Principles.²⁹ Some of the due diligence principles introduced via these instruments have been more recently adopted by several nation states, such as France, Germany, or the UK, as mandatory law at the national level.³⁰ A more serious attempt to regulate the liability of MNCs is currently taking place at the level of the UN, with the Binding Treaty on Business and Human Rights being drafted.³¹ But this UN measure (as is often the case) is being met with lukewarm support from "developed countries".³²

The European Union (EU) itself enters this space of business and human rights' relatively late.³³ It has introduced obligatory due diligence in specific high-risk sectors, such as timber,³⁴ and conflict minerals.³⁵ Furthermore, in 2014 the EU promulgated a more general measure, the 'non-financial reporting directive',³⁶ which required the largest corporations to publish 'non-financial information' related to environmental protection, the treatment of employees, human rights, anti-corruption, bribery, diversity on company boards, and any diligence procedures throughout the supply chain – if they had any.³⁷ The

---

[29] OECD, 'OECD Guidelines for Multinational Enterprises on Responsible Business Conduct' (2023), https://mneguidelines.oecd.org/mneguidelines/, last accessed 10 January 2024.

[30] Such laws have been promulgated in the UK, the Netherlands, or France, as committed to under UN principles: F. Anita Ramasastry, 'Corporate Social Responsibility Versus Business and Human Rights: Bridging the Gap Between Responsibility and Accountability', *Journal of Human Rights* 14, no. 2 (2015): 237–59.

[31] United Nations OEIGWG 'Legally Binding Instrument to Regulate, in International Human Rights Law, The Activities of Transnational Corporations and Other Business Enterprises' Third Revised Draft, www.ohchr.org/sites/default/files/Documents/HRBodies/HRCouncil/WGTransCorp/Session6/LBI3rdDRAFT.pdf, last accessed 10 January 2024.

[32] Lydia de Leeuwe, 'Progress and Challenges: Recap of 2023 UN Binding Treaty Negotiations on Business and Human Rights', *SOMO* (2023), www.somo.nl/recap-2023-un-biding-treaty-negotiations/, last accessed 10 January 2024.

[33] European Commission, A Renewed EU Strategy 2011–14 for Corporate Social Responsibility, COM(2011) 681 final.

[34] Regulation (EU) No. 995/2010 of the European Parliament and of the Council of 20 October 2010 laying down the obligations of operators who place timber and timber products on the market.

[35] Regulation (EU) 2017/821 of the European Parliament and of the Council of 17 May 2017 laying down supply chain due diligence obligations for Union importers of tin, tantalum, and tungsten, their ores, and gold originating from conflict-affected and high-risk areas.

[36] Council Directive 2014/95/EU of 22 October 2014 amending Directive 2013/34/EU as regards disclosure of non-financial and diversity information by certain large undertakings and groups.

[37] The reporting strategy proved not to be effective enough in reigning in the problems caused by transnational business activity – not least because of the low degrees of accountability and enforcement of reporting standards. To remedy at least the issue of

directive was primarily successful in revealing that very few large corporations actually undertook any due diligence across the chain at all.[38] Somewhat more promisingly, the EU has also started developing a 'green finance' package. While still a part of the "reporting paradigm", it contains some important tools for steering investments towards green initiatives.[39] All these initiatives found an overarching ambitious policy framework in the 2019 European Green Deal (EGD).[40]

With the launch of EGD, the question of the role of businesses in delivering (or not) the objectives of EGD became paramount.[41] The European Commission thus started a revision of its corporate governance framework in 2020, with a view of aligning it with the EGD. This action took place on two fronts. First, the Commission undertook the overhaul of the 2014 non-financial reporting directive, with the DG FISMA having prepared a new corporate sustainability reporting directive.[42] While the primary objective was to help investors make more sustainable investment decisions, the transparency element was also expected to have a broader disciplining effect on corporate behaviour. Somewhat later, the Commission also opened a 'due diligence' file, under the directorship of DG Justice.[43] Going beyond transparency of 'material information', the due diligence framework was expected to set material

---

standards, the EU later published more elaborate guidelines on environmental (2017) and climate (2019) reporting and proposed a revised directive in 2021: Directive (EU) 2022/2464 of the European Parliament and of the Council of 14 December 2022 amending Regulation (EU) No. 537/2014, Directive 2004/109/EC, Directive 2006/43/EC, and Directive 2013/34/EU, as regards corporate sustainability reporting.

[38] European Commission, Directorate-General for Justice and Consumers, Torres-Cortés, F., Salinier, C., Deringer, H. et al., *Study on Due Diligence Requirements through the Supply Chain: Final Report* (Publications Office, 2020).

[39] The EU Sustainable Finance Package includes several important elements, including Taxonomy Rules and corporate sustainability reporting and disclosures. For more, see https://ec.europa.eu/info/business-economy-euro/banking-and-finance/sustainable-finance_en. For a critical assessment, see Jennifer de Lange, 'Great Expectations of Sustainable Finance: A Critical Analysis of EU Sustainable Finance Strategy and Sustainable Finance Regulation', UVA Doctoral Thesis (2024). On file with the author.

[40] European Green Deal 2019.

[41] See the presentation by DG Justice Commissionaire Reynders, at https://?responsiblebusinessconduct?.eu/wp/2020/04/30/european-commission-promises-mandatory-due-diligence-legislation-in-2021/.directive.

[42] Directive (EU) 2022/2464 on corporate sustainability reporting.

[43] Proposal for a Directive of the European Parliament and of the Council on Corporate Sustainability Due Diligence and Amending Directive (EU) 2019/1937, COM(2022) 71 final.

standards on the corporate action of large European, and even larger non-European, firms.

However, the Commission's ambitions went further than just due diligence – something that became obvious from the preliminary stages of the due diligence proposal, starting with commissioning a report on the 'directors' duties and sustainable corporate governance'.[44] Tasking the reporter (Ernst & Young) to explore the impacts of 'short-termism' in corporate governance, the Commission appeared interested in tackling some elements of the fundamentals, namely the role of 'investment', in the interplay between financial markets and corporate governance. These efforts may have followed on from the European Banking Authority report of December 2019, which found some evidence of short-termism in relation to the corporate sector (and less so in the banking sector), precisely thanks to the changes in the underlying legal and governance framework: *'Changes in banking regulations since the financial crisis, notably on remuneration, have been designed specifically to counter undue short-termism, and the outcomes of these changes themselves are reflected in this report'*.[45]

The study on 'directors' duties and sustainable corporate governance' was delivered by Ernst & Young, in July 2020, finding that short-termism is indeed strongly present in the EU's corporate arena and leads to both unsustainable choices in terms of the company's bottom line (the lack of investment in innovation and people) and irresponsible behaviour towards all other stakeholders and environment.[46] In the same year, the European Parliament (in reaction to this and other studies and initiatives) also called on the European Commission to revise the Directive on non-financial reporting and propose a more robust 'sustainable corporate governance' framework that would solve some of the identified issues.[47]

---

[44] European Commission, Directorate-General for Justice and Consumers, 'Study on Directors' Duties and Sustainable Corporate Governance: Final Report' (Publications Office, 2020), https://data.europa.eu/doi/10.2838/472901, last accessed 10 January 2024.

[45] 'Final EBA Report on Undue Short-Term Pressures from the Financial Sector', European Banking Authority (2019), www.eba.europa.eu/file/461440/down, last accessed 10 January 2024.

[46] European Commission, 'Study on Directors' Duties and Sustainable Corporate Governance'.

[47] European Parliament Resolution of 17 December 2020 on sustainable corporate governance (2020/2137(INI), www.europarl.europa.eu/doceo/document/TA-9-2020-0372_EN.html, last accessed 10 January 2024.

In response, in Spring 2021 the Commission published a so-called inception impact assessment ('a roadmap') that outlined ideas of how to move forward in the field of corporate governance.[48] The roadmap was opened to public consultation and became a basis for the assessment of the first ideas by the Commission's 'regulatory watchdog', the RSB.

The inception impact assessment recognised short-termism as a systemic problem and envisaged a relatively broad range of interventions in the field of company law to ensure 'sustainable value creation'.[49] These interventions included several (previously unthinkable) hard law measures, including defining directors' duties and liabilities, the composition of company board(s) as well as the remuneration of their members, the inclusion of sustainability in business strategy, and the provision for stakeholder involvement. The Commission had thus intended to remedy several of the systemic constraints on the operation of public corporations via company law. Even if these constraints may not have originated in company law in a narrow sense, market operation could not be expected to remedy them – according to the European Commission – and resultantly hard law changes in company law were necessary.

However, the Commission's ambitious agenda faced notable opposition. According to the report of the Corporate Europe Observatory, during the preparation of the corporate governance file the DG Justice refrained from extensive consultation with the business community[50] – something that stands in contrast to other EU legislative proposals. In the wake of the inception impact assessment then, the industry and some member states (MSs) (especially Nordics, such as Denmark), as well as many corporate law and corporate finance scholars, set out a broad range of challenges to the Commission's proposal.

Still, in the end it was the Commission's RSB that actually forced it to cut back most of its more ambitious proposals. The RSB is an internal body established by the Juncker's Commission in 2015, with the US Office of Information and Regulatory Affairs (OIRA) in mind. As such,

---

[48] European Commission, 'Inception Impact Assessment: Sustainable Corporate Governance' (2020), https://ec.europa.eu/info/law/better-regulation/have-your-say/initiatives/12548-Sustainable-corporate-governance_en, last accessed 10 January 2024.
[49] Ibid., p. 3.
[50] Kenneth Haar et al., 'Inside Job: How Business Lobbyists Used the Commission's Scrutiny Procedures to Weaken Human Rights and Environmental Legislation' (Bund, Corporate Europe Observatory & Friends of the Earth Europe, June 2022), p. 6.

both its methodologies (economic/cost-benefit analysis[51]) and composition (it is populated mainly by members who have economics and business administration backgrounds)[52] are meant to limit the regulation – constraining the power of the government and giving more "breathing space" to commercial actors.[53] Due to its methods and composition, the RSB understands *better* regulation mainly as *less* regulation, and presents thus (another) layer of institutionalisation of neoliberal imaginary of privatised prosperity – enforced eventually long after other actors institutions may have moved on.

The RSB rejected the Commission's inception impact assessment on several grounds, the most important one being that the Commission had not shown that the problem – unsustainable corporate governance – existed at all.[54] It called on the Commission to provide evidence on both the problem description and its impacts. DG Justice thus went back to the drawing board and "strengthened" this time with the new co-lead Thierry Breton, from DG Internal Market, as a guarantor that industry interests will be better safeguarded.[55] And yet, a couple of months later, the newly drafted full impact assessment, in a quite exceptional move, was again rejected in November 2021,[56] on the grounds that it still did not sufficiently demonstrate the existence of the problem (unsustainable corporate governance) nor the solutions proposed (a need to change how businesses operate).[57] From within the imaginaries of privatised prosperity, both the Commission's problems and solutions appeared as gibberish.

---

[51] Frank Ackerman and Lisa Heinzerling, *Priceless: On Knowing the Price of Everything and the Value of Nothing* (The New Press, 2005).
[52] Haar et al., 'Inside Job', p. 20.
[53] The cases where the RSB has vetoed twice the measures are relatively scarce, and they concern, except for sustainable corporate governance, issues such as preventing and combating gender-based violence, or energy performance of buildings. See report 2021, Annex, https://ec.europa.eu/info/sites/default/files/rsb_report_2021_en.pdf, last accessed 10 January 2024.
[54] European Commission Regulatory Scrutiny Board, 'Opinion: Impact Assessment/ Sustainable Corporate Governance', Ares(2021)3065513.
[55] Haar et al., 'Inside Job', p. 28.
[56] Klaas Hendrick Elller and Ioannis Kampourakis, 'Through the Quantitative Lens: The EU Regulatory Scrutiny Board and the Sustainable Corporate Governance Initiative', Verfassungsblog (21 February 2022), https://verfassungsblog.de/quantifying-better-regulation/, last accessed 10 January 2024.
[57] European Commission Regulatory Scrutiny Board, 'Opinion: Impact Assessment/ Sustainable Corporate Governance' SEC(2022) 95, p. 1, https://eur-lex.europa.eu/legal-content/EN/TXT/PDF/?uri=PI_COM:SEC(2022)95&from=EN, last accessed 10 January 2024.

Ultimately then, the RSB has booked a half win. The Commission has still put forth a proposal, after the decision of the Board of Commissionaires. The reason for this decision was the recognition that '*[t]he market and competitive dynamics together with the further evolution of companies' corporate strategies and risk management systems are considered insufficient as regards the assumed causal link between using corporate sustainability tools and their practical effect in tackling the problems*'.[58] The published proposal is, however, a considerably watered-down version of its previous ideas: '*The Directive is more focused and targeted compared to the preferred option outlined in the draft impact assessment. The core of it is the due diligence obligation, while significantly reducing directors' duties by linking them closely to the due diligence obligation*'.[59]

What changes were introduced in the final version? To start, the title of the measure is not as broad – with 'sustainable corporate governance' being narrowed down to 'corporate sustainability *due diligence*'.[60] This signals the limited ambition to tackle fundamentals, including the incentives driving public companies towards 'short-termism'. Thus, directors' duties and liabilities, as well as management remuneration, are mentioned in a much more limited way. The stakeholder involvement has almost disappeared from the proposal. Also, the ideas on sustainable corporate strategy have been watered down, with no reference in the proposal to the need to include science-based targets nor inclusion of any specific requirements on the content of transition plans or strategies. As the Commission explains, '*Further reaching specific directors' duties that had been put forward in the impact assessment are not retained*'.[61]

The Proposal seemed to get another hit with the publishing of the Council position on 1 December 2022.[62] In terms of scope, the Council proposes to slow down the application, introducing a "phase in" approach, with only the largest corporations being expected to comply first (art. 2). The Council further proposed to abandon the concept of 'established business relationship', in favour of 'business partner', and to abandon 'value chain' in favour of 'chain of activities' – all in order to further limit the downstream partners falling within the due diligence

---

[58] Corporate Sustainability Due Diligence Proposal 2022, p. 22
[59] Corporate Sustainability Due Diligence Proposal 2022, p. 21.
[60] Corporate Sustainability Due Diligence Proposal 2022.
[61] Corporate Sustainability Due Diligence Proposal 2022, p. 22.
[62] See Council of the European Union, General Approach with regard to the Commission's proposal on the Sustainable Corporate Due Diligence Directive, of 30 November 2022, available at https://data.consilium.europa.eu/doc/document/ST-15024-2022-REV-1/en/pdf.

obligations (art. 3). In line with the international soft law instruments, the Council also proposes to strengthen the risk-based approach (art. 3), while it intended to leave to MSs the decision whether to apply the directive to regulated financial undertakings (art. 2 and ff). Some of the more remarkable changes concern the Council proposal to delete the provision linking the climate change obligation to the variable part of directors' remuneration (art. 15) as well as to delete two articles dedicated to directors' duty of care (art. 25 and art. 26). As it concerns civil liability, the Council held that the company should not be liable if the damage was caused only by business partners in its chain of activities, while also expressing concern that the 'full compensation for victims' should not lead to overcompensation (art. 22).[63]

If the Competitiveness Council thought gutting the proposal is what is necessary, the European Parliament considered that the proposal is not ambitious enough. Thus, on several levels it proposes a text that is more ambitious than the European Commission's proposal. According to the Parliament, the new rules should apply to a wider range of companies, from all sectors, including financial services (art. 6), if they have more than 250 employees and a worldwide turnover of more than €40 million (art. 2). The Parliament further demanded that companies engage in prevention, not only via contractual arrangements with partners with whom they have a business relationship but also by adapting their business models and strategies, including purchasing practices (art. 7), in order to prevent potential adverse impacts. Companies should monitor and assess the impact of their business partners, that is not only suppliers but also partners in areas such as sales, distribution, transport, storage, and waste management (art. 7). When negative impacts occur, companies should take steps to remedy or contribute to the remedying of any adverse impact, with a view to restore the affected individuals, groups, communities, and/or the environment to a situation equivalent to or as close as possible to that which existed prior to the adverse impact (art. 8). On the climate front, companies should implement 'a transition plan' to limit global warming to 1.5 Celsius, with specific content (art. 15). Companies with more than 1,000 employees on average should have an effective policy, ensuring that part of any variable remuneration for directors is linked to the company's transition plan (art. 15).

---

[63] Critically on the civil liability provisions, see Alessio M. Pacces, 'Civil Liability in the EU Corporate Sustainability Due Diligence Directive Proposal: A Law & Economics Analysis', European Corporate Governance Institute-Law Working Paper, no. 691 (2023).

Non-compliant companies would be liable for damages and could be sanctioned with fines worth at least 5 per cent of the company's net worldwide turnover (art. 20). The limitation periods for victims cannot be shorter than ten years (art. 22).

As the trialogue is ongoing at the time of writing, it is worth noting that the split we observe follows institutional (between different institutions – Commission, RSB, EP, Council etc.) rather than ideological (within institutions) lines. It could be that in the periods of change of a more "paradigmatic" nature, such as the current moment, the main division will emerge around whether one is *within* or *outside* a particular "paradigm" - a type of differentiation that is more likely to follow institutional lines.[64] Depending on what imaginary of prosperity one endorses, disagreements will be present at the most basal level: is there a **problem** at all, and if so of what nature; are the **solutions** we have relied upon until now sufficient to deal with the problem; what is the necessary **expertise** in order to assess and react to the situation; and, finally what is the **collective** interest (what is and how we get to prosperity) and what is the **individual** (corporate) responsibility.

6.2 New Problems, New Solutions

So, what are the problems that the RSB could have a hard time accepting? The European Commission framed the problem of the neoliberal corporation in this way: '*many companies, in particular those listed on regulated markets, face pressure to focus on generating financial return in a short timeframe and redistribute a large part of the income generated to shareholders, which may be to the detriment of the long-term development of the company, as well as of sustainability*'.[65] It continued, '*company as a whole, the company interest and directors duties are interpreted narrowly favouring maximisation of short-term financial value*'.[66] This leads to business strategies, the Commission suggested, which '*hamper investment crucial for the sustainability transition, into productive facilities, innovation, upgrading and employee retraining. It may also contribute to income inequality as short-termism creates*

---

[64] Thomas S. Kuhn, *The Structure of Scientific Revolutions*, 2nd ed. (The University of Chicago Press, 1970).
[65] European Commission, 'Inception Impact Assessment', p. 1.
[66] Inception Impact Assessment: Sustainable Corporate Governance 2020, p. 2.

pressure to depress non-executive wages and employees often do not benefit from shareholder payouts'.[67]

In the Ernst & Young study, which precedes the Commission's position, these dynamics are shown to have translated in several "drivers of short-termism":

'1. *Directors' duties and company's interest are interpreted narrowly and tend to favour the short-term maximisation of shareholder value;*
2. *Growing pressures from investors with a short-term horizon contribute to increasing the boards' focus on short-term financial returns to shareholders at the expense of long-term value creation;*
3. *Companies lack a strategic perspective over sustainability and current practices fail to effectively identify and manage relevant sustainability risks and impacts;*
4. *Board remuneration structures incentivise the focus on short-term shareholder value rather than long-term value creation for the company;*
5. *The current board composition does not fully support a shift towards sustainability;*
6. *Current corporate governance frameworks and practices do not sufficiently voice the long-term interests of stakeholders;*
7. *Enforcement of the directors' duty to act in the long-term interest of company is limited.'*[68]

The European Parliament concurred that even if company directors have the duty to act in the general interest of the company, this has so far too often been understood as the financial interests of shareholders.[69] This led both the European Parliament and the European Commission to conclude that what we need is a different kind of corporation. Society has created firms and markets that favour short-term interests, rather than long-term perspectives – even against companies' own best interests. Instead, as the European parliament suggests, '*companies should make*

---

[67] Inception Impact Assessment: Sustainable Corporate Governance 2020, p. 2.
[68] European Commission, 'Study on Directors' Duties and Sustainable Corporate Governance', p. 10.
[69] '*Company directors have the legal and statutory duty to act in the interest of their company; whereas this duty has been the subject of different interpretations in different jurisdictions and the interest of the company has often been equated with the financial interests of the shareholder; ... whereas a narrow interpretation of this duty with an excessive focus on short-term profit maximisation is detrimental to the company's long-term performance and sustainability, and hence the long-term interests of its shareholders*', European Parliament resolution of 17 December 2020 on sustainable corporate governance (2020/2137(INI)) www.europarl.europa.eu/doceo/document/TA-9-2020-0372_EN.html, last accessed 10 January 2024.

a more active contribution to sustainability as their long-term performance, resilience and even their survival may depend on the adequacy of their response to environmental and social matters'.[70]

Adopting this long-term horizon will require, according to the European Commission, '*encouraging businesses to frame decisions in terms of environmental (including climate, biodiversity), social, and human impact for the long-term, rather than on short-term gains*'.[71] Such responsible corporate behaviour cannot be driven, however, by '*[v]oluntary action* [that] *does not appear to have resulted in large scale improvement across sectors and, as a consequence, negative externalities from EU production and consumption are being observed both inside and outside EU*''.[72] It is both the impact of sustainability challenges on the company's long-term performance and the company's impact on the planet – double materiality – that should guide corporate behaviour.[73]

In order to get there, both the European Commission and the European Parliament in its 2021 position have proposed two sets of measures when it comes to 'sustainable corporate governance'. One set of measures, which are better at surviving pushback, are the due diligence measures. In line with a longer recent history of international (soft law) efforts to hold companies accountable for their supply chains, and several MSs regulating due diligence nationally, the EU had a responsibility to act in order to prevent distortions of the internal market. This time around, however, the due diligence was not meant to be only a voluntary commitment but be paired with administrative and civil liability (with the latter having a hard time currently, from the side of the Council).[74]

The other set of measures, which primarily tried to address some of the more systemic "drivers of short-termism" identified not least by the Ernst & Young study,[75] came under the heading of 'director's duties'.

---

[70] European Parliament resolution of 17 December 2020 on sustainable corporate governance, para. 18.
[71] European Commission, 'Inception Impact Assessment', p. 1.
[72] Corporate Sustainability Due Diligence Proposal 2022, p. 2.
[73] Proposal for a Directive 2021/0104 Amending Directive 2013/34/EU, Directive 2004/109/EC, Directive 2006/43/EC, and Regulation (EU) No. 537/2014, as regards corporate sustainability reporting.
[74] European Council, Position on the CSDDD Proposal, 2022/0051(COD) available at https://data.consilium.europa.eu/doc/document/ST-15024-2022-REV-1/en/pdf, last accessed 10 January 2024.
[75] The issue of short-termism comes up also in the European Banking Authority: 'Final EBA Report on Undue Short-Term Pressures from the Financial Sector', European Banking Authority (2019), www.eba.europa.eu/file/461440/down, last accessed 14 October 2022.

Alongside the articulation of the problem and the description of the corporation, it is these proposals that were placed under the most significant pressure – first from the RSB, and today being squeezed in the Council position.[76] The directors' duties included a whole package of issues, such as limiting the negative impact of remuneration incentives, the need for a serious integration of sustainability in business strategy, and a duty of care with regard to all stakeholders – that is, also workers, consumers, and communities at home. To put it in EP's own terms: *'whereas company directors have the legal and statutory duty to act in the interest of their company; whereas this duty has been the subject of different interpretations in different jurisdictions and the interest of the company has often been equated with the financial interests of the shareholder; whereas what is considered to be the interest of the company should also incorporate the interests of relevant stakeholders, including employees, and wider societal interests; whereas a narrow interpretation of this duty with an excessive focus on short-term profit maximisation is detrimental to the company's long-term performance and sustainability, and hence the long-term interests of its shareholders'.*[77]

This set of prescriptions that the Commission and the Parliament had in mind required a more significant departure from the neoliberal corporation, which was premised on the idea best formulated by Friedman, *'In a free-enterprise, private-property system, a corporate executive is an employee of the owners of the business. He has direct responsibility to his employers. That responsibility is to conduct the business in accordance with their desires, which generally will be to make as much money as possible while conforming to their basic rules of the society, both those embodied in law and those embodied in ethical custom'.*[78] But as the 'basic rules of the society' changed due to the pressures of globalisation, financialisation, and privatisation, the social norm of shareholder primacy became ever more onerous.

This is exactly what the European institutions thought was crucial to reverse – to expand the duties of care of the company directors to a range of 'social responsibility' obligations: to care for all its stakeholders, in value chains and at home, to care for the environment, in a scientifically credible way, and to implement serious monitoring as well as proper

---

[76] European Commission Regulatory Scrutiny Board, 'Opinion: Impact Assessment/Sustainable Corporate Governance' SEC(2022) 95; European Council, 'Position on the CSDDD Proposal'.

[77] European Parliament resolution of 17 December 2020 on sustainable corporate governance (2020/2137(INI)); Pascal Durand, 'Report on Sustainable Corporate Governance', European Parliament Report A9–0240/2020 (2020) (2020/2137(INI)), p. 7.

[78] Friedman, 'The Social Responsibility of Business Is to Increase Its Profits', p. 1.

mitigation strategies – under the (still very limited) threat of administrative and civil liability.[79]

Importantly, in terms of the legal imaginaries behind the proposal, even if (in continental Europe at least) the Commission recognised that the company law *stricto sensu*[80] has not ushered itself the "collective irresponsibility", it also realised that it needed law in order to engineer back the neoliberal transformation, as a change of discourse and the soft law measures relied upon until present were anything but successful.[81] Thus, the Commission argued that '*it will need to be established which issues would need to be laid down in legislation*',[82] announcing the return of legal strategies to repair corporate governance.

6.2.1 Wait a Bit – What Problems?

Immediately after publishing the inception impact assessment, which favoured a more serious intervention in corporate governance with hard company law rules,[83] a plethora of actors and voices came forward to challenge it. The industry, which had received relatively limited access to the Commission in the period of preparation, entered on a warpath. It mobilised all kinds of actors in support of its cause – including MSs and the RSB.[84] Several Nordic MSs, most notably Denmark (with its business associations very active on the issue), engaged in considerable "diplomacy" with a view to cut back on the Commission's ambitions.[85] In addition to this, many corporate governance and company law scholars organised academic events often critical of the proposals.[86]

---

[79] European Parliament resolution of 17 December 2020 on sustainable corporate governance.
[80] The core question here is whether the 'corporate governance codes', which have been strongly shaped by the shareholder primacy principles, are part of company law or not. But that discussion need not be taken up here.
[81] Corporate Sustainability Due Diligence Proposal 2022, p. 2.
[82] European Commission, 'Inception Impact Assessment', p. 4.
[83] Of course, the inception impact assessment also outlines 'no action', or 'self-regulation' as an option for dealing with the issue, but as with all impact assessments, the preference of the legislator is clearly noticeable in the articulation of the problem and constraints of action via market instruments. Some MSs (notably Denmark), industry, and the RSB all notice the same.
[84] Reference to Laura Wolters' group and evidence on many meetings with the industry. See here https://?responsiblebusinessconduct?.eu/wp/.
[85] Haar et al., 'Inside Job'.
[86] For example, at the 2022 Global Corporate Governance Colloquium in Oxford, June 2022 <https://ecgi.global/content/2022-global-corporate-governance-colloquium-gcgc>, and in Marvyn King et al., *Call to Action on Sustainable Corporate Governance* (Harvard Law School

But it is rather telling that the most consequential pushback against changing imaginaries of prosperity behind the sustainable corporate governance came, at least initially, from the RSB. Unsurprisingly, industry focused its efforts there – ultimately gaining the access it wanted and discussing the substance of the Commission's inception impact assessment with the RSB (arguably in violation of its own rules[87]).

The RSB has rejected the Commission proposal twice: first the inception impact assessment and then the full impact assessment. In its first opinion, the RSB argued that the Commission's inception impact assessment set out '*a very broad and intangible problem*' and did too little to show the existence of that same problem, since it was not '*substantiated with clear evidence that EU businesses do not sufficiently address sustainability*'.[88] Yet, it was not an issue of the *quantity* of information provided by the Commission. Even the ninety-seven-page impact assessment, put together by the Commission knowing the stakes and trying to make their most substantiated case, did not as much as introduce an element of hesitation in the second opinion of the RSB, who claimed the '*problem description remains vague and does not demonstrate the scale and likely evolution of the problems the initiative aims to tackle does not provide convincing evidence that EU businesses, in particular SMEs, do not already sufficiently reflect sustainability aspects or do not have sufficient incentives to do so*'.[89]

The RSB could build upon a number of academic contributions that have been submitted to the consultations that followed the publication of the inception impact assessment. While many academics contributed, to illustrate the academic contestation I will single out in this chapter the contributions by two larger groups of scholars that are likely to have had a bigger impact, that is the ECGI group of corporate governance

---

Forum on Corporate Governance, 2021) https://corpgov.law.harvard.edu/2021/03/09/call-to-action-on-sustainable-corporate-governance/.

[87] European Parliament Working Group on Responsible Business Conduct 'MEPS for Responsible Business Conduct' (RBC), 'MEPS Call For Transparency and Information Over the Independence Of the Commission's Regulatory Scrutiny Board' (2021), https://?responsiblebusinessconduct?.eu/wp/2021/12/15/meps-call-for-transparency-and-information-over-the-independence-of-the-commissions-regulatory-scrutiny-board/, last accessed 11 January 2024.

[88] European Commission Regulatory Scrutiny Board, 'Opinion: Impact Assessment/ Sustainable Corporate Governance', Ares(2021)3065513, pp. 1 and 2.

[89] European Commission Regulatory Scrutiny Board, 'Opinion: Impact Assessment/ Sustainable Corporate Governance' SEC(2022) 95, p. 1. All emphases in the quotes in this chapter were added by the author of this book

scholars (counting eighty-six people) and the (self-appointed group) of Nordic professors (counting twenty-seven people).

Both these groups have made public statements against the problem definition that the Commission puts forth. In a long piece article submitted to the consultation by the Nordic professors, it is suggested that the Ernst & Young study (and thus also the Commission's inception impact assessment) *'exaggerates the problem of climate change and neglects the many other, equally serious, problems facing both company directors and EU legislators in their obligations to their respective constituencies'*.[90] The Nordic professors advise the Commission to place more trust in the efforts businesses are already making, insofar as *'the regulatory options recommended by the Study would seriously harm European business and prevent it from continuing to contribute to the sustainable growth and prosperity that the Union needs to fulfil its overall policies'*.[91] The same group of Nordic professors also suggest that there was no need to change corporate law to address the non-existent problem: *'Just as the company interest includes a multitude of stakeholders so does the concept of directors' duties comprise the same multitude and **current company law needs not change to reflect this**'*.[92]

The bigger ESGI group, although more sympathetic to the environmental urgency, also did not share the enthusiasm for the company law reform and rather suggested that the *'regulation should instead focus on correcting market failure, through taxing externalities, curbing monopoly power and improving information disclosure'*.[93] In truth, for those who have followed the discussion in this field, such statements may sound a bit like a broken record. Information provision, taxation, and competition law – measures favoured in law and economics scholarship – have been shown as either ineffective (information provision),[94] insufficient, or impracticable in the context of globalisation (taxation),[95] or simply

---

[90] Nordic Company Law Scholars, 'Response to the Study on Directors' Duties and Sustainable Corporate Governance' LSN Research Paper Series No. 20–12, p. 2.
[91] Ibid.   [92] Ibid.
[93] Alex Edmans, Luca Enriques, Jesse Fried, Mark Roe, and Steen Thomsen, 'Call for Reflection on Sustainable Corporate Governance' (2021), https://ecgi.global/news/call-reflection-sustainable-corporate-governance, last accessed 11 January 2024. This call for reflection was based on the ECGI policy workshop on sustainable corporate governance, and it was supported by eighty-seven corporate governance scholars.
[94] Corporate Sustainability Due Diligence Proposal 2022, p. 2.
[95] Tax Justice Network, '"Tax us if you can" Briefing Paper', (2005), www.taxjustice.net/cms/upload/pdf/tuiyc_-_eng_-_web_file.pdf, last accessed 11 January 2024.

inapplicable to the issues of concern (competition law came to endorse monopoly power).[96]

6.2.2 Wait a Bit – What Solutions?

6.2.2.1 How Capable Are Directors?

Perhaps the strongest pushback was mounted against the Commission's idea to introduce changes regarding director's duties. The Council expressed 'the strong concerns expressed by Member States that considered Article 25 to be an inappropriate interference with national provisions regarding directors' duty of care, and potentially undermining directors' duty to act in the best interest of the company'.[97] On what intellectual basis does the Council, and RSB before it, base their concerns about placing a more demanding set of duties and responsibilities on the directors?

The positions of both groups of the abovementioned scholars provide a hint. Thus, the group of Nordic professors write in their position paper: 'Strangely, the [Commission's] Study appears to believe that directors as opposed to shareholders have an incentive to act in the long-term interest of the company and would do so if not restrained by shareholders [...]. rude experience that directors are in fact not long-term oriented, but motivated by short-time enrichment and if left unsupervised prone to **divert company funds to their own pockets or use them for self-aggrandising projects like unnecessary investments and empire-building takeovers**'.[98] The ECGI group adds that placing more duties on the managers would lead to an even 'bigger danger for stakeholder value [which] is not shareholder capitalism but **"managerial capitalism,"** where unaccountable managers shrink the pie for both shareholders and stakeholders'.[99]

One may ask, why now this demonisation and infantilisation of directors? Fifty years ago, Milton Friedman was in no way concerned that corporate executives were *not able* to take the interests of workers, the environment, or inflationary pressures into account, but rather that they have done so too *eagerly* – and at the *expense* of the shareholders. That is, Friedman was concerned that the social responsibility of directors

---

[96] Michelle Meagher, *Competition Is Killing Us: How Big Business Is Harming Our Society and Planet-and What to Do about It* (Penguin UK, 2020).

[97] European Council, Proposal for a Directive of the European Parliament and of the Council on Corporate Sustainability Due Diligence and Amending Directive (EU) 2019/1937 – General Approach, ST 15024 2022 REV 1, p. 10.

[98] Nordic Company Law Scholars, 'Response to the Study on Directors' Duties and Sustainable Corporate Governance', p. 12.

[99] Edmans et al., 'Call for Reflection on Sustainable Corporate Governance', section 3.

amounted to not acting "in the interest of their employers"[100] [ie. shareholders] and it meant "spending" someone else's [ie. shareholders'] money.[101]

After many years of discussing how to align the agency of managers to that of shareholders, however, this corporate governance constituency became distrustful not only of the willingness but also the capacity of corporate leaders to act responsibly. But if the directors so eagerly assumed the obligation to balance very complex sets of interests in the past – much to the dismay of Friedman – why could they not do it today? All the more so given that their personal capacities must have grown multiple times – judging by the fact that they earn some ten to fifteen times more than their colleagues in the 1960s and 1970s.[102]

The obvious irony here is that the preoccupation of corporate scholarship with constraining the power of managers meant that managers grew considerably richer, while their responsibilities grew thinner. The pay gap between managers and workers increased more than tenfold over the past forty years[103] – with huge bumps usually justified with a "war for talent" type of argument,[104] or with the lack of willingness to take the job without large pay.[105] And yet, these highly paid talented people were considered as not being capable of caring for more than one thing only (i.e. profit) and had to be accountable only to one group of stakeholders (i.e. shareholders). This development is perhaps one of the most notable shifts that has taken place from the time that Friedman wrote his famous article.

6.2.2.2 The Conflicting Imaginaries of Prosperity

To the credit of the abovementioned critical groups of participants in the public consultations, they have not missed the fact that 'sustainable corporate governance' starts from a very different imaginary of political economy, a very different imaginary of prosperity. Not unsimilar to Friedman decades ago, this is how Nordic professors present the

---

[100] Friedman, 'The Social Responsibility of Business Is to Increase Its Profits', p. 2.
[101] Ibid.   [102] Piketty, *Capital in the Twenty-First Century*.
[103] James Suzman, *Work: A History of How We Spend Our Time* (Bloomsbury Publishing, 2020).
[104] Kibum Kwon and Soebin Jang, 'There Is No Good War for Talent: A Critical Review of the Literature on Talent Management', *Employee Relations: The International Journal* 44, no. 1 (2021): 94–120.
[105] Rutger Betlem, Mathijs Rotteveel, and Pieter Couwenbergh, 'Opvolging bij banken steeds groter problem', FD (2022), https://fd.nl/financiele-markten/1444588/opvolging-bij-banken-steeds-groter-probleem, last accessed 11 January 2024.

Commission's synthesis: '*We are surprised of the apparent hostility to shareholders as a group and the idea that to serve shareholders' interest is to increase inequality and somehow unfairly benefit the ultra-rich "1 per cent." It is sentiments that we mostly associate with anti-market ideologies that are difficult to reconcile with the framework of a **free market** economy, **private** ownership rights and **innovation** and **progress** through **competition** upon which the European Union is based*'[106] [emphasis added].

The 'framework' (or imaginary) of prosperity they allude to is premised on a different synthesis of political economy, which places the 'free market economy', 'private property', and 'competition' in the driving seat of 'innovation' and 'progress'. Nordic professors thus outline (succinctly and effectively) the imaginary of neoliberal imaginary of prosperity and corporation that has become hegemonic, across the political spectrum and society,[107] from the 1990s.

The Commission's proposal presents a different imaginary of prosperity and corporation, which sees social responsibility rather than market forces as the drivers of prosperity, while resting on a different relationship between public and private, political and economic, individual and collective. The Commission's imaginary resembles in part the post-WWII imaginary of corporation that Friedman identified as 'collectivist': '*the doctrine of "social responsibility" taken seriously would (...) not differ in philosophy from the most explicitly collective doctrine. It differs only by professing to believe that collectivist ends can be attained without collectivist means*'.[108] The new synthesis adds, however, at least two new irritants – the allegedly exaggerated concern with climate, and (if too carefully) the concern with the prosperity of people abroad. '*This Directive aims to ensure that companies active in the internal market contribute to sustainable development and the sustainability transition of economies and societies by respecting human rights and the environment, through the identification, prevention and mitigation, bringing to an end remediation and minimisation, and where necessary, prioritisation, of potential or actual adverse human rights and environmental impacts connected with companies' own operations, subsidiaries and value chains, and ensuring that those affected by a failure to respect this duty have access to justice and legal remedies*'.[109]

---

[106] Nordic Company Law Scholars, 'Response to the Study on Directors', p. 15.
[107] Martin Gelter, 'EU Company Law Harmonization between Convergence and Varieties of Capitalism', ECGI, 2017.
[108] Friedman, 'The Social Responsibility of Business Is to Increase Its Profits', p. 6.
[109] European Parliament, Amendments adopted by the European Parliament on 1 June 2023 on the proposal for a directive of the European Parliament and of the

6.3 Paradigm Shift in Knowledge and Expertise

The new imaginary of prosperity will often be preceded by the observation of problems and developments that usually (but not always[110]) translate into the production of academic knowledge aiming to systematise and provide answers to the problems uncovered. This has also been the case for the sustainable corporate governance file, as we have learnt through the backdoor. Namely, many of the criticisms levelled at the Commission for its reassessment of the complex problem seemed to stem from the knowledge used in the preparation of the Ernst & Young report, as well as consequent Commission and Parliament positions.

The Ernst & Young study (serving as the basis for the Commission's initial impact assessment, the Parliament's recommendation, and the final proposal of the Directive) seems to draw primarily on green finance and corporate (law) scholarship regarding business and human rights on the one hand and the climate and environment on the other. Such a choice is not immediately a surprising one. Given the subject matter of the report, the Ernst & Young consultants reached out to what dealt with the questions they were tasked to explore. However, the considerable outcry in the wake of the inception impact report made clear that there was far more to the story.[111]

Scholars who usually claim ownership of the field of 'company law' and 'corporate governance' are company law scholars, law and economics scholars, and law and finance scholars. These fields are white and male dominated,[112] something that any participant in a conference who

---

Council on Corporate Sustainability Due Diligence, www.europarl.europa.eu/doceo/document/TA-9-2023-0209_EN.html, last accessed 11 January 2023, Recital 14.

[110] Marija Bartl, 'Contesting Austerity: On the Limits of EU Knowledge Governance', *Journal of Law and Society* 44, no. 1 (3 February 2017): 150–68.

[111] One can find a plethora of very critical contributions on the Oxford Business Law Blog and in the *Harvard Business Law Review*; see Mark Roe, Holger Spamann, Jesse Fried, and Charles Wang, 'The European Commission's Sustainable Corporate Governance Report: A Critique', Harvard Business School, Working Paper 21-056 (2020), www.hbs.edu/ris/Publication%20Files/21-056_51410b50-5488-477a-9aa3-df8f81138e53.pdf, last accessed 14 January 2024; Marcello Bianchi, Mateja Milič, 'EC Corporate Governance Initiative Series: "European Companies are Short-Term Oriented: The Unconvincing Analysis and Conclusions of the Ernst & Young Study,"' Oxford Business Law Blog (2020), https://blogs.law.ox.ac.uk/business-law-blog/blog/2020/10/ec-corporate-governance-initiative-series-european-companies-are, last accessed 14 January 2024.

[112] For instance, if one looks at the list of scholars who represent themselves as the 'Nordic Professors of Company Law', the group is comprised of twenty (out of twenty-one) male academics. But that will be a perception of everyone who has ever attended the

does not fit the suit would realise upon entering the room. These fields also often include a large proportion of practising corporate lawyers. Now, given that these fields have led the way on the study of problems raised by the neoliberal corporation – shareholder primacy, shareholder activism, and agency problems (at times with the ESG flavour)[113] – the knowledge they produced failed to provide an obvious source that a consultancy firm such as Ernst & Young would look to when trying to identify the "root causes" of corporate short-termism.[114]

The omission of this mainstream knowledge precipitated an offence, best illustrated by the group of Nordic company law scholars who, when responding to the Commission's (and Ernst & Young's) claim that the position in the report presents the mainstream in the field of corporate law and sustainability, say: 'In legal discourse, silence is not acquiescence, but more likely reflects genuine disinterest'.[115] By implication, these company lawyers admit that they were neither interested in the topics that were taken as relevant by Ernst & Young (climate or human rights) nor were they bothering to engage with scholars dealing with these matters.

However, while the owners of the corporate governance field remained concerned with perfecting the alignment between shareholders' and managers' interests, something shifted. Much to their surprise. When the European Commission came to explore how corporate law and governance relate to some of the problems it increasingly identified – from the perspective of sustainability (as articulated by natural and social sciences)[116] and inequality (as articulated by an ever-growing

---

conferences organised in this field. Nordic Company Law Scholars, 'Response to the Study on Directors'.

[113] Today, with a growing concern for impending environmental catastrophe, this type of scholarship is still strongly shareholders/investors focused, exploring often whether and how shareholders and investors can bring about more environmentally friendly behaviour. The most prominent venue for this kind of scholarship is www.ecgi.global/.

[114] While most corporate scholars claim the shareholder perspective to be a long-term orientation, the problem is that this characteristic does not really convince in contemporary financial markets and globalised economy. See Robé, *Property, Power and Politics*.

[115] Nordic Company Law Scholars, 'Response to the Study on Directors', p. 3.

[116] See, for instance, B. Sjåfjell and C. Bruner (eds.), *Cambridge Handbook on Corporate Law, Corporate Governance and Sustainability* (Cambridge University Press, 2019). For two important collective proposals for the transformation of corporate governance, see Johnston, J. Veldman et al., 'Corporate Governance for Sustainability' (2020), available at https://papers.ssrn.com/sol3/papers.cfm?abstract_id=3502101, last accessed 14 January 2024; Beate Sjåfjell, Jukka Mähönen, Tonia Novitz, Clair Gammage, and Hanna Ahlström, 'Securing the Future of European Business: SMART Reform

body of economic, social, and legal sciences) – the types of scholarship produced by the aforementioned corporate law groups appeared irrelevant. In a world where corporations produce 50 per cent of CO_2 emissions and inequality has become rampant (much to the advantage of large shareholders and managers), aligning the interests of managers and shareholders may seem somewhat redundant.

Fortunately for this group of scholars, they still found a sympathetic ear in the RSB, which also based its extraordinary double rejection on the fact that it did not recognise either the problems or the solutions as discussed earlier and instead advised that the *'report should be revised to present the evidence in a more balanced and neutral way'*.[117] Or, in the second round, that *'the report should present more systematically the views of different stakeholder categories. It should find a better balance between supportive and critical views expressed'*.[118]

The famous philosopher of science Thomas Kuhn argued decades ago that it is the accumulation of anomalies and contradictions that will drive "normal science" – such as that of mainstream corporate (law and finance) scholarship today – increasingly out of its dominant position.[119] The inability of traditional corporate governance scholarship to provide answers to the problems plaguing the corporate world leaves this scholarship, and by extension the RSB, only with the option of interpreting away any problems. But that gets one only so far.

6.4 The Contours of New Imaginary of Prosperity

What kinds of different understandings of political economy are being instituted via the EU's attempts to change what corporation stands for? In whatever final form the CSDDD will take effect, it will present important discursive and normative building blocks for the new imaginary of prosperity – if and when it is instituted. In what follows, I will first outline shifts that have taken place thus far and then turn to discuss some rather conspicuous omissions.

Proposals', University of Oslo Faculty of Law Legal Studies Research Paper Series No. 2020–11 (2020), https://ssrn.com/abstract=3595048, last accessed 14 January 2024.
[117] European Commission Regulatory Scrutiny Board, 'Opinion: Impact Assessment/ Sustainable Corporate Governance', Ares(2021)3065513, p. 3.
[118] European Commission Regulatory Scrutiny Board, 'Opinion: Impact Assessment/ Sustainable Corporate Governance' SEC(2022) 95, p. 5.
[119] Kuhn, *The Structure of Scientific Revolutions*.

To start, the European Commission has produced the CSDDD proposal on the basis of a very different understanding of how the economy, law, politics, government, society, and nature work and ought to work together, in order to bring us into a more prosperous future. The Nordic academics accurately point to this paradigmatic shift, by suggesting that the Commission's proposal departs from the neoliberal understandings of '*free market economy, private ownership rights and innovation and progress through competition*'[120] that have been prevalent in the EU until the present. Rather, the Commission (and European Parliament) reappraise the problems economies and societies face today– social and environmental – and propose a different mix of solutions that move beyond reliance on markets and shareholders alone, and suggest that law and government have a more important role to play.

Starting with legal imaginaries, in the CSDDD proposal, law is not a laggard behind technology or business. Rather, it is seen as *constitutive* of social and economic relations, also in its absence (!), and thus at the same time capable of reshaping those relations. The room for manoeuvre that company law leaves today for private parties to fill – for instance, by social norms of shareholder value – should be supplanted by public norms that embrace more constructive pursuits. Soft law, which has been so popular in the neoliberal imaginary of prosperity, is out of the picture – not only did it not work (like in the case of the non-financial reporting directive)[121] but it also makes far less sense to leave the questions of collective good entirely to the decisions of private actors.

What fundamentally distinguishes the contemplated imaginary of prosperity from both the neoliberal imaginary of prosperity and the welfare state imaginary of shared prosperity is the rearticulation of the relationship between nature and society. If the neoliberal imaginary of prosperity did not see either nature (at all) or society (viewing it only as a collection of individuals), the welfare state imaginary of shared prosperity mainly linked questions of nature to that of precaution.[122] The 'sustainable corporate governance', inspired by the EGD, aims to reshape society in a much more nature-centric way. It is thus no surprise that 'sustainable corporate governance' placed sustainability and the

---

[120] Nordic Company Law Scholars, 'Response to the Study on Directors', p. 15.
[121] Directive (EU) 2022/2464 on corporate sustainability reporting, Explanatory Memorandum.
[122] See Timothy O'Riordan and James Cameron, 'The History and Contemporary Significance of the Precautionary Principle', in *Interpreting the Precautionary Principle* (Routledge, 1994), p. 12.

6.4 THE CONTOURS OF NEW IMAGINARY OF PROSPERITY

directors' duties of care at the centre.[123] The final trimming down of the ambition, prompted by commentary that climate and nature played too dominant a role,[124] only underscores this ambition.

When it comes to the conception of the "corporate self", the set of concerns, interests, and duties that the corporation embraces are to *expand* (via legal intervention) beyond the narrow, profit-driven neoliberal corporate self. Companies in this new imaginary are certainly not there to further "shareholder value" alone, and shareholders themselves are not seen as the only, or the best, "accountability mechanism" for the corporation. Instead, it is clear to lawmakers that the ethics of corporate conduct needs to change. Again, it is responsible directors that Friedman so abhorred, and current corporate scholars' mistrust, that need to be committed by *hard law* to social responsibility. Currently, both their socialisation[125] and their financial incentives[126] work against responsible conduct. The new rules should expand the gaze of directors towards all stakeholders as well as a bigger chunk of the supply chain.

Profit (which has come to mean "shareholder value"), celebrated first by Friedman and later by much corporate law scholarship for its relative "clarity"[127] and "precision" in directing directors action,[128] cannot be the main guiding star for managerial conduct. If anything, the shareholder perspective must be paired with 'stakeholder' perspectives,[129] which in turn need to account for our interdependence with nature – a complex ecosystem that cannot be controlled, but instead approached with respect, precaution, and care.

Finally, the exasperation of EU institutions with waiting for voluntary action by corporations has led to a shift in enforcement strategies. In this proposal, we see a growing role for the administrative enforcement that, next to courts, must ensure that companies are socially responsible. And while civil liability has been trimmed down due to pressures exerted

---

[123] See the summary at the website of the European Commission, at https://ec.europa.eu/info/law/better-regulation/have-your-say/initiatives/12548-Sustainable-corporate-governance_en.
[124] Nordic Company Law Scholars, 'Response to the Study on Directors', p. 5.
[125] Winter, 'Dehumanisation of the Large Corporation'.
[126] Beate Sjåfjell, 'Redefining the Corporation for a Sustainable New Economy', *Journal of Law and Society* 45, no. 1 (2018): 29–45.
[127] Friedman, 'The Social Responsibility of Business Is to Increase Its Profits', p. 1.
[128] Ibid.
[129] Stakeholders' involvement was maintained in the Proposal in a very limited fashion, as the obligation to consult with regard to the prevention and mitigation plans 'where relevant' (Corporate Sustainability Due Diligence Proposal 2022, arts. 7 and 8).

upon the Proposal, administrative liability has remained mostly untouched.

This is certainly not to say that this is the most ambitious way of socialising the corporation – either in the Commission's, Parliament's, or the Council's version. Many NGOs have argued that the proposal is not ambitious enough in terms of scope (i.e. which companies are subject to due diligence rules), the breadth of directors' duties, the engagement with the distribution of value in the economy, the rights of workers, the participation of other stakeholders in governance, etc.[130]

My more specific concern is that the current proposal fails to engage with the 'fundamentals' of corporate activity – be it ownership or governance, power or profit. This is particularly problematic because this proposal aims to tackle the grossly unfair "terms of trade" between Europe and "developing' countries",[131] which gets expressed in HR violations, exploitation, and tax evasion.[132] The attempt to solve the problems of global maldistribution by increasing the administrative capacity of MNCs can be seen as optimistic (at best) and cynical (at worst). While the proposal makes an identifiable shift on what corporation is and ought to be, the response to the question of whether this is going far enough, quickly enough, remains doubtful.

6.5 Going Beyond: *Pluralising Economy, Transforming Imaginaries*

If transforming the "mainstream" business is difficult to achieve, is there perhaps an alternative way forward that would instead work *around* mainstream business? In this section, I want to argue that not only is there such an alternative path, but that it is also an obvious choice for the EU institutions to take up, as it has become clear in various policy fields that there is such a "low hanging fruit" for achieving various EU objectives.

One way to make the economy "work for people" is to facilitate and support those businesses that today (want to) operate on the basis of different principles than represented by the mainstream model. Such

---

[130] Robé, *Property, Power and Politics*.
[131] Daniela Caruso, 'Non-Parties: The Negative Externalities of Regional Trade Agreements in a Private Law Perspective', *Harvard International Law Journal* 59 (2018): 389.
[132] Robé, *Property, Power and Politics*.

6.5 GOING BEYOND: PLURALISING ECONOMY

enterprises exist, and have existed for a long time,[133] and they are recognised in the EU under a broader term of 'social economy'. These organisations share a couple of traits. First, they have social purpose, that is, they are committed to *'the primacy of people as well as social and/or environmental purpose over profit'*.[134] Second, when they make a surplus, they do not extract it as profit. Rather, they *'reinvest most of the profits and surpluses to carry out activities in the ("collective interest") or ("general interest")'*. Finally, they have and embrace more *'democratic and/or participatory governance'*.[135]

These social economy organisations are social or non-extractive by design. Not being motivated by the extraction of profits, they have more space to care both for people and the planet, inside and outside of the enterprise. Such organisations usually have numerous positive impacts: not only do they *not* create social, labour, and environmental harm in order to increase their profits, but – as the European Commission itself underscores – they have positive effects on providing resilience in crises[136] while further increasing social inclusion, creating social innovations as well as innovations in circularity, and caring for nature.[137] They are particularly important today, when the benefits of economic cooperation accrue to the lucky few – either because of their geographical location, age, or their social status – while the harms of economic activity are distributed broadly.[138]

Social economy entities are often highly innovative, not only on the technological but also on the social and legal plain. Just consider the degree of social and legal innovations within the so-called Miethausersyndikat in Germany. This cooperative housing network ensures that people on all budgets can live in affordable (cooperative rentals), sustainable (they build with sustainable technologies), and inclusive (they ensure that residents are mixes of various groups) housing, developing new social and legal designs in order to guarantee the continuous decommodification of these properties, while further investing in building more non-extractive housing projects, to house more people.[139]

---

[133] As (social) cooperatives, steward owned (foundation or association owned) enteprises and social enterprises more narrowly understood.
[134] European Commission, Building an economy that works for people: an action plan for the social economy, COM(2021) 778 final, p. 5.
[135] Social Economy Action Plan 2021, p. 3.   [136] Social Economy Action Plan 2021, p. 9.
[137] Social Economy Action Plan 2021, p. 10.   [138] Piketty, *Capital and Ideology*.
[139] David Bollier and Silke Helfrich, *Free, Fair, and Alive: The Insurgent Power of the Commons* (New Society Publishers, 2019).

The most encouraging news is that we are not only talking about the fringes when we talk about social economy in Europe. According to the European Commission, 'there are 2.8 million social economy enterprises, representing 10% of all businesses in the EU. Almost 13.6 million people – about 6.2% of the EU's employees – work for social economy enterprises'.[140] And many more people engage in voluntary work in social economy. Social economy organisations are often not legally and publicly seen and recognised, but in countries where they have received some public support, such as in Italy, they present a serious economic force.[141]

What is rather surprising is that despite the fact that the Commission clearly recognises the vast benefits of social economy in providing resilience in the face of crises, inclusion, innovation, etc., the EU institutions have shown very little "public leadership" to promote social economy. In fact, the EU has been developing 'action plans' for social economy for more than a decade, but not much actual support has come from those efforts.[142] So why not take a logical step and provide public support to social economy – just as we are providing it today to clean technologies?

6.5.1 Mainstreaming Non-extractive Organisations

What would it take to provide public support for social economy? I want to argue here for using the tools of industrial policy to support social economy. This would certainly not be an exceptional way of supporting a certain sector of the economy – as we have seen some of those tools in Chapter 5, with regard to, most recently, clean technology. In order to make it easier and more attractive for emerging and existing organisations to become social organisations, many facilitations can and should be proposed:[143]

---

[140] See Commission's website, https://single-market-economy.ec.europa.eu/sectors/proximity-and-social-economy/social-economy-eu_en.
[141] Antonio Fici, 'The New Italian Code of the Third Sector. Essence and Principles of a Historic Legislative Reform', in *The Law of Third Sector Organizations in Europe*, ed. Fici (Springer Nature Switzerland, 2023), 115–39.
[142] See Commission's website https://single-market-economy.ec.europa.eu/sectors/proximity-and-social-economy/social-economy-eu_en.
[143] These proposals build on the extensive empirical research within the framework ERC N-EXTLAW project (no. 852990), which mapped various legal and non-legal obstacles that social economy enterprises face. The research is on file with the author; it will be made available as country reports at the end of project.

(A) Giving legal recognition to social economy entities. Social economy organisations that respect the principles mentioned earlier cannot be distinguished from mainstream enterprises in many of the EU MSs. Nor can they easily find a legal form that would foster their social purpose. Thus, Europe and its MSs should in the first instance provide a recognisable legal form, or distinguishable public label, and thus both increase recognition while lowering the costs of setting up and running this type of organisation.

(B) Another traditional way of supporting a sector would be to provide social economy organisations with privileged access to public procurement. Giving such privileged access to social economy organisations would also help the EU MSs to fulfil the environmental and social aspirations that they have within the framework of procurement policy, while at the same time help social economy to become more useful to European economy.

(C) One could also consider giving social economy organisations various subsidies, guarantees, tax benefits, and rebates – as we have just seen in the industrial policy chapter in relation to clean technologies. Some countries already do this (such as Italy and Germany), but this should ideally become a rule across Europe.

(D) Importantly, it is crucial to ease the administrative burden on social economy enterprises. Given that many administrative requirements today are intended for mainstream economy, they may be at times less necessary, or necessary in a modified form, for social economy organisations. Just like we have seen before, we need to create 'one-stop-shops', national agencies for social economy that would not only promote social economy, but also help social economy organisations fulfil, or eventually dispose of, administrative requirements that serve no purpose in relation to their operation.

(E) Finally, ensuring effective public and private financing for social economy is fundamental. As social economy organisations need small-scale financing, they are usually commercially uninteresting. Alternatively, they are seen by banks as too risky, given that they are not oriented to profit extraction. They are also commercially uninteresting to investors, including impact investors, who still expect high returns. In order to foster truly socially responsible economy, the governments have to play a much more prominent role – and like in the case of the Net Zero Industry Act – provide loans and guarantees, in exchange for social economy delivering various necessary products and services, etc. Thus, not only a Hydrogen Bank, but a Social Economy Bank, is what Europe needs today.

6.5.2 Transforming Imaginaries

There are several ways in which social economy can help pluralise the way we think about, and do, economy. First, and the most obvious one, is that the proliferation of organisations with different motivations and ways of operating would not only have positive environmental and social impacts, as the Commission underscores at present, but would also provide a different way of thinking about economic activity along with the people that populate it. Social economy enterprises show a different face of the "corporate self", demonstrating that narrow self-interest is not the only reason why people want to engage in entrepreneurship, and in turn, whatever gains entrepreneurship brings, it is not dependent on oversized profit. Economic activity is possible and also beneficial on the basis of more caring and less extractive relations with both human and non-human nature.

Second, as the European Commission itself suggests, *'Social economy business models can influence and create spill-overs to mainstream business. A growing number of mainstream businesses are moving closer to social economy goals. For example, "benefit corporations" and "impact enterprises" incorporate sustainable ambitions in their missions, while other enterprises are adopting ad hoc measures to improve transparency and engage more actively with communities. This and the gradual incorporation of environmental, social and corporate governance (ESG) criteria in the governance of mainstream businesses and the investment policies of financial institutions and investment funds, are creating new opportunities for cooperation and cross-fertilization as well as access to new markets. The Commission will also reinforce the interactions between social economy entities and mainstream businesses by promoting best practices such as in the field of social intrapreneurship'*.[144]

Third, the visibility of social economy would also make new policy solutions available. Perhaps one of the most remarkable proposals on this front was Elisabeth Warren's 'Accountable Capitalism Act', which put forward how to make gigantic corporations more socially responsible. According to this proposal, every gigantic corporation (worth 1 billion or more) would have to take the form of a 'public benefit corporation' (the equivalent of 'social enterprise' in Europe). Such corporations would then be able to reinvest most of its surplus in advancing socially beneficial purposes, while submitting to being governed more democratically. The proposal did not make it through Congress, but

---

[144] Social Economy Action Plan 2021, p.13.

perhaps the conditions in the US were not ripe. With a stronger presence and visibility of social economy, this may change.[145]

The legislator could also actively create more spillovers and interactions between the 'social economy' file and the corporate governance file. First, one could consider expanding the purpose of business, going beyond 'due diligence' or even the more ambitious 'sustainable value creation' of the inception impact assessment, to making social and environmental impacts the central goals of business activity. Second, the Proposal could tackle profits, to make sure that for the most part they are reinvested in the company and its social purposes – instead of being privatised by those paying them out either to shareholders or management. Third, the corporate governance needs to go beyond identifying, mitigating, and remedying violations of human rights and aspire to greater democratic governance of companies, which by extension would influence how the benefits and costs of cooperation are both made and distributed.[146]

Last but not least, supporting social economy would have benefits also at the level of imagination, helping us to reimagine what corporation, and economy, can stand for. Economic activity is possible also on the basis of a more caring and less extractive attitude with regard to both human and non-human nature, helping to pluralise value-making practices and enabling private action to be both sustainable and distributive by design.[147]

---

[145] Colin Mayer, Leo E. Strine Jr., and Jaap Winter, 'Fifty Years Later, Milton Friedman's Shareholder Doctrine Is Dead', *Fortune* (13 September 2020), https://phyleon.com/wp-content/uploads/2021/03/Fortune-Milton-Friedmans-shareholder-doctrine-is-dead-on-its-50th-anniversary-20200913.pdf, last accessed 11 January 2024.

[146] These organisations include in the Netherlands, for instance, Buurtzorg (see www.buurtzorg.com), Triodos (see www.triodos.nl), or Odin (see www.odin.nl).

[147] Kate Raworth, *Doughnut Economics: Seven Ways to Think Like a Twenty-first-Century Economist* (Chelsea Green Publishing, 2017).

7 Conclusion

Towards a New Imaginary of Prosperity in the EU

Social integration in European countries seems increasingly dependent on the "we" that draws on tribal markers of identity. This type of belonging, in good times flatteringly called demos,[1] tends to resurface in its far uglier exclusionary versions when times get more difficult and resources more scarce – and at the same time, the horrors of previous wars are either forgotten or strategically rehashed. The European Union (EU),[2] however, still has a window to change these dynamics and reorient Europe towards prosperity. For Europe, this is both a task and a necessity: the EU cannot socially integrate but via the imaginaries of

---

[1] For a famous debate on the need for demos in Europe, see Dieter Grimm, 'Does Europe Need a Constitution?', *European Law Journal* 1, no. 3 (1995): 282–302; J. Habermas, 'Remarks on Dieter Grimm's "Does Europe Need a Constitution?"', *European Law Journal* 1, no. 3 (1995): 303–7.

[2] Who is the EU I discuss in this book? I focus on the European institutions: the European Commission, the European Parliament, the Councils of the EU, and occasionally the European Courts, the ECB, as well as more opaque institutions such as the 'Regulatory Scrutiny Board' or various standardisation bodies. Importantly, after more recent attempts of the EU institutions to move beyond privatised prosperity, I am somewhat more confident than before (Marija Bartl, 'Internal Market Rationality, Private Law and the Direction of the Union: Resuscitating the Market as the Object of the Political', *European Law Journal*, 21, no. 5 (15 January 2015), 572–98) in the responsiveness and democratic potential of these (surely imperfect) European institutions. At the same time, this is not to deny the contribution of the EU institutions to the very same problems that now threaten democratic institutions in Europe and beyond. Foremost, the incapacity of EU institutions to move beyond privatising prosperity post-2008, and instead doubling down on it, shows the EU's limits – its deficient institutional framework, the misalignment between the economic interests of its MSs or the strong influence of industry and capital on its policymaking. But especially in the face of irrelevance or dissolution, the EU is more likely to develop an imaginary of shared prosperity, showing us hereby also – as Habermas once hoped – what the post-national democracy and solidarity could look like.

prosperity, all the while it emerged with a task to prevent the excesses of tribalism.

As I have tried to show above, the EU is not limited to privatised prosperity, with consumerism and neo/ordoliberal imaginaries as the only credible route to a better future. Rather it can, and has already started to, develop a thicker understanding of *shared* prosperity. Such a conception of prosperity will have to be built around the recognition of interdependence, collective institutions, public values centred on sharing and inclusion, and effective problem-solving. It is, however, not a conflict-free imaginary. Rather, political mobilisation and conflict will centre around questions of political economy and its constitutive outsides,[3] as well as questions of economic (including market) structures and their distributive outcomes. The collectives that engage in such political struggles are also constructed around shared interests and values (such as farmers, workers, practically educated, social movements, millennials, etc.), rather than tribal markers.

The possibility of developing a conception of shared prosperity in the EU, as a supranational entity, may go against some received wisdom on the capacity of "interstate federation" to generate solidarity. Writing in the 1930s, Hayek, later followed by a number of other brilliant political economists,[4] suspected that an "interstate federation" would be mostly incapable of redistribution or effective regulation – making thus sure that all individuals and groups living in such a federation would be permanently consigned to privatised prosperity. But the history of the EU to date, I would argue, proves them at least partially wrong.

First, from its inception, the EU has had a mixed set of "Ideological commitments"[5], with different values and normative concerns dominating EU's policy and action in each subsequent imaginary of prosperity. For instance, in the field of consumer law and policy, discussed in Chapter 3, this played out as a focus on protection, empowering weaker parties and restructuring market dynamics and distributive outcomes in the welfare state imaginary of prosperity.[6] At a later point, the has EU embraced a

---

[3] I discuss those in Section 2.4.1.
[4] Friedrich A. Hayek, 'The Economic Conditions of Interstate Federalism'. *New Commonwealth Quarterly* 5 (1939): 131–49. For important revisions of this claim, for the context of the EU and global context, see Wolfgang Streeck, 'The Crises of Democratic Capitalism', *New Left Review* 71, no. 5 (2011): 5–29; Dani Rodrik, *The Globalization Paradox: Democracy and the Future of the World Economy* (W. W. Norton & Company, 2011).
[5] Clemens Kaupa, *The Pluralist Character of the European Economic Constitution* (Bloomsbury Publishing, 2016).
[6] See Chapter 3, Section 3.3.

neoliberal imaginary of prosperity, with its focus on market liberalisation and optimisation, making consumers the main vehicles of internal market building. Finally, privatised prosperity came to seem increasingly untenable in the face of the current challenges, with the EU institutions hesitantly moving beyond privatised prosperity and its focus on overconsumption.[7]

Second, after a prolonged period of privatisation, such as that which we have seen in recent decades (or in the pre-war period in Europe for that matter), discontent will mount. These pressures could either be channelled towards the transformation of political economy (as was the case in the US or Sweden in the 1930s), or they could be channelled to tribal collectivism (as was the case in Italy, Germany, and a significant part of Europe during the same period) and is threatening to be the case in Europe today.[8]

Third, given that the EU cannot easily produce a thick tribal identity, it can only respond to these collectivising pressures by transforming its imaginary of prosperity, by rearticulating the relations between the state, capital, labour, society and so forth. At the same time, by remaining within the ambit of prosperity, the EU would be (as its founders envisaged) an important force in preserving democratic institutions, knowledge governance and ultimately peace on the continent.

The success of the EU in delivering shared prosperity will require political courage, however. To start, the EU institutions cannot replace their aspirations of "knowledge governance" with fear or prejudice. There is no such thing as losing (or gaining) legitimacy with those embracing tribal logics, as there is no place for European integration worth its name in a tribal Europe. Furthermore, the EU institutions will have to be able to stand up for those pulling the short straw in the integration process – something they failed to do in 2008. In order to help institutionalise a new imaginary of shared prosperity, they will have to stand up, on the one hand, to the (well-resourced) interests of the capital, driven more by the unhealthy pressures of the financial markets than societal and long-term interests. And, on the other hand, they will also have to stand up to influential EU member states (MSs), especially when they push for paths that are clearly damaging to peripheral EU MSs (today, for instance, the new push for austerity that would

---

[7] See Chapter 2, Section 2.3.
[8] Daron Acemoglu and James A. Robinson, *Why Nations Fail: The Origins of Power, Prosperity, and Poverty* (Broadway Business, 2013), chapter 13.

decimate welfare and infrastructural investment in these countries).[9] Finally, the EU institutions will have to take rule of law issues more seriously and intervene in a timely manner. If democracy-undermining conduct continues to spread, soon there may not be sufficiently large majorities to safeguard democracy and rule of law – and we may see, again, loud minorities destroy the institutions that have at least partially delivered equality, justice, and prosperity in Europe.

7.1 Changing Background Assumptions

As this book shows, the EU has already taken the first steps towards a new imaginary of shared prosperity in Europe. Apart from macro measures such as the European Green Deal and the Next Generation Europe, the EU has made significant strides in redesigning microeconomic institutions, including consumption, technology, industrial development, and the corporation. These various policy and legislative measures, put in place over the past couple of years, depart from a different background understanding of how central elements of its political economy – law, politics, government, economy, nature and society – fit together, setting thus grounds to shift to an imaginary of political economy that would be better able to include various contemporary constitutive outsides (such as nature, care, inequality, or prosperity abroad).

In Table 7.1, I try to capture what these background shifts are. They concern the assumptions as to (a) ontology, that is, how the political economy (economy, law, politics, government, society and nature) fit together, (b) epistemology, that is what frameworks one should use in order to know and act on the political economy, and finally (c) different values, both public and intersubjective ones, that ought to ground our moral, cultural, and political intuitions. Importantly, this table captures background assumptions rather than any specific 'policy solutions' that aim to address the problems the EU faces. These assumptions *set ground* for a different way of thinking about problems and possible solutions. The actual transition to a new imaginary, however, requires more: implementing laws and policies that can deliver on material, social, and institutional fronts, while grounding a real hope in a prosperous

---

[9] Wester Van Gaal, '"A Prosperous New Year"? EU Heads for Austerity in 2024', *EU Observer* (2024), https://euobserver.com/green-economy/157852, last accessed 16 January 2024.

Table 7.1 Modern Social Imaginaries: Background Assumptions

	'HOW DOES THE WORLD FIT TOGETHER?'			'HOW SHOULD WE KNOW AND ACT ON THE WORLD'?			'WHAT VALUES GROUND THE FUTURE'?		
	Privatised Prosperity	Shared Prosperity	Tribal Imaginaries	Privatised Prosperity	Shared Prosperity	Tribal Imaginaries	Privatised Prosperity	Shared Prosperity	Tribal imaginaries
ECON	Self regulating 'Human-nature given'	'Human-made' institution	'Ours'	Positivist	Constructivist	Made by native people	Self-interest, growth	Collective action, sharing	Tribal interest
POL	Centrality of private/corporate actors	Centrality of collective & public institutions	'Deep state'/elites	Technocratic	Political + technocratic	Identity focused; we/they	Trust in private/corporate actors	Trust in democracy collective action	Protect identity, nativism
GOV	Smaller	Bigger	Serving own tribe	Outsourcing, neutral arbiter	Capable, deciding, redistributing	Distinguishing/discriminating	Service provider	Responsible	Choosing sides
LAW	Private Autonomy, Self regulation	Hard law, Liability	Disregard for the Rule of Law	Exogenous, 'add on' to social processes	Endogenous Constitutive Transformative	Elitist judges, the enemy of people	Facilitative rather than interventionist	Intervenes, shapes, transforms	Keeping out
NATURE	Resources	Ecosystem, complex	Traditional lands	Technological fixes	Uncertainty and risks	Adaptation	Efficient use	Care	Anti-environmentalism
SOCIETY	Only individuals, no society	Pluralist and inclusive society	Traditionalism, nativism	Aggregation of preferences	Social norms, values, trust, justice	Community needs, hierarchies	We don't owe to others, inclusive	We owe to others, inclusive	We owe only to the ingroup, exclusive
SELF/SUBJECT	Thin subjects	Thick subjects, complex	Reduced to a particular identity marker	Narrowing of "Self" and self-interest	Expanding of "Self" Interest	Group interest, the 'real' people	Competitive, responsible	Cooperative	Soldier, tribal identification

future. On that front, the new imaginary of prosperity is only in its infancy.

The caveat is that the table itself presents 'ideal' types of social imaginaries, with respect to which the shift in the EU at present may still be incomplete. As it concerns the imaginaries of prosperity, the ideal types are distilled from the empirical work behind this book, including the previous transformation of the welfare state imaginary of prosperity to the neoliberal one, as well as the slow change of the neoliberal imaginary to the present more amorphous imaginary, as read in the light of the longer history of modernity. I articulate the tribal imaginaries, in contrast, on the basis of the secondary literature (dealing with contemporary and historical matters) only, without studying them empirically. The reason is that in the context of the fields I study, I have not (and likely could not have) found them expressed in any discernible form.

On the basis of the four case studies, I submit that the EU has made at least partial shifts in all aspects of political economy that I have examined. The EU has increasingly started to recognise that the (internal) market is a gullible institution, rather than a natural self-regulating system, which thus needs more than just facilitation (via information obligations, for instance) to operate in socially useful ways.[10] What is more, if the EU wants growth, it has to be green – and green growth is always steered growth: celebrating economic activity as such will not do.[11] The transition that the EU is contemplating requires restructuring the economy, away from the production of consumer goods towards the services to maintain goods,[12] while replacing throw-away consumer culture with a more caring – that is repairing, refurbishing, and reusing – consumption.[13]

This transforming imaginary of the economy hinges on the EU's changing conception of politics. We can see that the EU starts recognising distributive conflicts to a greater degree than was the case before, with different groups struggling over the shape of the economy and its distributive outcomes – rather than being staged in a common project of optimising markets.[14]

The shift in the imaginary of prosperity in the EU has also implied a shift in the role of government – the EU institutions in our case – who must assume more political responsibility going forward. The

---

[10] More institutionalist approach to the economy can be seen in Chapters 3–6.
[11] A shift from taking to steering economy and markets can be seen in Chapters 3–6.
[12] See Chapters 3 and 4. [13] Mostly Chapters 3 and 4
[14] Foremost Chapter 4, but also Chapter 6.

government increasingly has to choose between different products,[15] between different sectors,[16] and even between different ways of producing,[17] in order to bring about a more sustainable and equitable economy. Hiding behind (often regressive) 'horizontal measures' of cutting labour rights or lowering taxes in order to create a "good investment climate" will not do any longer.[18] This embrace of political responsibility from the side of the EU institutions has, however, only been partial. For instance, in industrial policy, the EU still does not impose many conditionalities, remaining in the paradigm where benefits are privatised while costs are socialised.[19] Gabor has critically called this a 'de-risking state' – de-risking private capital investment, without corresponding benefit on the side of the public.[20] But the EU position goes even further, I would argue: the EU seems to suffer from a certain aversion to public voice or public ownership – even though the new imaginary of prosperity will likely have to ensure that many services are provided either publicly or via some other collective route.[21]

There have been changes also in the EU's legal imaginaries. The law is becoming more clearly 'normative' – relying on its own normativity rather than the one borrowed from "efficient markets", while aiming to *reshape* the economy rather than just optimise it.[22] In most examined fields, law is moving away from self-regulation[23] and returning to the language of protection[24] and institutional experimentation, designing at times even new institutional and legal forms.[25] However, the issues of distributive justice and the inequality of (bargaining) power remain in very early infancy.[26]

In relation to nature, we see somewhat more humility, recognising the complexity of natural ecosystems and human (inter)dependence on them. Rather than only *intervening on* nature, it is recognised that we need to extract less (via consumption and production)[27] and return more (via care and nature laws).[28] This is, however, not an entirely consistent position.[29]

---

[15] Foremost Chapter 4.   [16] Foremost Chapter 5.   [17] Foremost Chapter 6.
[18] Foremost Chapter 5.   [19] See Chapter 5.
[20] Daniela Gabor, 'The (European) Derisking State', *Stato e mercato* 1 (2023): 53–84.
[21] Foremost Chapters 3 and 5.   [22] See Chapters 3–6.   [23] See Chapters 3–6.
[24] Foremost Chapter 3.   [25] Foremost Chapter 5, partially also Chapter 6.
[26] Some references in Chapters 3–6.   [27] See Chapters 3–6.
[28] Foremost Chapters 3–5.
[29] In Chapter 5, for instance, "competitiveness" and "extractiveness" sometimes have an upper hand.

Finally, we see also the transformation of the subject. The EU is moving beyond the thin subject interested only in price and profit.[30] The subject rather has more interests and more complex rationality, they are more interdependent with their social and natural environment, and finally they carry more responsibility for others and for nature.[31] This thicker subject is also what, going forward, may ground a different conception of society, which places interdependence and sharing more centrally.[32]

7.2 The Road Ahead

The shift in the background assumption sets preconditions for instituting a new, post-neoliberal society. For that to happen, however, many new struggles, new movements, new programmes, measures, policies, and laws will have to be taken up and implemented. Some of these transformations are already incipient and thus imaginable going forward. In what follows, on the basis of previous chapters, I want to propose a couple of 'compossible futures' that would help usher in a new imaginary of prosperity and thus, to paraphrase Acemoglu and Robinson, help the EU and its MSs to "stay in the corridor".[33]

To start, the EU is working towards making consumption both slower and less wasteful. However, the paradigm is still that of individual consumption. Public infrastructures and services (e.g. 'European public goods')[34] as well as via public and collective ways of consumption (including enabling forms of co-housing, sharing of consumer goods, public transport, etc.) will be a must if we indeed intend to keep the quality of life while lowering material throughput. The EU already opens up towards restructuring consumption, away from mass consumption, towards reuse, services, and repair, but it still does not venture into encouraging more public or communal forms of consumption that would be beneficial both environmentally and socially.[35] This connects

---

[30] Foremost Chapters 3 (consumer), 4 (product), and 6 (corporation).
[31] Foremost Chapters 3 and 6.   [32] See Chapters 5 and 6.
[33] Acemoglu and Robinson, *Why Nations Fail*.
[34] Marco Buti and Marcello Messori, 'European Public Goods Are Key to Tackle the Economic Challenges of 2023', EUIdeas (2023), https://euideas.eui.eu/2023/02/01/european-public-goods-are-key-to-tackle-the-economic-challenges-of-2023/, last accessed 16 January 2024.
[35] Jefim Vogel et al., 'Safeguarding Livelihoods against Reductions in Economic Output', *Ecological Economics* 215 (1 January 2024): 107977.

to a wider problem, namely that the emergent imaginary is still a "fair weather" imaginary, more easily embraced by those who are economically and socially secure. To be truly an imaginary of *shared* prosperity, the new imaginary of prosperity should be increasingly thought of from the perspectives of *have not's* rather than *have's* – that ought to convey, I would argue, the primary meaning of GED's '*just* transition'.

The imagination of the EU institutions also remains limited concerning the relationship between technology and labour – even if the EU sees itself as a regulatory champion.[36] Neither data legislation, industrial policy, nor ecodesign takes up the role of steering technological progress in a direction that would ensure safer labour futures. The EU remains reactive, making workers, consumers, and citizens *fit for* market-made technologies rather than the reverse. The EU will need to become more proactive in democratically shaping the technological futures that would actually live up to the needs of humans rather than capital.[37] The prosperous future requires a credible promise that it will not be a purposeless or dystopic future – a promise that has to be delivered via more democratic steering of technology and/or via modes of social provision (like universal basic income, citizen dividend, or work guarantee).[38]

When it comes to relationships with the so-called third countries, we see two sets of developments, each pulling in a different direction. On the one hand, the EU is very carefully attempting to reign in its own multinationals from causing social and environmental harm abroad. The solidarity, however, does not go as far as to demand *fairer pricing* as a condition of non-extractive relations,[39] and at this point, it is also unclear whether even fair purchasing practices have made it through the last round of negotiations of the CSDDD between the EU parliament and the Council. On the other hand, within the framework of its industrial policy and the Critical Raw Materials Act, the EU remains in a competitive mode that we associate with privatised prosperity. If and when the EU actually takes the question of interdependence with "third

---

[36] Anu Bradford, *The Brussels Effect: How the European Union Rules the World* (Oxford University Press, USA, 2020).
[37] Simon Johnson and Daron Acemoglu, *Power and Progress: Our Thousand-Year Struggle Over Technology and Prosperity* (Hachette UK, 2023).
[38] Vogel et al., 'Safeguarding Livelihoods against Reductions in Economic Output'.
[39] See Chapter 6.

countries" more seriously, it has to go further on many levels: the impact of multinationals, the sharing of benefits of cooperation, the questions of debt, climate adaptation funds, or sharing technologies in a way that tries to empower local populations rather than European capital.[40] It is crucial to see that with regard to these developing countries, it is perhaps the first time that the conflict between European capital and European society is there for everyone to see: the lack of even elementary prosperity abroad (due to the extraction of minerals, land, profits, tax, liveable climate, etc.) will increasingly contribute to migration pressures.

Currently, perhaps the lowest hanging fruit in EU policymaking, which could be a game changer in instituting a new imaginary of shared prosperity, is to strengthen the so-called 'social economy'.[41] Social economy organisations engage in economic activity for the "right reasons", creating on the way various kinds of "positive externalities", such as providing a range of affordable services, ensuring resilience in the face of crises, increasing inclusion, and strengthening local communities.[42] While the EU has had social economy on the radar for a long time, due to all these positive externalities, it has not done much to actually create a level playing field for such organisations. If it does so, as I suggest in Chapter 6, social economy could be an instrument of economic development that would eventually limit anxiety with stagnating economic growth and at the same time support people, via individual and collective efforts, to make the economy that can be fun – and still work for people. Also in relation to the 'third countries', international trade via social economy or steward-owned enterprises would result in a fairer distribution of the surpluses of economic cooperation, increasing prosperity abroad in the interest of us all.

Together, these proposals may seem utopian, but I have tried to argue that they present a *realistic utopia*,[43] because they are both imaginable (within the framework instituted today) and necessary. They are imaginable inasmuch as the EU has already partially shifted its background

---

[40] Isabel Feichtner, Markus Krajewski, and Ricarda Roesch, eds., *Human Rights in the Extractive Industries: Transparency, Participation, Resistance*, vol. 3, *Interdisciplinary Studies in Human Rights* (Springer International Publishing, 2019).
[41] See Chapter 6, Section 6.5.
[42] European Commission, Building an economy that works for people: an action plan for the social economy, COM(2021) 778 final, pp. 4–6.
[43] Rutger Bregman, *Utopia for Realists* (Bloomsbury Publishing, 2018).

understandings, having prepared grounds for a new understanding of prosperity. They are also necessary, since both peace and the relevance of the EU depend on ushering in a credible imaginary of prosperity. Such imaginary, which would be both more shared and sustainable, can address the problems societies face, while offering a credible prospect of a prosperous future.

Select Bibliography

Aalbers, Manuel B. 'The Variegated Financialization of Housing'. *International Journal of Urban and Regional Research* 41, no. 4 (1 July 2017): 542–54.

Acemoglu, Daron, and James A. Robinson. *Why Nations Fail: The Origins of Power, Prosperity and Poverty*. Profile Books, 2012.

Ackerman, Frank, and Lisa Heinzerling. *Priceless: On Knowing the Price of Everything and the Value of Nothing*. The New Press, 2005.

Adam, Smith. *The Wealth of Nations*. Aegitas, 2016.

Adams, Suzi. *Ricoeur and Castoriadis in Discussion: On Human Creation, Historical Novelty, and the Social Imaginary*. Rowman & Littlefield, 2017.

Aimaer, Karl, and Dani Rodrik. 'Rebirth of Industrial Policy and an Agenda for the Twenty-First Century'. *Journal of Industry, Competition and Trade* 20, no. 2 (6 January 2020): 189–207.

Anderson, Benedict. *Imagined Communities: Reflections on the Origin and Spread of Nationalism*. Verso Books, 2006.

Andre, Thomas J., Jr. 'Cultural Hegemony: The Exportation of Anglo-Saxon Corporate Governance Ideologies to Germany'. *Tulane Law Review* 73, no. 1 (1998): 104–16.

Anghie, Antony. *Imperialism, Sovereignty and the Making of International Law*. Cambridge University Press, 2007.

Atiyah, P. S. *The Rise and Fall of Freedom of Contract*. Oxford University Press, 1985.

Augenstein, Daniel. *'Integration through Law' Revisited: The Making of the European Polity*. Ashgate Publishing, 2013.

Balanyá, Belén. *Europe Inc: Regional and Global Restructuring and the Rise of Corporate Power*. Pluto Press (UK), 2000.

Barkhausen, Robin, Antoine Durand, and Katharina Fick. 'Review and Analysis of Ecodesign Directive Implementing Measures: Product Regulations Shifting from Energy Efficiency towards a Circular Economy'. *Sustainability* 14, no. 16 (19 August 2022): 10318.

Barry, John M. 'Green Republicanism and a "Just Transition" from the Tyranny of Economic Growth'. In *Green Politics and Civic Republicanism*, edited by Ashley Dodsworth and Iseult Honohan, 59–76. Routledge, 2022.

Bartl, Marija. 'The Affordability of Energy: How Much Protection for the Vulnerable Consumers?' *Journal of Consumer Policy* 33, no. 3 (9 February 2010): 225–45.

Bartl, Marija. 'Contesting Austerity: On the Limits of EU Knowledge Governance'. *Journal of Law and Society* 44, no. 1 (3 February 2017): 150–68.

Bartl, Marija. 'Hayek Upside-Down: On the Democratic Effects of Transnational Lists'. *German Law Journal* 21, no. 1 (1 January 2020): 57–62.

Bartl, Marija. 'Imaginaries of Progress as Constitutional Imaginaries'. In *European Constitutional Imaginaries: Between Ideology and Utopia*, edited by Jan Komárek, 360–77. Oxford University Press, 2021.

Bartl, Marija 'Internal Market Rationality, Private Law and the Direction of the Union: Resuscitating the Market as the Object of the Political', *European Law Journal* 21, no. 5 (15 January 2015), 572–98.

Bartl, Marija 'Internal Market Rationality: In the Way of Re-imagining the Future'. *European Law Journal* 24, no. 1 (1 January 2018): 99–115.

Bartl, Marija 'Making Transnational Markets: The Institutional Politics behind the TTIP'. *Europe and the World* 1, no. 1 (1 June 2017): 1–37.

Bartl, Marija 'Regulatory Convergence through the Back Door: TTIP's Regulatory Cooperation and the Future of Precaution in Europe'. *German Law Journal* 18, no. 4 (1 July 2017): 969–92.

Bartl, Marija 'Towards the Imaginary of Collective Prosperity in the European Union (EU): Reorienting the Corporation'. *European Law Open* 1, no. 4 (2022): 957–86.

Bartl, Marija 'The Way We Do Europe: Subsidiarity and the Substantive Democratic Deficit'. *European Law Journal* 21, no. 1 (1 January 2015): 23–43.

Bartley, Tim. 'Transnational Corporations and Global Governance'. *Annual Review of Sociology* 44, no. 1 (30 July 2018): 145–65.

Bedjaoui, Mohammed. *Towards a New International Economic Order*. Holmes & Meier, 1979.

Berman, Elizabeth Popp. *Thinking Like an Economist: How Efficiency Replaced Equality in U.S. Public Policy*. Princeton University Press, 2022.

Blokker, Paul. 'The Imaginary Constitution of Constitutions'. *Social Imaginaries* 3, no. 1 (1 January 2017): 167–93.

Blyth, Mark. *Austerity: The History of a Dangerous Idea*. Oxford University Press, 2013.

Boas, Ingrid, Carol Farbotko, Helen Adams, Harald Sterly, Simon R. Bush, Kees Van Der Geest, Hanne Wiegel et al. 'Climate Migration Myths'. *Nature Climate Change* 9, no. 12 (2019): 901–3.

Bogoeski, Vladimir. 'The Aftermath of the Laval Quartet: Emancipating Labour (Law) from the Rationality of the Internal Market in the Field of Posting'. PhD diss., Hertie School, Berlin, 2021. https://opus4.kobv.de/opus4-hsog/frontdoor/index/index/docId/3717.

Bollier, David, and Silke Helfrich. *Free, Fair, and Alive: The Insurgent Power of the Commons*. New Society Publishers, 2019.

Bradford, Anu. *The Brussels Effect: How the European Union Rules the World*. Oxford University Press, 2020.

Bruna, Natacha. 'A Climate-Smart World and the Rise of Green Extractivism'. *The Journal of Peasant Studies* 49, no. 4 (2022): 839–64.

Bruszt, László, and Višnja Vukov. 'Making States for the Single Market: European Integration and the Reshaping of Economic States in the Southern and Eastern Peripheries of Europe'. *West European Politics* 40, no. 4 (2017): 663–87.

Bundgaard, Anja Marie, Mette Mosgaard, and Arne Remmen. 'From Energy Efficiency towards Resource Efficiency within the Ecodesign Directive'. *Journal of Cleaner Production* 144 (1 February 2017): 358–74.

Burgers, Laura. 'Private Rights of Nature'. *Transnational Environmental Law* 11, no. 3 (1 November 2022): 463–74.

Callon, Michel. 'Introduction: The Embeddedness of Economic Markets in Economics'. *The Sociological Review* 46, no. S1 (1 May 1998): 1–57.

Calvin, Katherine, Dipak Dasgupta, Gerhard Krinner, Aditi Mukherji, Peter Thorne, Christopher H. Trisos, José Romero et al. 'IPCC, 2023: Climate Change 2023: Synthesis Report, Summary for Policymakers. Contribution of Working Groups I, II and III to the Sixth Assessment Report of the Intergovernmental Panel on Climate Change'. *IPCC* (25 July 2023): 1–34.

Cappelletti, Mauro, Monica Seccombe, and Joseph Weiler. *Integration through Law: Europe and the American Federal Experience*. De Gruyter, 1985.

Caruso, Daniela. 'Non-parties: The Negative Externalities of Regional Trade Agreements in a Private Law Perspective'. *Harvard International Law Journal* 59 (2018): 389–430.

Castoriadis, Cornelius. *The Imaginary Institution of Society*. MIT Press, 1997.

Chamorel, Patrick. 'Macron versus the Yellow Vests'. *Journal of Democracy* 30, no. 4 (1 January 2019): 48–62.

Chandhoke, Neera. *Democracy and Revolutionary Politics*. Bloomsbury Publishing, 2015.

Chomsky, Noam. 'The Corporate Takeover of U.S. Democracy'. *Chomsky.info* (24 January 2010). https://chomsky.info/20100124/.

Christodoulidis, Emilios. 'Europe's Donors and Its Supplicants: Reflections on the Greek Crisis'. In *Constitutional Sovereignty and Social Solidarity in Europe,* edited by Johan ven der Walt and Jeffrey Ellsworth, 241–66. Bloomsbury Publishing, 2015.

Christodoulidis, Emilios. *The Differentiation and Autonomy of Law*. Cambridge University Press, 2023.

Closa, Carlos, Dimitry Kochenov, and Joseph H. H. Weiler. 'Reinforcing Rule of Law Oversight in the European Union'. *Robert Schuman Centre for Advanced Studies Research Paper*, No. 2014/25 (2014).

Colgan, Jeff D., and Robert O. Keohane. 'The Liberal Order Is Rigged: Fix It Now or Watch It Wither'. *Foreign Affairs* 96, no. 3 (2017): 36–44.

Copeland, Paul, and Mary E. Daly. 'The European Semester and EU Social Policy'. *JCMS: Journal of Common Market Studies* 56, no. 5 (28 February 2018): 1001–18.

Cremaschi, Simone, Paula Rettl, Marco Cappelluti, and Catherine E. De Vries. 'Geographies of Discontent: Public Service Deprivation and the Rise of the Far Right in Italy'. *Harvard Business School Working Paper*, No. 24-024 (1 November 2023).

Crouch, Colin. 'Privatised Keynesianism: An Unacknowledged Policy Regime'. *The British Journal of Politics and International Relations* 11, no. 3 (1 August 2009): 382–99.

Dahl, Robert A. *On Democracy*. Yale University Press, 2020.

Dani, Marco, Edoardo Chiti, Joana Mendes, Agustín José Menéndez, Harm Schepel, and Michael Wilkinson, 'At the End of the Law: A Moment of Truth for the Eurozone and the EU,' *University of Luxembourg Working Paper* (2020). https://orbilu.uni.lu/bitstream/10993/45861/1/Weiss-VB.pdf.

Dari-Mattiacci, Giuseppe, Oscar Gelderblom, Joost Jonker, and Enrico Perotti. 'The Emergence of the Corporate Form'. *The Journal of Law, Economics, and Organization* 33, no. 2 (24 March 2017): 193–236.

Dawson, Mark. 'New Governance and the Displacement of Social Europe: The Case of the European Semester,' *European Constitutional Law Review* 14, no. 1 (2018): 191–209.

Domurath, Irina, and Chantal Mak. 'Private Law and Housing Justice in Europe'. *The Modern Law Review* 83, no. 6 (2020): 1188–220.

Dukes, Ruth. *The Labour Constitution: The Enduring Idea of Labour Law*. Oxford University Press, 2014.

Duyvendak, Jan Willem, and Josip Kesic. 'The Return of the Native: Can Liberalism Safeguard Us against Nativism?' In *Oxford Studies in Culture and Politics*. Oxford University Press, 2023.

Eco, Umberto. 'Ur-Fascism'. *The New York Review of Books* 22 (1995): 12–5.

Ellinas, Antonis A. 'Media and the Radical Right'. In *The Oxford Handbook of the Radical Right*, edited by Jens Rydgren, 269–84. Oxford University Press, 2018.

Esposito, Roberto. *Institution*. John Wiley & Sons, 2022.

Esposito, Roberto. *Politics and Negation: For an Affirmative Philosophy*. John Wiley & Sons, 2020.

European Banking Authority. 'Final EBA Report on Undue Short-Term Pressures from the Financial Sector'. *European Banking Authority* (2019) www.eba.europa.eu/sites/default/files/document_library/Final%20EBA%20report%20on%20undue%20short-term%20pressures%20from%20the%20financial%20sector%20v2_0.pdf.

European Economists for an Alternative Economic Policy in Europe, 'EuroMemorandum 2020: A Green New Deal for Europe – Opportunities and Challenges'. *Euromemo Group* (2019) www.euromemo.eu/euromemorandum/euromemorandum_2020/index.html.

Feichtner, Isabel, Markus Krajewski, and Ricarda Roesch, eds. *Human Rights in the Extractive Industries: Transparency, Participation, Resistance*, vol. 3, Interdisciplinary Studies in Human Rights. Springer International Publishing, 2019.

Fennis, Bob M., and Wolfgang Stroebe. *The Psychology of Advertising*. Psychology Press, 2015.

Ferrari, Valeria. 'The Platformisation of Digital Payments: The Fabrication of Consumer Interest in the EU FinTech Agenda'. *Computer Law & Security Review* 45 (1 July 2022): 1–20.

Fetzer, Thiemo. 'Did Austerity Cause Brexit?' *American Economic Review* 109, no. 11 (1 November 2019): 3849–86.

Fici, Antonio. 'The New Italian Code of the Third Sector. Essence and Principles of a Historic Legislative Reform'. In *The Law of Third Sector Organizations in Europe*, edited by Antonio Fici, 115–39. Springer Nature Switzerland, 2023.

Flamant, Eloi, Sarah Godar, and Gaspard Richard. 'New Forms of Tax Competition in the European Union: An Empirical Investigation'. *EU-Tax Observatory* (2021).

Folbre, Nancy. 'The Unproductive Housewife: Her Evolution in Nineteenth-Century Economic Thought'. *Signs: Journal of Women in Culture and Society* 16, no. 3 (1 April 1991): 463–84.

Føllesdal, Andreas, and Simon Hix. 'Why There Is a Democratic Deficit in the EU: A Response to Majone and Moravcsik'. *JCMS: Journal of Common Market Studies* 44, no. 3 (16 August 2006): 533–62.

France, Alan. *Understanding Youth in the Global Economic Crisis*. Policy Press, 2016.

Fraser, Nancy, and Rahel Jaeggi. *Capitalism: A Conversation in Critical Theory*. Polity, 2018.

Frey, Carl Benedikt. *The Technology Trap: Capital, Labor, and Power in the Age of Automation*. Princeton University Press, 2019.

Funke, Manuel, Moritz Schularick, and Christoph Trebesch. 'Going to Extremes: Politics after Financial Crises, 1870–2014'. *European Economic Review* 88C (1 September 2016): 227–60.

Gabor, Daniela. 'The (European) Derisking State'. *Stato e mercato* 1 (2023): 53–84.

Gabriel, Ricardo Duque, Mathias Klein, and Ana Sofia Pessoa. 'The Political Costs of Austerity'. *The Review of Economics and Statistics* (27 September 2023): 1–45. https://direct.mit.edu/rest/article-abstract/doi/10.1162/rest_a_01373/117705/The-Political-Costs-of-Austerity?redirectedFrom=fulltext.

Galofré-Vilà, Gregori, Christopher M. Meissner, Martin McKee, and David Stuckler. 'Austerity and the Rise of the Nazi Party'. *The Journal of Economic History* 81, no. 1 (11 January 2021): 81–113.

Geertz, Clifford. 'Common Sense as a Cultural System'. *The Antioch Review* 33, no. 1 (1 January 1975): 5–26.

Gelter, Martin. *EU Company Law Harmonization between Convergence and Varieties of Capitalism*. ECGI, 2017.

Ghodsee, Kristen R. *Everyday Utopia: What 2,000 Years of Wild Experiments Can Teach Us about the Good Life*. Simon & Schuster, 2023.

Ging, Debbie. 'Alphas, Betas, and Incels: Theorizing the Masculinities of the Manosphere'. *Men And Masculinities* 22, no. 4 (10 May 2017): 638–57.

Green, Andy. *The Crisis for Young People: Generational Inequalities in Education, Work, Housing and Welfare*. Springer, 2017.

Greve, Bent. *Welfare, Populism and Welfare Chauvinism*. Policy Press, 2020.

Grimm, Dieter. 'Does Europe Need a Constitution?' *European Law Journal* 1, no. 3 (1995): 282–302.

Grundmann, Stefan. 'The Concept of the Private Law Society: After 50 Years of European Business and European Business Law'. *European Review of Private Law* 16, no. 4 (2008): 553–81.

Guriev, Sergei, and Elias Papaioannou. 'The Political Economy of Populism'. *Journal of Economic Literature* 60, no. 3 (1 September 2022): 753–832.

Habermas, Jürgen. *A New Structural Transformation of the Public Sphere and Deliberative Politics*. John Wiley & Sons, 2023.

Habermas, Jürgen. *Between Facts and Norms: Contributions to a Discourse Theory of Law and Democracy*. Polity Press, 1997

Habermas, Jürgen. *Communication and the Evolution of Society*. Beacon Press, 1979.

Habermas, Jürgen. 'Remarks on Dieter Grimm's "Does Europe Need a Constitution?"' *European Law Journal* 1, no. 3 (1 November 1995): 303–7.

Haldane, Andrew. 'Whose Recovery?' Speech at the Bank of England (30 June 2016). www.bankofengland.co.uk/speech/2016/whose-recovery.

Hale, Robert L. 'Coercion and Distribution in a Supposedly Non-Coercive State'. *Political Science Quarterly* 38, no. 3 (1 September 1923): 470–94.

Harremoes, Paul, David Gee, Malcom MacGarvin, Andy Stirling, Jane Keys, Brian Wynne, and Sofia Guedes Vaz. *The Precautionary Principle in the Twentieth Century: Late Lessons from Early Warnings*. Routledge, 2013.

Hartley, Kris, Ralf Van Santen, and Julian Kirchherr. 'Policies for Transitioning towards a Circular Economy: Expectations from the European Union (EU)'. *Resources, Conservation and Recycling* 155 (1 April 2020): 1–10.

Harvey, David. *A Brief History of Neoliberalism*. Oxford University Press, 2005.

Hayek, Friedrich A. 'The Economic Conditions of Interstate Federalism'. *New Commonwealth Quarterly* 5 (1939): 131–49.

Hermann, Christoph, and Koen Verhoest. 'Varieties and Variations of Public-Service: Liberalisation and Privatisation in Europe'. *PIQUE Policy Paper* 1 (2008): 1–12.

Hess, David J., and Benjamin K. Sovacool. 'Sociotechnical Matters: Reviewing and Integrating Science and Technology Studies with Energy Social Science'. *Energy Research & Social Science* 65 (1 July 2020): 1–17.

Hesselink, Martijn W. 'Alienation Commodification: A Critique of the Role of EU Consumer Law'. *European Law Open* 2, no. 2 (1 June 2023): 405–23.

Hesselink, Martijn W. 'Common Frame of Reference & Social Justice'. *European Review of Contract Law* 4, no. 3 (1 January 2008): 248–69.

Hesselink, Martijn W. *Justifying Contract in Europe: Political Philosophies of European Contract Law*. Oxford University Press, 2021.

Hickel, Jason, and Giorgos Kallis. 'Is Green Growth Possible?' *New Political Economy* 25, no. 4 (2019): 469–86.

Hinteregger, Monika. 'Civil Liability and the Challenges of Climate Change: A Functional Analysis'. *Journal of European Tort Law* 8, no. 2 (2 November 2017): 238–60.

Hirschman, Albert O. *The Rhetoric of Reaction: Perversity, Futility, Jeopardy*. Harvard University Press, 1991.

Hishiyama, Izumi. 'The Tableau Economique of Quesnay'. *Kyoto University Economic Review* 30, no. 1 (1960): 1–46.

Hüller, Thorsten, and Beate Kohler-Koch. 'Assessing the Democratic Value of Civil Society Engagement in the European Union'. in *EU Governance to Civil Society – Gains and Challenges*, edited by Beate Kohler-Koch, Dirk de Bièvre, and William Maloney, CONNEX Report Series 05 (1 January 2008): 145–81.

Ireland, Paddy. 'Corporate Schizophrenia: The Corporation as a Separate Legal Person and an Object of Property', University of Bristol Working Paper (2016).
Irion, Kristina, Svetlana Yakovleva, and Marija Bartl, 'Trade and Privacy: Complicated Bedfellows?,' *How to Achieve Data Protection-Proof Free Trade Agreements* (13 July 2016). Available at SSRN: https://ssrn.com/abstract=2877166 or http://dx.doi.org/10.2139/ssrn.2877166.
Jaakkola, Jussi. 'Taming the Leviathan or Dismantling Democratic Government? Evolving Political Ideas on Spontaneous Income Tax Integration in the European Union'. *European Law Open* 2, no. 3 (2023): 575–615.
Jabko, Nicolas. *Playing the Market: A Political Strategy for Uniting Europe, 1985–2005*. Cornell University Press, 2006.
Jackson, Tim. *Prosperity without Growth: Foundations for the Economy of Tomorrow*. Taylor & Francis, 2016.
Janoski, Thomas, and Brian Gran. 'Political Citizenship: Foundations of Rights'. In *Handbook of Citizenship Studies*, edited by Engin F. Isin and Bryan S. Turner, 13–52. SAGE Publications Ltd, 2002.
Jasanoff, Sheila. *The Fifth Branch: Science Advisers as Policymakers*. Harvard University Press, 1998.
Jasanoff, Sheila, and Sang-Hyun Kim. 'Containing the Atom: Sociotechnical Imaginaries and Nuclear Power in the United States and South Korea'. *Minerva* 47, no. 2 (1 June 2009): 119–46.
Joerges, Christian, and Karl Polanyi. *Globalisation and the Potential of Law in Transnational Markets*. Hart Publishing, 2011.
Joerges, Christian, and Navraj Singh Ghaleigh. *Darker Legacies of Law in Europe: The Shadow of National Socialism and Fascism over Europe and Its Legal Traditions*. Hart Publishing, 2003.
Joerges, Christian, Yves Mény, Joseph Weiler, Inge Burgess, Chris Engert, and Fritz W. Scharpf. 'Mountain of Molehill? A Critical Appraisal of the Commission White Paper on Governance'. *Jean Monnet Working Papers, Harvard Law School* (2001).
Johnson, Simon, and Daron Acemoglu. *Power and Progress: Our Thousand-Year Struggle Over Technology and Prosperity*. Hachette UK, 2023.
José Menéndez, Agustín. 'The Existential Crisis of the European Union,' *German Law Journal* 14, no. 5 (2013): 453–526.
Judt, Tony. *Postwar: A History of Europe since 1945*. Penguin, 2006.
Kaupa, Clemens. 'Has (Downturn-)Austerity Really Been "Constitutionalized" in Europe? On the Ideological Dimension of Such a Claim'. *Journal of Law and Society* 44, no. 1 (2017): 32–55.
Kaupa, Clemens. *The Pluralist Character of the European Economic Constitution*. Bloomsbury Publishing, 2016.
Kellij, Sara, and Ester Hilhorst. 'Negen Op Tien Nederlanders: Sprake van "wooncrisis"'. Ipsos I&O (2 November 2023). www.ioresearch.nl/actueel/negen-op-tien-nederlanders-sprake-van-wooncrisis/.
Kelton, Stephanie. *The Deficit Myth: Modern Monetary Theory and How to Build a Better Economy*. Hachette UK, 2020.

Kennedy, David. *A World of Struggle: How Power, Law, and Expertise Shape Global Political Economy*. Princeton University Press, 2016.

Kennedy, Duncan. 'Three Globalizations of Law and Legal Thought: 1850–2000'. In *The New Law and Economic Development*, edited by Alvaro Santos and David M. Trubek, 19–73. Cambridge University Press, 2006.

Keune, Maarten 'Not Balanced and Hardly New: The European Commission's Quest for Flexicurity'. *ETUI, The European Trade Union Institute* (2007).

Keynes, John Maynard. 'The End of Laissez-Faire'. In *Essays in Persuasion*, 272–94. Palgrave Macmillan UK, 2010.

Kjaer, Poul F. 'The Law of Political Economy: An Introduction'. In *The Law of Political Economy: Transformation in the Function of Law*, 1–30. Cambridge University Press, 2020.

Klein, Ezra. *Why We're Polarized*. Simon & Schuster, 2020.

Klein, Peter G. *The Capitalist & The Entrepreneur*. Ludwig von Mises Institute, 2010.

Knill, Christoph, and Jale Tosun. *Public Policy: A New Introduction*. Red Globe Press, 2020.

Komárek, Jan. *European Constitutional Imaginaries: Between Ideology and Utopia*. Oxford University Press, 2023.

Komárek, Jan. 'European Constitutional Imaginaries: Utopias, Ideologies and the Other,' *SSRN Scholarly Paper* (29 October 2019).

Koskenniemi, Martti. *From Apology to Utopia: The Structure of International Legal Argument*. Cambridge University Press, 2006.

Krugman, Paul. 'Competitiveness: A Dangerous Obsession Essay'. *Foreign Affairs* 73, no. 2 (1994): 28–44.

Kuhn, Thomas S. *The Structure of Scientific Revolutions*. 2nd ed., University of Chicago Press, 1970.

Kukovec, Damjan. 'Law and the Periphery'. *European Law Journal* 21, no. 3 (20 November 2015): 406–28.

Kwon, Kibum, and Soebin Jang. 'There Is No Good War for Talent: A Critical Review of the Literature on Talent Management'. *Employee Relations* 44, no. 1 (2021): 94–120.

Laclau, Ernesto, and Chantal Mouffe. *Hegemony and Socialist Strategy: Towards A Radical Democratic Politics*. Verso Books, 2014.

Leaman, Jeremy *The Bundesbank Myth: Towards a Critique of Central Bank Independence*. Springer, 2000.

Leino-Sandberg, Päivi. 'Constitutional Imaginaries of Solidarity: Framing Fiscal Integration Post-NGEU,' *University of Helsinki Working Paper* (2023). https://helda.helsinki.fi/bitstreams/6c044fbd-a8ee-4bb1-a884-baf52446888a/download;.

Leone, Candida. 'The Missing Stone in the Cathedral: Of Unfair Terms in Employment Contracts and Coexisting Rationalities in European Contract Law'. PhD diss., University of Amsterdam, 2022. https://pure.uva.nl/ws/files/48074023/Thesis_complete_.pdf.

Leone, Candida. 'Transparency Revisited – On the Role of Information in the Recent Case-Law of the CJEU'. *European Review of Contract Law* 10, no. 2 (1 January 2014): 312–25.

Leone, Candida, and Joanna M. L. Van Duin. 'The Real (New) Deal: Levelling the Odds for Consumer-Litigants: On the Need for a Modernization, Part II'. *European Review of Private Law* 27, no. 6 (2019): 1227–50.

Lesniewska, Feja, and Katrien Steenmans. *Circular Economy and the Law: Bringing Justice into the Frame.* Taylor & Francis, 2023.

Liverman, Diana. 'Who Governs, at What Scale and at What Price? Geography, Environmental Governance, and the Commodification of Nature,' *Annals of the Association of American Geographers* 94, no. 4 (1 December 2004): 734–38.

Ragnar E. Lofstedt. The 'Plateau-ing' of the European Better Regulation Agenda: An Analysis of Activities Carried Out by the Barroso Commission 1,' *Journal of Risk Research, Taylor & Francis Journals* 10, no. 4 (June 2007):423–447.

Loos, Marco B. M. 'Full Harmonisation as a Regulatory Concept and Its Consequences for the National Legal Orders. The Example of the Consumer Rights Directive'. *Centre for the Study of European Contract Law Working Paper Series,* No. 2010/03 (2010).

MacKenzie, Donald, and Yuval Millo. 'Constructing a Market, Performing Theory: The Historical Sociology of a Financial Derivatives Exchange'. *American Journal of Sociology* 109, no. 1 (1 July 2003): 107–45.

Magnuson, William. *For Profit: A History of Corporations.* Hachette UK, 2022.

Mak, Chantal. 'Gutiérrez Naranjo – On Limits in Law and Limits of Law'. *Amsterdam Law School Research Paper,* No. 2017-38 (2017).

Mak, Chantal. 'Giving Voice: A Public Sphere Theory of European Private Law Adjudication'. *European Law Open* 2, no. 4 (2023): 697–723.

Mak, Chantal, and Betül Kas. *Civil Courts and the European Polity: The Constitutional Role of Private Law Adjudication in Europe.* Bloomsbury Publishing, 2023.

Mak, Vanessa, and Evelyne Terryn. 'Circular Economy and Consumer Protection: The Consumer as a Citizen and the Limits of Empowerment through Consumer Law'. *Journal of Consumer Policy* 43, no. 1 (2020): 227–48.

Mańko, Rafał, Martin Škop, and Markéta Štěpáníková, 'Carving Out Central Europe as a Space of Legal Culture: A Way Out of Peripherality?,' *Wroclaw Review of Law, Administration & Economics* 6, no. 2 (1 December 2016): 4–28.

Marchart, Oliver. *Post-Foundational Political Thought: Political Difference in Nancy, Lefort, Badiou and Laclau.* Edinburgh University Press, 2007.

Markovits, Daniel. *The Meritocracy Trap: How America's Foundational Myth Feeds Inequality, Dismantles the Middle Class, and Devours the Elite.* Penguin, 2020.

Maruyama, Warren H. 'A New Pillar of the WTO: Sound Science'. *International Lawyer* 32, no. 3 (1 January 1998): 651–77.

Marx, Karl, and Friedrich Engels. 'The German Ideology' (1845). In *Cultural Theory: An Anthology,* edited by Imre Szeman and Timothy Kaposy. John Wiley & Sons, 2010.

Mazzucato, Mariana. *Mission Economy: A Moonshot Guide to Changing Capitalism.* Penguin UK, 2021.

Mazzucato, Mariana. *The Entrepreneurial State: Debunking Public vs. Private Sector Myths,* 1st ed. Anthem Press, 2013.

Mazzucato, Mariana. *The Value of Everything: Making and Taking in the Global Economy.* Penguin UK, 2019.

Mazzucato, Mariana, and Dani Rodrik. 'Industrial Policy with Conditionalities: A Taxonomy and Sample Cases'. *Working paper WP 2023/07, Institute for Innovation and Public Purpose* (2023).

Mazzucato, Mariana, and Rosie Collington. *The Big Con: How the Consulting Industry Weakens Our Businesses, Infantilizes Our Governments and Warps Our Economies*. Penguin Press, 2023.

Meagher, Michelle. *Competition Is Killing Us: How Big Business Is Harming Our Society and Planet – and What to Do About It*. Penguin UK, 2020.

Mellink, Bram, Merijn Oudenampsen, and Naomi Woltring. *Neoliberalisme: Een Nederlandse Geschiedenis*. Boom Amsterdam, 2022.

Meuwese, Anne C. M. 'EU–US Horizontal Regulatory Cooperation: Mutual Recognition of Impact Assessment?' In *Transatlantic Regulatory Cooperation: The Shifting Roles of the EU, the US and California*, edited by David Vogel and Johan F. M. Swinnen, Edward Elgar Publishing, 2011.

Michel, Anaïs. 'Premature Obsolescence: In Search of an Improved Legal Framework'. PhD diss., KU Leuven, 2022.

Micklitz, Hans-W. 'A "Certain" Future for the Optional Instrument'. In *A European Optional Contract Law: Policy Choices*, edited by Sanne Jansen, 181–94. De Gruyter, 2011.

Micklitz, Hans-W. 'The Measuring of the Law through EU Politics'. In *The Politics of European Legal Research*, 223–38. Edward Elgar Publishing, 2022.

Micklitz, Hans-W. *The Politics of Justice in European Private Law: Social Justice, Access Justice, Societal Justice*. Cambridge University Press, 2018.

Micklitz, Hans-W. 'The Visible Hand of European Regulatory Private Law – The Transformation of European Private Law from Autonomy to Functionalism in Competition and Regulation'. *Yearbook of European Law* 28, no. 1 (1 January 2009): 3–59.

Micklitz, Hans-W., and Dennis Patterson. 'From the Nation State to the Market: The Evolution of EU Private Law'. In *The EU's Role in Global Governance: The Legal Dimension*, edited by Bart van Vooren, 59–78. Oxford University Press, 2013.

Micklitz, Hans-W., and Norbert Reich. 'The Court and Sleeping Beauty: The Revival of the Unfair Contract Terms Directive (UCTD)'. *Common Market Law Review* 51, no. 3 (1 June 2014): 771–808.

Milanovic, Branko. *Global Inequality: A New Approach for the Age of Globalization*. Harvard University Press, 2016.

Miller, Toby. 'Michel Foucault, the Birth of Biopolitics: Lectures at the Collège de France, 1978–79'. *International Journal of Cultural Policy* 16, no. 1 (1 February 2010): 56–7.

Moore, Jason W. *Capitalism in the Web of Life: Ecology and the Accumulation of Capital*. Verso Books, 2015.

Moravcsik, A. 'The Myth of Europe's Democratic Deficit'. *Intereconomics* 43, no. 6 (2008): 331–40.

Morvillo, Marta, and Maria Weimer. 'Who Shapes the CJEU Regulatory Jurisprudence? On the Epistemic Power of Economic Actors and Ways to Counter It'. *European Law Open* 1, no. 3 (1 September 2022): 510–48.

Mouffe, Chantal. *The Return of the Political*. Verso Books, 2006.
Mouffe, Chantal. *Agonistics: Thinking the World Politically*. Verso Books, 2013.
Mounk, Yascha. *The Identity Trap: A Story of Ideas and Power in Our Time*. Penguin Press, 2023.
Myrdal, Gunnar. *Economic Theory and Under-Developed Regions*. Methuen & Co. Ltd, 1964.
Niglia, Leone. *The Structural Transformation of European Private Law: A Critique of Juridical Hermeneutics*. Bloomsbury Publishing, 2023.
O'Riordan, Timothy, and James Cameron. 'The History and Contemporary Significance of the Precautionary Principle'. In *Interpreting the Precautionary Principle*, 1–19. Routledge, 1994.
O'Toole, Fintan. 'Review of *Defying Tribalism*, by Susan Neiman'. *The New York Review of Books* (2 November 2023).
Pacces, Alessio M. 'Civil Liability in the EU Corporate Sustainability Due Diligence Directive Proposal: A Law & Economics Analysis,' *European Corporate Governance Institute – Law Working Paper*, No. 691 (2023).
Pargendler, Mariana. 'The Corporate Governance Obsession'. *Journal of Corporation Law* 42 (2016): 359–402.
Pelkmans, Jacques. 'The New Approach to Technical Harmonization and Standardization'. *Journal of Common Market Studies* 25, no. 3 (1987): 249–69.
Petersmann, Ernst-Ulrich. 'Neoliberalism, Ordoliberalism and the Future of Economic Governance'. *Journal of International Economic Law* 26, no. 4 (December 2023): 836–42.
Pianta, Mario. 'An Industrial Policy for Europe'. *Seoul Journal of Economics* 27 (2014): 277–305.
Piketty, Thomas. *Capital and Ideology*. Harvard University Press, 2020.
Piketty, Thomas. *Capital in the Twenty-First Century*. Harvard University Press, 2014.
Pistor, Katharina. *The Code of Capital: How the Law Creates Wealth and Inequality*. Princeton University Press, 2019.
Polanyi, Karl. *The Great Transformation: The Political and Economic Origins of Our Time*. Beacon Press, 2001.
Polverini, Davide. 'Regulating the Circular Economy within the Ecodesign Directive: Progress so Far, Methodological Challenges and Outlook'. *Sustainable Production and Consumption* 27 (1 July 2021): 1113–23.
Ponticelli, Jacopo, and Hans-Joachim Voth. 'Austerity and Anarchy: Budget Cuts and Social Unrest in Europe, 1919–2008'. *Journal of Comparative Economics* 48, no. 1 (2020): 1–19.
Přibáň, Jiří. *Constitutional Imaginaries: A Theory of European Societal Constitutionalism*. Routledge, 2021.
Putnam, Robert D. *Bowling Alone: The Collapse and Revival of American Community*. Simon & Schuster, 2000.
Putnam, Robert D. *The Upswing: How America Came Together a Century Ago and How We Can Do It Again*. Simon & Schuster, 2020.
Rau, Thomas, and Sabine Oberhuber. *Material Matters: Developing Business for a Circular Economy*. Taylor & Francis, 2022.

Raworth, Kate. *Doughnut Economics: Seven Ways to Think Like a Twenty-first-Century Economist*. Chelsea Green Publishing, 2017.

Read, Rupert, and Tim O'Riordan. 'The Precautionary Principle under Fire'. *Environment: Science and Policy for Sustainable Development* 59, no. 5 (18 August 2017): 4–15.

Reich, Norbert, and Hans-Wolfgang Micklitz. 'Crónica de una muerte anunciada: The Commission Proposal for a "Directive on Consumer Rights"'. *Common Market Law Review* 46 (2009): 471–519.

Rhode, Deborah L. 'Access to Justice'. *Fordham Law Review* 69 (2000): 1785–819.

Ricoeur, Paul. *Lectures on Ideology and Utopia*. Columbia University Press, 1986.

Robé, Jean-Philippe. *Property, Power and Politics: Why We Need to Rethink the World Power System*. Policy Press, 2020.

Rodrik, Dani. *The Globalization Paradox: Democracy and the Future of the World Economy*. W. W. Norton & Company, 2011.

Rosenberg, Anat. 'Exaggeration: Advertising, Law and Medical Quackery in Britain, c. 1840–1914'. *The Journal of Legal History* 42, no. 2 (4 May 2021): 202–31.

Rosset, Jan, Nathalie Giger, and Julian Bernauer. 'More Money, Fewer Problems? Cross-Level Effects of Economic Deprivation on Political Representation'. *West European Politics* 36, no. 4 (1 July 2013): 817–35.

Samson, David R. *Our Tribal Future: How to Channel Our Foundational Human Instincts into a Force for Good*. St. Martin's Press, 2023.

Sandel, Michael J. *The Tyranny of Merit: What's Become of the Common Good?* Allen Lane, 2020.

Sanders, Senator Bernie. *It's OK to Be Angry about Capitalism*. Crown, 2023.

Sauer, Hanno. *Moral Teleology: A Theory of Progress*. Taylor & Francis, 2023.

Scharpf, Fritz W. 'Monetary Union, Fiscal Crisis and the Preemption of Democracy'. *MPIfG Discussion Paper, No. 11, 2011, Max Planck Institute for the Study of Societies, Cologne.*

Scharpf, Fritz W. *Governing in Europe: Effective and Democratic?* Oxford University Press, 1999.

Scharpf, Fritz W. 'The Asymmetry of European Integration, or Why the EU Cannot Be a "Social Market Economy"'. *Socio-Economic Review* 8, no. 2 (24 December 2010), 211–50.

Schepel, Harm. 'The Bank, the Bond, and the Bail-Out: On the Legal Construction of Market Discipline in the Eurozone'. *Journal of Law and Society* 44, no. 1 (1 March 2017): 79–98.

Schmid, Christoph U. 'The Instrumentalist Conception of the Acquis Communautaire in Consumer Law and Its Implications on a European Contract Law Code,' *European Review of Contract Law* 1, no. 2 (July 2005): 211–27.

Schmidt, Vivien A., and Mark Thatcher. 'Why Are Neoliberal Ideas so Resilient in Europe's Political Economy?' *Critical Policy Studies* 8, no. 3 (3 July 2014): 340–47.

Schmitter, Philippe C. 'Neo-Neofunctionalism'. In *European Integration Theory*, 1st ed., edited by Antje Wiener and Thomas Diez, 46–74. Oxford University Press, 2003.

Schularick, Moritz. 'Public and Private Debt: The Historical Record (1870–2010)'. *German Economic Review* 15, no. 1 (1 February 2014): 191–207.

Shaw, Kate Alexander. *Baby Boomers versus Millennials: Rhetorical Conflicts and Interest*. Shefffield Political Economy Research Institute (SPERI) (2018).
Siems, Mathias M. 'Shareholder Protection around the World ('Leximetric II')'. *Centre for Business Research, University of Cambridge Working Paper*, No. 359 (December 2007).
Silva, Margarida. 'The European Union's Revolving Door Problem'. In *Lobbying in the European Union*, edited by Doris Dialer and Margarethe Richter, 273–89. Springer, 2019
Sjåfjell, Beate. 'Redefining the Corporation for a Sustainable New Economy'. *Journal of Law and Society* 45, no. 1 (2018): 29–45.
Sjåfjell, Beate, Andrew Johnston, Linn Anker-Sørensen, and David K. Millon. 'Shareholder Primacy: The Main Barrier to Sustainable Companies'. In *Company Law and Sustainability*, edited by Beate Sjåfjell and Benjamin J. Richardson, 79–147. Cambridge University Press, 2015.
Slobodian, Quinn. *Globalists: The End of Empire and the Birth of Neoliberalism*. Harvard University Press, 2020.
Şorman, Alevgül H. 'Deceitful Decoupling: Misconceptions of a Persistent Myth'. In *Studies in Ecological Economics*, edited by R. Kerry Turner, Robert Costanza, and Joshua Farley, 165–77. Springer, 2023.
Soroka, Stuart, and Stephen McAdams. 'News, Politics, and Negativity'. *Political Communication* 32, no. 1 (2 January 2015): 1–22.
Srinivasan, Amia. *The Right to Sex: Feminism in the Twenty-First Century in the United States*. Farrar, Straus and Giroux, 2021.
Stiglitz, Joseph E. 'Government Failure vs. Market Failure: Principles of Regulation'. In *Government and Markets: Toward a New Theory of Regulation*, edited by Edward J. Balleisen and David A. Moss, 13–51. Cambridge University Press, 2009.
Streeck, Wolfgang. 'The Crises of Democratic Capitalism'. *New Left Review*, no. 71 (January 1, 2011): 5–29.
Sum, Ngai-Ling, and Bob Jessop. *Towards a Cultural Political Economy: Putting Culture in Its Place in Political Economy*. Edward Elgar Publishing, 2013.
Suzman, James. *Work: A History of How We Spend Our Time*. Bloomsbury Publishing, 2020.
Taylor, Charles. *Modern Social Imaginaries*. Duke University Press, 2004.
Teubner, Gunther. 'Societal Constitutionalism: Alternatives to State-Centred Constitutional Theory'. In *Transnational Governance and Constitutionalism*, edited by Christian Joerges, Inge-Johanne Sand, and Gunther Teubner, 3–28. Oxford University Press, 2004.
Teubner, Gunther. 'Substantive and Reflexive Elements in Modern Law'. *Law & Society Review* 17, no. 2 (1 January 1983): 239–86.
Thompson, Edward Palmer. *Whigs and Hunters: The Origin of the Black Act*. Pantheon, 1975.
Tørsløv, Thomas, Ludvig Wier, and Gabriel Zucman. 'The Missing Profits of Nations'. *The Review of Economic Studies* 90, no. 3 (2023): 1499–534.
Trentmann, Frank. *Empire of Things: How We Became a World of Consumers, from the Fifteenth Century to the Twenty-First*. Penguin UK, 2016.

Van Apeldoorn, Bastiaan. 'Transnational Class Agency and European Governance: The Case of the European Round Table of Industrialists'. *New Political Economy* 5, no. 2 (1 July 2000): 157–81.

Van Dam, P. 'The Entangled Consumer: Rethinking the Rise of the Consumer after 1945'. *Journal of Nonprofit & Public Sector Marketing* 33, no. 2 (2021): 212–38.

Van Hoek, Aukje A. H. 'Re-Embedding the Transnational Employment Relationship: A Tale about the Limitations of (EU) Law?,' *Common Market Law Review* 55, no. 2 (2018): 449–87.

Venzke, Ingo. 'Possibilities of the Past: Histories of the NIEO and the Travails of Critique,' *Journal of the History of International Law/Revue d'histoire Du Droit International* 20, no. 3 (2018): 263–302.

Vogel, Jefim, Gauthier Guérin, Daniel W. O'Neill, and J. Steinberger. 'Safeguarding Livelihoods against Reductions in Economic Output'. *Ecological Economics* 215 (1 January 2024): 107977.

Vukov, Visnja. 'Growth Models in Europe's Eastern and Southern Peripheries: Between National and EU Politics'. *New Political Economy* 28, no. 5 (3 September 2023): 832–48.

Wagner, Wendy. 'Administrative Law, Filter Failure, and Information Capture'. *Duke Law Journal* 59, no. 7 (1 January 2010): 1321–1432.

Weatherill, Stephen. 'Competence Creep and Competence Control'. *Yearbook of European Law* 23, no. 1 (1 January 2004): 1–55.

Weber, Max. *Economy and Society: An Outline of Interpretive Sociology, vol. 2*. University of California Press, 1978.

Wettstein, Florian. 'The History of Business and Human Rights and Its Relationship with Corporate Social Responsibility'. In *Research Handbook on Human Rights and Business*, edited by Surya Deva and David Birchall, 23–45. Edward Elgar Publishing, 2020.

Whitehouse, Senator Sheldon. *Captured: The Corporate Infiltration of American Democracy*. The New Press, 2019.

Wolf, Martin. *The Crisis of Democratic Capitalism*. Penguin Press, 2023.

World Bank. *Doing Business – an Independent Evaluation: Taking the Measure of the World Bank-IFC Doing Business Indicators*. World Bank Publications, 2008.

Young, J. Michael. 'Kant's View of Imagination'. *Kant-Studien* 79, nos. 1–4 (1 January 1988): 140–64.

Zeitlin, Jonathan, and Bart Vanhercke. 'Socializing the European Semester: EU Social and Economic Policy Co-ordination in Crisis and Beyond'. *Journal of European Public Policy* 25, no. 2 (2018): 149–74.

Žižek, Slavoj. *The Sublime Object of Ideology*. Verso Books, 1989.

Index

2008 crisis, 1, 21, 34, 37, 47–8, 54, 57–8, 145, 151, 162–3

Aarhus Convention, 103
access to finance, 147
Acemoglu, Daron, 211
Action Plan on Critical Raw Materials, 150
Action Plan to implement the European Pillar of Social Right, 127
Africa
   migration pressures, 69
   Sustainable Investment Facilitation Agreements (SIFA), 150
AI, 113
allocative efficiency, 33
Amazon
   destruction of unsold goods, 136
Anderson, Benedict, 23
   'Imagined Communities', 23
artificial intelligence, 122
austerity, 2
Austria
   European Core, 57
authoritarian modes of government, 64

Bank of England. See Haldane, Andrew
Batteries Act, 142
Batteries Regulation
   due dilegence obligations, 149
Battery Regulation, 118, 138
Bcorps, 128
Better Regulation agenda, 156
Better Regulation package, 158
Binding Treaty on Business and Human Rights, 176
Blair, Tony, 37
blockchain, 122
Breton, Thierry, 180
Brexit, 34

Bundgaard, Anja Marie, 133
Carbon Border Adjustment Mechanism, 164
Castoriadis, Cornelius, 23
CE conformity marking, 129
China, 44
   foreign capital, 58
Chips Act, 142, 146, 149, 160
   Chips Joint Undertaking, 149
   European Chips Infrastructure Consortium, 149
circular economy
   informational requirements, 118
   planned obsolesce, 118
   principles, 119
   standards, 118
Circular Economy Action Plan (CEAP), 105, 118, 124, 127, 134
circular economy principles, 43
clean technology, 139
Codex Alimentaris, 96
co-habitation, 110
collective rights, 83
collective self-determination, 35
company law, 172
competition law, 172
competitiveness
   industrial, 155
Competitiveness Council, the, 182
competitiveness, 155–6
compossible futures, 43
compossible technological futures, 114
Conference on Europe, 170
constitutive outsides, 5
   prosperity's, 13
consumer
   agenda, 100
   contracts, 79
   interests, 79
   law, 80, 95

230   INDEX

consumer (cont.)
  movement, 85
  policy
    internal market, the, 87
    policy objectives, 91
  policy, 75, 80
  protection, 73, 80
  purchasing, 90
  welfare, 124
consumer agenda 1998, 93
Consumer Agenda 2020, 91
consumer credit directive, 88, 91
consumer law, 37
consumer policy
  of 1975, 81, 84
  of 1981, 84, 88
  of 1990, 88
  of 1998, 75
Consumer Rights Directive, 99
consumers
  interests of, 95
  rationality of, 95
  vulnerable, 96
consumers, 40
consumption, 5, 72
  communal forms of, 211
  individuation of, 73
  mass, 22, 77
  sustainable, 105
contract law
  formal equality, 78
  private autonomy, 78
Corporate Europe Observatory (CEO), 152, 179
corporate governance framework, 177
corporate social responsibility initiatives, 100
corporate sustainability due diligence, 181
corporation, 171
  limited liability, 172
  privatised, 172
Court of Justice of the European Union, 73
Covid-19, 2, 10, 16, 163
crisis
  care, 1
  energy, 2
  housing, 1, 70
  migration, 1
Critical Minerals Act, 142
Critical Minerals Action Plan, 146, 168
Critical Raw Material Strategy, 146
Critical Raw Materials Act, 146, 168
cross-border transactions, 90
CSDDD, 138, 195
  proposal, 196

democracy, 51
Democracy, 35

democratic and expert institutions, 9
democratic and/or participatory governance, 199
democratic capitalism, 29, 39
democratic institutions, 2–5
Denmark
  industry, 179
de-risking, 210
destruction of unsold goods, 124
DG Energy and Enterprise, 117
DG FISMA, 177
DG Internal Market, 180
DG Justice, 177
digital economy, 122
digital market, 102
  Digital Markets Act, 102
  Digital Services Act, 102
Digital Markets Act
  gate keepers, 102
Directive on Collective Redress, 103
distance selling, 73
distributive conflicts, 123
doorstep selling directive, 73, 90

East, the
  socialisms, 32
EBRD, the, 148
ECGI group of corporate governance scholars, 175–90
ecodesign, 43, 112
  2005 ecodesign framework directive, 116
  2009 directive, 116
  2016 Ecodesign Working Plan, 121
  2022 revision of ecodesign framework with the New Proposal, 130
    conformity assessment bodies, 131
    eco-vouchers and green taxation, 131
    green public procurement, 131
    notified bodies, 130
    surveillance and cooperation obligations on online platforms, 130
  Consultation Forum, 129
    market surveillance mechanisms, 129
  Ecodesign Forum, 130
  ecodesign framework 2022, 119
  Ecodesign Working Plan, 117
  framework, 114, 128
  hard law, 132
  implementing measure
    impact assessment, 129
  standards, 133
e-commerce, 124
economic exploitation, 108
Economist, the, 153
Emissions Trading Scheme, 163
England, 30
Enlightenment ideology, 61

environmental dangers, 108
environmental degradation, 66
environmental regulation, 156
Ernst & Young, 178
  study, 184–5, 189, 193–4
Esposito, Roberto, 34
  Institution, 28
Espositol, Roberto
  Institution
    instituting praxis, 28
Europe, 1
  banking sector, 34
  financial and industrial capital, 68
  post-war, 4
  tribalism, 8
European Banking Authority, 178
European Chips Infrastructure Consortium, 160
European Commission
  'green paper' on consumer policy, 72–97
  Communication on Shaping Europe's digital future, 105
  inception impact assessment, 179
  Proposal for a Sustainable Products Regulation, 114
European Core, 57
European Court of Justice, 44
European Green Deal, 44, 71
  Green growth, 71
European Green Deal (EGD), 10, 104, 174
  growth strategy, 153
European Green Paper on Integrated Product Policies, 116
European Parliament, 8
European Peripheries, 57
European public goods, 59, 110
European Roundtable of Industrialists and Business Europe, 152
European Roundtable of Industrialists, 58
European Social Entrepreneurship Funds, 168
European Sovereignty Fund, 148, 164
European Structural and Investment Funds, 144
The European Union (EU), 1, 8, 69
  austerity, 70
  common agricultural policy, 43
  constitutional construction, 70
  consumer policy, 36
  industrial law and policy, 142
  technocratic bureaucracy, 70
European Venture Capital Funds, 168

far and extreme right, 1
  parties, 40
finance
  control of public, 57
  growth of, 33

financial law, 172
financialisation, 66
foreign direct investment, 58
France
  trade unions, 79
Freedman, Milton, 172
freedom of contract, 42
Friedman, Milton, 186, 190

Gabor, Daniela, 210
Geertz, Clifford, 26
General Exception and the Temporary Crisis and Transition Framework, 142
General State Aid exception, 147
Germany, 37, 201
  European Core, 57
  third way social democrats, 37
Global Gateway, 168
global interdependence, 69
Global North, 13, 46, 66, 111
Global South, 66, 175
  New International Economic Order, 175
globalization, 112
goods
  institutional, 6
  material, 6
  social and institutional, 49
  social, 6
great financial crisis, 1. *See* 2008 crisis
Greece
  austerity, 58
  internal devaluation, 58
  unemployment, 58
Green Claims Directive, 106
Green Deal Industrial Plan for Net Zero Age. See Net Zero Plan
green extractivism, 12, 151, 167
green finance, 177
Gross Domestic Product (GDP), 31

Haldane, Andrew, 54
Hayek, Friedrich, 55
  ordoliberals, 56
hegemonies in democratic societies, temporary, 53
Horizon Europe, 147
housing, 48
Hungary, 33

Ideology, 26–8
  productive imagination, 26
imaginaries
  collective, 42
  collectivist, 62
  conservative, 3
  of consumption, corporation, technological governance, 59

232 INDEX

imaginaries (cont.)
  of consumption, 101
  industrial, 156
  of law, 83
  nativist, 3, 68
  nativist and conservative, 3
  of privatised prosperity, 13
  of prosperity, 4, 46
  of shared prosperity, 13
  social, 3, 12, 23
  tribal, 3, 17, 21, 68
imaginaries of prosperity
  patriarchal
    women, 67
  privatised, 13
  shared, 13
imaginary
  of consumption, 101, 107, 124
  of corporation, 172
  of the economy, 87
  of law, 96
  of prosperity, privatised, 21
  of shared prosperity, 9, 68, 205
imaginary of prosperity, 2, 4
  neoliberal, 37
Impact Assessment Board, 157
Important Projects of Common European Interest (IPCEI), 148
individual rights, 83
industrial food production, 112
industrial policy
  circular economy model, 145
  green, 164
  laissez-faire, 140
  NET ZERO, 141
  of the new growth strategy, 154
  to support social economy, 200
  vertical, 140
  welfare state, 140
Industrial Policy 2010, 142
industrial policy, 12, 59, 139
Industrial Renaissance policy, 144, 152
  Growth-Friendly Public Administration, 161
industrialisation, 77
inequality, 1
Injunction Directive, 103
intellectual property rights, 42
internal market, 36, 55
InvestEU, 148
Italy, 163, 201

Jessop, Bob, 24
  economic imaginaries, 24
Just Transition Fund, 147

Kaupa, Clemens, 57
Keynes, John Maynard, 31–2

laissez-faire, 31–2
Keynesianism
  privatised, 7
  public, 7
Kuhn, Thomas, 195

labelling directive, 115
  for household appliances, 115
labour productivity, 113
laissez-faire, 4, 30
language
  of competitiveness, 154
  of protection, 83, 86, 210
law, 17, 40
  institution of, 29
  juridification, 41
  labour and tenancy, 43
  rule of law, 40
Leone, Candida, 79
lighting regulations, 118
Lisbon Agenda, 97

Macron, Emmanuel, 139
Mannheim, Karl, 25, 27
market regulation, 71
market surveillance, 128
Marx, Karl, 25
Mazzucato, Mariana, 164
  Entrepreneurial State
    public-private partnerships, 155
media, non-partisan, 64
Micklitz, Hans W, 34, 80
The Middle Ages, 28
Miethausersyndikat
  cooperative housing, 199
migration, 68
millennials, 47
Minimum Corporate Tax directive, 162
modernity, 23
Moore, Jason W., 151
mortgage contracts, 42
Mortgage Directive, 44, 110
multinational corporations (MNCs), 175

neoliberal imaginary of privatised prosperity, 76
neoliberal imaginary of prosperity and corporation, 192
neoliberal imaginary of prosperity, 196
neoliberalism, 1, 20, 33
  deregulation, 33
  financialization, 33
  flexibilization, 33
  liberalisation, 33
  privatisation, 33
  privatised prosperity, 33
Net Zero Industry Act, 44, 142, 146, 160

Net Zero Academies, 148
Net Zero Plan, 145, 160
Netherlands, the
  housing crisis, 70
Netherlands, the, 80
New Consumer Agenda, 72–104
New Deal for Consumers, 72–101
New Impetus to Consumer Policy, 86
Next Generation EU, 10, 145
Ngai-Ling, Sum
  economic imaginaries, 24
Niglia, Leone, 44
non-financial reporting directive, 176–7
Nordic countries
  European Core, 57
Nordic Member States
  Denmark
    business associations, 187
Nordic professors, 175–90
nuclear families, 67
nuclear family dwellings, 72

O'Toole, Fintan, 63
OECD Principles, 176
one-stop-shop, 126, 146
Orban, Viktor, 58
output legitimacy, 5

Patterson, Dennis, 34
pharmaceutical industry, 42
platform economy
  Airbnb, 102
  Amazon, 102
  uber, 102
Polanyi, Karl, 29
precautionary principle, 157
Přibáň, Jiří
  European Consitutional Imaginaries, 55
Priorities for Consumer Policy 1996–1998, 91
private rule-making processes
  CEN, CENELEC, 93
privatisation
  of basic services, 66
  of power, 42
Prodi Commission, 157
product as service, 138
product liability directive, 90
Profit, 197
Proposal for a Net Zero Industrial Act, 146
prosperity
  neoliberal privatised, 38
  privatised, 4, 56
Prosperity, 6
protection of health and safety, 83
public procurement, 201

Recovery and Resilience plans, 163
regenerative growth, 121
regressive fiscal pact, 18
regulatory sandboxes, 146, 201
Regulatory Scrutiny Board, 126, 175–81, 186, 195
REPower EU, 10, 148
revolution
  digital, 112
  in transport, 112
  Industrial, 112
Ricoeur, Paul, 23
  Lectures on Ideology and Utopia, 25
'Right to Repair' Directive, 106
Robinson, James A., 211
Rodrik, Dani, 150
rule of law, 9

Schroder, Gerhard, 37
self-regulation
  measures, 133
  processes, 133
self-regulation agreements, 96
self-regulation, 132
services of general economic interest (SGEI), 77
shared prosperity, 4, 205
shareholder primacy, 173–4, 186
sharing economy, 106
Single European Act, 86, 115
Smart Specialisations, 144
SME Strategy, 159, 169
social and environmental extraction, 7
Social Economy Bank, 202
social economy, 127, 138, 168, 199, 213
social enterprises, 128
social imaginaries of "prosperity", 13
social integration, 12, 204
social intrapreneurship, 202
social market economy, 56
social media, 113
social purpose, 199
socially integrative function, 20
societal disintegration, 15
Stability and Growth Pact, 12
'stakeholder' perspectives, 197
strategic autonomy, 139
strategic partnerships, 147
Strategic Technologies for Europe Platform, 148
Sum, Ngai-Ling, 24
surveillance, 109
sustainable corporate governance, 191, 196
sustainable economy, 114
Sustainable Products Regulation Proposal, 135–7
  product passports, 135

Sustainable Products, 105
sustainable value creation, 203

tax
  competences, 57
  competition, 57, 162
  credits and subsidies, 166
  cutting of, 33
  harmonisation, 57, 162
  incentives for R&D, 140
taxation, 161
Taylor, Charles, 24
  modern social imaginary, 24
  Western modern social imaginary, 29
technocratic institutions, 54
technological development, 66, 114
  Silicon Valley, 67
technology, 112
Temporary Crisis and Transition Framework, 147
Timmermans, Frans, 153
tribal
  collectivism, 206
tribal imaginaries, 5
tribal societies
  output legitimacy, 64
tribal violence
  Yugoslavia, 62
tribalism, 1, 62
Trump, Donald, 34
twin green and digital transitions, 145

UK, the, 33, 37
  Melony Report (1960), 80
  third way social democrats, 37
UN Convention on the Rights of Persons with Disabilities, 105
UN Principles, 175
unfair terms directive, 44
unfair terms protection, 88
unfair terms, 86
unfair trading practices, 86

United Nations' 2030 Agenda for Sustainable Development, 105
United Nations' sustainable development goals, 154
USA, the, 33, 44
  Inflation Reduction Act, 147, 149, 166
  Kennedy's Consumer Bill of Rights, 80
  OIRA (Office of Information and Regulatory Affairs), 179
USA, 15
Utopia, 26–8
  imaginaries of prosperity, 27
  productive imagination, 26

von der Leyen, Ursula, 148

war, 5, 65
  growth strategy, 5
  in Ukraine, 10, 139
Warren, Elisabeth
  Accountable Capitalism Act, 202
weather events, 69
Weber, Max, 26
  Herrschaft, 26
Weimar, 1
West, the
  welfare states, 32
White Paper for the Competition of the Internal Market, 86, 115
White Paper on Governance, 97
Wigger, Angela, 144, 151
Wilders, Geert, 64
Wolf, Martin
  The Crisis of Democratic Capitalism, 45
World Bank's Doing Business Index, 152
WTO, 149
WWII imaginary of corporation, 192
WWII imaginary of shared prosperity, 196

Yugoslavia, 33

For EU product safety concerns, contact us at Calle de José Abascal, 56–1°,
28003 Madrid, Spain or eugpsr@cambridge.org.

www.ingramcontent.com/pod-product-compliance
Ingram Content Group UK Ltd.
Pitfield, Milton Keynes, MK11 3LW, UK
UKHW030805150425
457293UK00016B/241